# The A-B-C's of Human Experience

## An Integrative Model

**Wallace J. Kahn**

*West Chester University*

TECHNICAL COLLEGE OF THE LOWCOUNTRY
LEARNING RESOURCES CENTER
POST OFFICE BOX 1288
BEAUFORT, SOUTH CAROLINA 29901-1288

Brooks/Cole • Wadsworth

**I T P**® an International Thomson Publishing Company

Belmont, CA • Albany, NY • Boston • Cincinnati • Johannesburg • London • Madrid • Melbourne
Mexico City • New York • Pacific Grove, CA • Scottsdale, AZ • Singapore • Tokyo • Toronto

ECHNICAL COLLEGE OF THE LOWCOUNTRY
EARNING RESOURCES CENTER
POST OFFICE BOX 1288
BEAUFORT, SOUTH CAROLINA 29901-1288

Sponsoring Editor: Eileen Murphy
Editorial Assistant: Julie Martinez
Marketing Team: Ron Shelly, Jean Thompson,
  Steve Catalano, and Aaron Eden
Permissions Editor: Elaine Jones
Design Editor: Roy R. Neuhaus

Production Editor: Mary Anne Shahidi
Copy Editor: Frank Hubert
Interior and Cover Designer: Ellen Pettengell
Art Editor and Illustrator: Jennifer Mackres
Compositor: Forbes Mill Press
Printer: Webcom

COPYRIGHT ©1999 by Wadsworth Publishing Company
A division of International Thomson Publishing Inc.
I(T)P  The ITP logo is a registered trademark under license.

*For more information, contact:*
Wadsworth Publishing Company, 10 Davis Drive, Belmont, CA 94002, or electronically at http://www.wadsworth.com

International Thomson Publishing Europe
Berkshire House
168-173 High Holborn
London, WC1V 7AA, United Kingdom

International Thomson Editores
Seneca, 53
Colonia Polanco
11560 México D.F. Mexico

Nelson ITP, Austrailia
102 Dodds Street
South Melbourne
Victoria 3205 Australia

International Thomson Publishing Asia
60 Albert Street #15-01
Albert Complex
Singapore 189969

Nelson Canada
1120 Birchmount Road
Scarborough, Ontario
Canada M1K 5G4

International Thomson Publishing Japan
Hirakawa-cho Kyowa Building, 3F
2-2-1 Hirakawa-cho, Chiyoda-ku
Tokyo 102, Japan

International Thomson Publishing Southern Africa
Building 18, Constantia Square
138 Sixteenth Road, P.O. Box 2459
Halfway House, 1685 South Africa

All rights reserved. No part of this work covered by the copyright hereon may be reproduced or used in any form or
by any means—graphic, electronic, or mechanical, including photocopying, recording, taping, or information storage
and retrieval systems—without the written permission of the publisher.

Printed in Canada
1 2 3 4 5 6 7 8 9 10

Library of Congress Cataloging-in-Publication Data
Kahn, Wallace J. [date]
    The A-B-C's of human behavior : an integrative model / Wallace J.
Kahn.
        p.      cm.
    Includes bibliographical references and index.
    ISBN 0-534-35981-7 (pbk. : alk. paper)
    1. Psychology.   2. Human behavior.   3. Change (Psychology)
I. Title.
BF121.K24   1999                          98-38401
150—dc21

This book is printed on acid-free recycled paper.

To those who renew my life and love every day

Bev

Wal

Cass

Edie

Wally, Sr.

# About the Author

Wallace J. Kahn (PhD, counselor education and child counseling, University of Maryland) is professor of counseling and teacher education at West Chester University, Pennsylvania. He is a licensed psychologist and certified school counselor who has served as an elementary school teacher, counselor, and maintained a clinical practice specializing in child and family counseling. Professor Kahn has published in the areas of self-management, cognitive-behavioral group work, school and systems-based consultation, and expressive writing techniques in counseling. His current interests include conflict resolution and anger management with children and attention deficit-hyperactivity disorder, with which he is intimately familiar.

# Contents

~~~~~~~~~~~~~~~~~~~~

## Chapter 9

# Our Covert a-b-c's: What We Think About  132

## Chapter 10

# Personalizing Our A-B-C's: The a-b-c's of the Self  153

# Preface

## For the Instructor

I have often heard that nothing is more practical than a good theory. Most frequently, this has been noted by experienced school counselors or mental health workers who are struggling to maintain an explicit, consistent, and predictable connection between what they believe, what the value, and what they actually do in their work. The beliefs and values that they hold concerning the lives of their clients, their own reality, and ultimately, what it means to be human form the core of their theory of the human experience and the process of change. Assumptions, beliefs, and expectations emanating from their theory provide the rationale and direction for what counselors and mental health workers actually do when engaged in the process of helping others.

For theory to inform actions, it must survive empirical validation within the scientific community as well as demonstrate the empirical face validity of our everyday experience. This scientific and personal validation requires a theory that incorporates the universe of social, physical, emotional, cognitive, behavioral, and even spiritual elements that comprise our human experience. Consequently, the theory from which we attempt to understand our counselees, our clients, and ultimately, ourselves must truly integrate all of these elements. This comprehensive integration of these disparate elements into a dynamic, synergistic whole is the purpose of this book. I refer to this integrative theory as the A-B-C model: a simple name, but a rich, comprehensive framework for helping our students understand, diagnose, and successfully intervene in the lives of others.

The A-B-C model that I present is not the definitive theory of human behavior, but it is a theory. From a social constructionist orientation, this model represents one person's construction of reality. My A-B-C paradigm represents my metaphor for how we might go about the business of being human within the many social and physical environments that make up our world. This metaphor draws from the rich social, psychological, physiological, cognitive, and behavioral research that exists within our scientific community. Readers will recognize many theories, principles, dynamics, and paradigms that they have encountered in their introductory coursework in the behavioral and social sciences. What they will find as new, innovative, exciting, and heuristic is the manner in which these varied pieces are woven into a complex, integrative whole called the A-B-C model. The model presented in this book demonstrates that operant behavior, emotion, physiology, neurology, cognition, social learning, and culture all have a place in our understanding of the human experience.

The A-B-C model is not a theory of counseling or therapy, but rather it is a way to conceptualize the human experience and the many mechanisms in which that experience can change extemporaneously or purposely. Although this book presents an integrative model for understanding the human experience, the model offers vast implications and directions for purposeful behavior change. The student of psychology, counseling, or education will readily appreciate the utility of the A-B-C model and easily use it as a conceptual framework and point of departure for purposeful change. Rather than offer any theory of counseling, this book presents an integrative model that can explain the theory and practice of many of the counseling and educational approaches employed today.

The scope of the A-B-C model is broad, integrating as much as we currently know about how our thoughts, feelings, physiology, behavior, and environment interact to create our unitary, conscious, and often unconscious experience of ourselves in the world. To achieve this formidable objective, I have tried to weave established and contemporary conclusions from the social, biological, and behavioral sciences with personal anecdotes. Personalization and user-friendliness are further enhanced by my conversational writing style. Although the content of my exposition on the A-B-C model is academically sound, thorough, and occasionally quite complex, the style of my communication is generally informal, direct, and experiential. Through numerous examples and reader applications, I have tried to incorporate experiential learning and guided discovery into my teaching of the A-B-C model. Key concepts, principles, and dynamics of the model are illustrated with cartoons appearing throughout the book. As well as stimulating an emphatic laugh, each cartoon demonstrates why a picture is worth a thousand words.

The greatest challenge in organizing this text was presenting an integrative, holistic, and synergistic model within the linear, reductionist structure imposed by writing. While the single visual Gestalt of "Figure 1, The A-B-C Model," illustrates the interrelationship of the various components of the model, the cogent, lucid explanation of each component required a sequential presentation. Consequently, I choose to present the components of the A-B-C's in the order in which I have used the model for diagnostic purposes. After a general introduction and orientation to the model in Chapter 1, I present the most salient aspect of our A-B-C's in Chapter 2. In Chapters 3 and 4, I move to an investigation of the consequences of our behavior, with particular emphasis on the contingency relationship of our actions (and inactions) and our external environment. From this behavior-consequence interaction, we begin to see the synergistic nature of the A-B-C model. Chapter 3 looks at desirable consequences that motivate us to action, and Chapter 4 presents undesirable consequences that cause pain, grief, and disappointment. The environmental context of our thoughts, feelings, and actions is explored in Chapter 5. As the antecedent factors are considered within the dynamic of our behavior and its consequences, we come to appreciate the influence of our physical and social environment on every aspect of our being. This complex world of people, places, things, sounds, colors, textures, images, smells, sensations, and temperatures forms the context of our life and, as antecedents, informs our behavior and the consequences that result.

As important as our purposeful actions (i.e., operant behavior) are to our human experience, we are biological beings and could not exist without a physiology that is generally involuntary. Rather than attempt to encompass all of human biology as it relates to the A-B-C model, I narrow my focus to respondents and our automatic nervous system. Thus, Chapter 6 provides an overview of our autonomic nervous system and its relationship to our thoughts, actions, and external environment. With the inclusion of our central nervous system in our understanding of the A-B-C's, we shift our attention to covert behavior and devote the remaining chapters, 7–12 to cognition and the covert world that exists in our head. Within this covert world, all of our A-B-C's finally come together to form our experience of understanding and purpose. The covert component of the model serves as the point of convergence for all that we know, experience, and remember about our A-B-C's. Within the subjective, cognitive realities of our thought, we give form and meaning to our antecedents, behavior, and consequences, and thus, it is not until Chapters 7–12 that we can truly understand and appreciate the integrative quality of the A-B-C model. Because of the superordinate position of thought (i.e., our covert behavior) in influencing every other component of the model, it was pedagogically and experientially appropriate that I address cognition last. Correspondingly, the mechanisms with which we process, understand, plan, and execute our actions (based on the A-B-C's of our mind) are extraordinarily complex and warrant extensive explanation.

Consequently, I devote the entire second half of this book to the cognitive aspect of the cognitive-behavioral model. After an introduction to the nature of thought and cognition in Chapter 7, I discuss innate covert structures and processes in Chapter 8. The basic mechanisms that prescribe how we think provide the framework for studying the context (or the what) of our thinking in Chapter 9. Chapter 10 explores aspects of our A-B-C's that we personalize. This universe of covert a-b-c's that we associate with us (our a-b-c's) provides our personal identity and ultimately our concept of self. The mechanisms through which we place value and render judgments about this self (or our many selves) are the focus of Chapter 11. The ultimate integration and yet most intimate experience of our A-B-C's occur with our experiences of emotion. Thus, the inclusion of emotion in the model provides a natural culmination to my presentation of the A-B-C's of our experience. Including emotion illustrates the essential quality of the A-B-C model: placing the most personal and idiosyncratic nature of our own reality within a holistic, universal framework of understanding.

## A Word to Students

This book attempts to integrate relevant principles from many diverse disciplines. Since each discipline has its own terms, concepts, paradigms, and vocabulary, you will run into unfamiliar terms and nomenclature (jargon). Although definitions of new terms can often be gleaned from the context, some nomenclature will have to be researched elsewhere. Laborious as this might be, the effort will reap rich rewards in clarity and sustained comprehension of the text. I have also provided an extensive summary for each chapter to aid in your review of the most salient points about each component of the A-B-C model.

As you read about the many principles and dynamics described by the A-B-C model, I hope you apply each one to personal experience. With each dynamic described in this text, ask yourself: Is this dynamic a part of my experience? What is it like to be me? This book is about you, and its value rests in your affirmative answer to these questions.

## Acknowledgments

A book of this magnitude represents the toil and inspiration of many others. Beyond the many scientists and practitioners who have contributed directly to the content, I wish to thank those who have supported, encouraged, and at times cajoled me to get this book done! First and foremost, I wish to thank my family who was always there to reinforce my progress and guide me out of periodic crises of confidence. To my wife, Beverly, whose confidence in me never faltered, and whose love is unceasing. Her keen insight and knowledge of the A-B-C model, attention to detail, and willingness to endure multiple drafts of my writing have been significant forces in the creation of this book. What a joy to have such a loving colleague and editor. To my son, Wally, and daughter, Cassie, who have allowed their personal experience to enter the pages of this text. In spite of the many hours denied them by writing this book, they let me know that it was "Okay, dad." To my parents, Wally, Sr. (yes, the original one) and Edie, I wish to express my love and gratitude for maintaining an environment full of "green lights" and "C+'s." My belief in the power of positive reinforcement has been sustained by their daily expressions of love and generosity.

During the 25 years that I have been formulating this work in progress called the A-B-C model, I have had assistance and validation from hundreds of students, colleagues, and counselees. My A-B-C model attained increasing complexity and validation as each person shared perceptions and experiences with me. Although too numerous to name here, those of you who have shared your A-B-C's with me will recognize your contributions and my expression of gratitude.

I wish to thank the following folks who have inspired, read, edited, or in some way influenced the product before you: Linda Adams, Michael Altekruse, Terry Bordon, Jay Friedman, Susan Graham, Jeffrey S. Haber, John Henning, Tracey Kesselman, George Maxim, Kathy Nagar, Rick Parsons, Jennifer and Dave Reinheimer, Margaret Shannon, Lesley Welsh, Robert W. Wildblood, Shannon Wright, and Geoffrey Yager. I also wish to recognize the support so generously offered by the folks of West Chester University. Without the sabbaticals granted to pursue this project, it never would have materialized into this text.

I sincerely thank Claire Verduin, her successor, Eileen Murphy, and the Brooks/Cole family. Claire's faith in the project got me started, and Eileen's enthusiasm and constructive editing kept me going. And finally, my appreciation goes to my production editor, Mary Anne Shahidi, and my copyeditor, Frank Hubert, for his accurate attention to detail.

*Wally Kahn*

# Chapter 1

~~~~~~~~~~

# Orienting Ourselves to the A-B-C Model

~~~~~~~~~~

## A Personal Introduction

Since 1971, I have been both a counselor and a counselor educator. Equally as relevant to my message, I am a husband, father of two children, and a human being trying to navigate a successful and happy path through life. In each of these endeavors, I have found the struggle much easier, the navigation more successful, and the tiller more under my own control when I have a clear awareness and understanding of myself and my environment. As Wally the husband, father, neighbor, and person, this awareness and understanding are usually intuitive and unconscious. My thoughts and actions are fairly consistent and predictable, appearing almost automatic. On Sunday evening, I take out the trash. I pay the monthly mortgage on time so the house remains secure. I say "no" when my 17-year-old son requests to try out his new curve ball in our family room.

In these situations, I don't think about my thinking (a process often referred to as *metacognition*). Rather, I quickly size up the situation and act. The more routine the situation, the less I consciously analyze the what, when, where, and how of my behavior. Fortunately, I have lots of habitual thoughts and actions (e.g., fixed action patterns) that serve me through the day. If I had to constantly think about my thinking, I would quickly become immobilized, and this book would never get written. Only when conditions are novel or I am really unsure about what is going on do I analyze the what, when, where, and how in any particularly conscious way.

As a psychologist, counselor, and counselor educator, when trying to help others navigate their own journeys successfully, I can't just rely on my own intuitive patterns of thinking and acting. The particular thoughts and actions that work well for me may be totally inappropriate for someone else. To help others, I cannot dictate the specific thoughts and actions that will work best for them. What I can do, however, is use and share the model that I use in deciding what thoughts and actions work best for me. This model is a conceptual framework for understanding ourselves (our thoughts and our actions) in the context of our social and physical environment. Since the model incorporates Antecedent conditions, Behavior, and Consequences into an integrated description and explanation of the human experience, I refer to it as the A-B-C model. These A-B-C's of experience help me understand (describe, explain, predict, and sometimes even control) why I and others think, feel, and behave as we do.

Because this representational system is personal, it can be called the Wally Kahn theory of behavior. (Perhaps I should say the Wally Kahn, Jr., theory, as my father and my son, also named Wally, possess their own theories.) In any case, the model or theory presented in this book serves as the basis of my clinical work, my teaching, and most pervasively, my day-to-day encounters with the world. This model manifests my answer to three very basic questions: (a) How are people at their best? (b) How are people at their worst? and (c) How does change occur? All three of these questions are particularly pertinent to anyone in the helping professions, where answers are called for with each helping intervention. When I am counseling others, I often share this model as a framework for self-awareness and purposeful behavior change. In teaching prospective counselors, I use this model as the basis for diagnosis, remediation, and purposeful behavior change. This latter application reflects my belief that the least (and perhaps even the most) that I can teach my students about counseling is the conceptual, or theoretical, model that I use in my own counseling practice.

This comprehensive A-B-C model represents the integration and synthesis of many disparate principles, processes, dynamics, and strategies researched and described by others. A vast array of empirically validated data has been compiled and selectively incorporated into the fabric of this model. You may recognize many familiar concepts, principles, laws, and theorems as you read this book. What you may not recognize is the way they have been pieced together into a broad, coherent, integrative framework. This framework can be used to describe, explain, and predict behavior. This piecing together of cognitive, environmental, physiological, emotional, behavioral, and even spiritual aspects of human functioning into a macroperspective of humans is the unique quality and contribution of this book.

This paradigm for conceptualizing human behavior incorporates established principles and concepts of psychological and behavioral functioning into a coherent pattern of how we think, feel, behave, and experience. Although some of these principles and concepts may be familiar, others may be totally new, even if fairly well recognized within the behavioral sciences. What I hope will be new, practical, and provocative to your own understanding of your human experience is the integrative, unitary framework offered by the A-B-C model.

As the A-B-C model attempts to integrate all of the factors involved in an entire experience or pattern of behavior, it can best be understood and appreciated when all of the parts (A's, B's, and C's) are fit together into a whole picture. Consequently, as we study behavior, we cannot help but bring in its related antecedents and consequences. All of the components and parts are interdependent; the expected consequences determine which antecedents we discriminate, and subsequently, the thinking and acting behavior produces the most desirable consequence. All of this is an attempt to explain why it is so difficult to understand any one part of the A-B-C model without bringing in all of the other parts. I now illustrate this unity by analyzing an experience common to most of us.

## A Preview Example of the A-B-C Model

**A**lthough the entire text describes the theoretical framework of this A-B-C model, a simple example illustrates how the components fit together into an integrated whole, or system. First, take a look at the ABC (cognitive–behavioral) model depicted in Figure 1. The following analysis shows how you might use this basic A-B-C model to analyze making a dental appointment. Since the A—B—C follows a linear or chronological sequence, we start with the A component, the external environment or context in which our example begins.

> A = This is the antecedent stimulus or external environmental event that starts the behavioral episode. The A is something (time, place, person, object, event) in the external environment that signals the start of your thinking and acting behavior. Since we are analyzing the behavior of making a dental appointment, the antecedent stimulus could be:

> **1.** A postcard from your dentist that reminds you it is "checkup time again."

> **2.** A notation on your calendar or refrigerator to "have teeth checked."

> **3.** A severe toothache.

> **4.** Bumping into your dentist at the local supermarket.

> **5.** An available telephone (you are making the appointment by phone).

> **6.** The time is 5:00–5:30 P.M. (the only time available to make the call).

**Note:** Some antecedents signal or enable you to make the appointment—these are "green light A's." Others prevent you from making the appointment or signal you not to—these are "red light A's." Let us assume that the green light A's occur and stimulate the next component of our A-B-C model—the covert/thinking behavior. The thoughts stimulated by these antecedents are as follows:

> B/Covert = The covert behavior represents the content and process of how we think. It is the subjective world that exists in your head. I call these thoughts *covert behaviors* because, although you cannot see or measure them directly, they can be purposely generated or eliminated much like our actions (acting behaviors or operants). Many of our thoughts consist of our interpretation of the messages sent from our external environment (i.e., A), the array of responses we could give to these messages (i.e., B), and the consequences that result from the behavioral responses we choose to make (i.e., C). We might experience these thoughts as images or self-talk that essentially informs us: "When this A occurs, I had better do this B if I want this C to result." Applying this to our example, our thought might be any of the following:

> **1.** "Uh-oh! I better make the appointment now, or I will never get to it. And I don't want to risk another cavity. I have the phone number right here."

> **2.** "Darn! Not again?! I'll wait awhile. My teeth seem okay for now."

> **3.** "Darn! Not again?! I am never going back. It hurts too much."

**Note:** Each covert response is probably based on some past experience, and each will elicit its own behavior. Also, these thoughts provoke your emotional experiences of this situation. How do you feel in this situation? What emotional or feeling label(s) would you use? Will your feelings differ depending on your covert response? How would you feel in response to 1? 2? and 3? I might feel brave in conjunction with 1, perhaps relieved in 2, and probably angry in 3. How about you?

Thus, our emotions are a critical dimension of our covert experience and represent the subjective meaning and associated label that we use for the feeling or emotion connected to any particular experience. Emotions are the meaning or interpretation we give to the composite A-B-C of an experience. And the affective labels (typically formed as adjectives) that we use, such as sad, frightened, angry, excited, worried, guilty, and so forth, are the language symbols that we use to convey the A's, B's, and C's of our immediate experience. The feeling words or emotional labels that we might apply in our example could be scared, worried, courageous, brave, guilty, ashamed, childish, optimistic, or strong—all depending on how we experience the A's, B's, and C's of the situation. I will say much more on this feeling aspect of the A-B-C's in Chapter 5. Now let's see how our thoughts and feelings might affect our body—that is, how we feel physically.

> B/Respondent = Respondents are our involuntary physiological/biochemical responses to either antecedent stimuli or the covert expectation of a particular consequence (i.e., C). In the expectation of a punishing or aversive consequence (C–), our body mobilizes itself physically (i.e., increasing muscle tension and arousal) in preparation to cope (fight or flight) with the perceived threat. We often call this increased mobilization *anxiety*. In our example, any of the three covert responses predicts pain or punishment as a consequence to making the appointment. Consequently, the immediate respondent or physiological arousal will be experienced as the *alarm reaction*: muscle tension, increased heart rate, rapid and shallow breathing, perspiration, dry mouth, and so on. These physical/biochemical changes increase in intensity as we dwell upon the aversive consequence. As total avoidance, response 3 may elicit the least anxiety in the short term, but the most pain and suffering overall. The first response produces immediate anxiety, but the best long-term consequence. Response 2 is a short-term solution (i.e., procrastination) with an unknown future.

**Note:** The decision to actually make the dental appointment depends on the covert expectation generated. The action taken to either make or avoid the appointment also depends somewhat on the level of anxiety experienced in the respondent (body). A manageable level of anxiety accompanying the covert expectation of a successful outcome motivates the operant behavior of making the appointment. Let's see what we actually do in response to our thoughts and feelings about this dental appointment.

> B/Operant = Behavior that is voluntary and operates on the environment to produce desirable consequences is referred to as *operant behavior*. We choose operant behavior because we expect (covert expectations stored in our head) that it will either get us something desirable or enable us to avoid/escape something

undesirable. Returning to our example, in response to covert expectation 1, we pick up the telephone, dial the dentist's number, and proceed to make an appointment for as soon as possible. Covert expectation 2 motivates us to walk away from the telephone, pursue some other distracting activity, and postpone making the appointment indefinitely or until we actually experience a painful toothache. Covert expectation 3 causes us to deny the very existence of dental treatment. Our operant behavior in this instance of total denial may be to proclaim the value of false teeth. After all, they were good enough for George Washington.

**Note:** Just as the action or operant behavior that we choose derives from our covert behavior, the consequence that we experience most probably results from the operant behavior that we choose. The following are some of the consequences that might follow our behavior.

> C = Consequences represent the immediate or long-term results of the operant behavior preceding them. Consequences can occur as either objects, events, or activities that we experience as desirable or undesirable. We tend to engage in behaviors that produce desirable consequences (i.e., positive reinforcement, or the symbol C+) or prevent undesirable consequences (i.e., negative reinforcement, or the symbol C̸). Unfortunately, in the case of our dental appointment behavior, the more immediate consequence may be some anxiety accompanied by some pain in the dentist's office. Ideally, the longer-term consequence of healthy teeth will far outweigh this short-term discomfort. The consequence of putting the appointment off until sometime in the future is really unknown. With luck and good teeth, the damage may be minor. With incipient tooth and gum disease, the consequences could be severe dental problems, which is precisely the consequence to expect from a coping strategy of total denial of the problem. The consequence that maintains both procrastination and the denial operant behaviors is that of avoiding anticipated pain, a short-term gain at best.

## Analysis and Prescription for Change

**A**s you can see, our analysis revealed much information about how we respond (or choose not to respond) to the challenge of scheduling an appointment for a relatively unpleasant experience. If we wanted, we could use the data obtained from our analysis to change our behavior in making this appointment. The information that is revealed when we do an A-B-C analysis of behavior provides many implications for purposeful behavior change. Based on the data obtained from our A-B-C analysis, here are some strategies that get to the task of resolving our immediate dental appointment problem.

Our A-B-C analysis of the dental appointment reveals two potential problem behaviors (i.e., responses to the A that will result in undesirable consequences). The procrastination behavior in response to the covert thought "I'll postpone this appointment until later" as well as the total avoidance behavior stemming from the thought

"I am never going back . . ." are both setting up the possibility of a severe dental problem in the future. If we choose to change these problematic responses and face up to the need for an appointment now, we might:

1. Change dentists if past encounters with this dentist were exceptionally unpleasant. (This involves changing the A and ideally the C.)

2. Change our covert behavior (images and/or self-talk) to the most positive aspects of making the appointment now. This strategy involves changing the covert B to such thoughts as, "With lots of Novocain and my Walkman radio, I won't feel a thing."

3. Break the process of scheduling (and making) the appointment as well as completing the treatment plan into small steps; then establish strong positive reinforcement contingencies for following through on each step. For example, schedule with the dentist to have only the examination or the teeth cleaning on the first visit. Subsequent treatments, if necessary, would be done in small steps (e.g., one cavity treated per visit). (This involves many B–C contingency management strategies such as shaping, behavioral rehearsal, contracting, etc.)

4. Have a supportive friend make the appointment and accompany us on our first visit. This friend might also help maintain our positive reinforcement contingencies for each step in the appointment/treatment process. (I will discuss the significance of positive reinforcement and social support for behavior change later in this book.)

5. Learn anxiety reduction techniques such as deep breathing, imagery, and muscle relaxation that we can use as we make the appointment and then throughout the treatment process. (This involves changing the B's.)

These purposeful actions are just a few of the many strategies that we could employ in overcoming our fear of the dentist. They all use data obtained from our A-B-C analysis. These data can be used to assess the ABC's of the problem, how we would really like to respond, and changes we could make in the A's, B's, and C's that will enable us to think and act as we would like.

When we wish to make changes in our thinking or acting behavior, the specific parts of the A-B-C model that we choose to manipulate depend on the behavior we wish to change as well as the antecedents and consequences that are influencing that behavior. At times, a simple change in the antecedent condition causes the behavior to change, as in placing the dentist's phone number by the telephone or even changing dentists. Often, a change in the consequences induces behavior change, as when we built in lots of positive consequences for making the appointment. In still other instances, we might directly alter the thoughts or actions, as when we learned relaxation skills and positive cognition about making the appointment.

Any situation that you encounter can be analyzed and understood with respect to the A-B-C's that are occurring during that situation. Your A-B-C's might be very different than someone else's A-B-C's, even in the same situation (e.g., in a classroom), and your own A-B-C's can even vary in similar situations (e.g., in one classroom compared with another classroom). As a teacher or counselor, your understanding of your

A-B-C's and the A-B-C's of others (students, counselees, etc.) helps you in facilitating learning and change.

My goal of this book is to help you understand the basic components, principles, and dynamics of the A-B-C model. Here is how the scope and organization of the book will unfold.

## Scope of the Book

The A-B-C model presented in this book is drawn from numerous disciplines including psychology, sociology, anthropology, as well as developments in the fields of medicine, mental health, and education. Like all theories of personality and human behavior, it attempts to extrapolate from the most valid data known about the human experience to hypotheses, models, and paradigms that describe, explain, predict, and ultimately control human thought and action. And as with all theories, it falls short of these conscientious goals. This worthy, yet futile and embryonic, effort at encapsulating this total human experience into a comprehensive, unified model is analogous to seven blind people trying to describe a large elephant. In this ancient parody of our limited capacity to experience and understand our world, seven blind people were asked to describe an elephant. Each person was brought to a different part of the elephant and given 10 min to experience the elephant. After the 10-min inspection, each was asked to answer the question, "What is an elephant?" The individual in the very front said that an elephant was "long, round, and curled up and down like a fire hose twisting under the pressure of water." The two standing beside each ear said that an elephant was "soft and flat like a huge pancake flapping in the wind." Those standing on either side said that an elephant was "hard, firm, and flat like a rough stuccoed wall." The person standing by the elephant's leg said that an elephant was "vertical, firm, and round with skin like the rough bark of a tree." The poor individual in back inspected the tail and proclaimed the elephant to be in the "snake family."

Each blind person was right, but yet so wrong in an attempt to characterize the total elephant. Most of our theories of personality and human behavior are correct within the limits of their narrow perspective, but they all fail to encompass the totality of the human experience. The A-B-C model presented in this book attempts to integrate as many pieces of the human experience as possible, but does not pretend to offer the definitive statement on what it means to be human.

This microperspective of seven blind people each trying to describe an elephant is analogous to most of our extant models of human behavior and personality. All models or theories emphasize certain variables or constructs (e.g., cognitive, operant or respondent behaviors, affective, social/environmental), and researchers draw on certain populations to establish, validate, and apply their theories. Empirical evidence supports some theories more than others. But regardless of their cogency, the parameters of their consideration are narrow, encompassing only a part of the human experience. The ABC model attempts to integrate many of the most empirically supported parts into a whole. Rather than describing the elephant from the perspective of a single part, this book attempts to understand the entire elephant as an integrated whole.

Intuitively, we know that we think, feel, act, maintain our physiology, engage others, and sustain a spiritual life. These are ingredients of our human experience. No one ingredient can exist without some reciprocal influence from each of the others. The essence of any experience, and thus our understanding of that experience, is the interaction of our thoughts, emotions, physiology, and behavior within the context of our social and physical environment. We can no more understand the human experience by isolating a single ingredient than we can understand and appreciate an elephant by describing its leg, ear, or tail. Yet many of our theories of personality and human behavior attempt to describe and explain the human experience in just such a microscopic manner. Not surprisingly, these elemental models have failed to effectively describe, explain, or ultimately control what we know to be the human experience. Only when we attempt to integrate all of the parts can we expect to understand and appreciate what it means to be human. This book offers such an integration: the A-B-C model. In humans, as in elephants, the whole is greater than the sum of its parts.

Although each part (cognitive, emotional, etc.) influences all of the others, my own bias and study of the literature leads me to emphasize certain elements. For example, I give greater importance to the cognitive component of the A-B-C model, but only in emphasis, never losing sight of the totality. Without all of the components of the A-B-C model working synchronously, an understanding of human functioning is impaired.

Synchronization and interdependence have become the *zeitgeist* of contemporary behavioral sciences. The A-B-C model characterizes a system in that it is composed of interdependent parts that consume resources (input) to create action/behavior (process) to produce consequences (output). With the advent of a systems perspective in studying (and changing) individual and social behavior, attempts have been made to integrate mind/body/environment. From the earliest pronouncements of Plato that the mind and body were entirely separate through Descartes' belief in mind/body dualism, the unity of the mind/body/environment system has gradually evolved.

The work of Prigogine (1984), Pert (1987), Churchman (1979), and Hanson (1995) has given strong credence to this systems approach. Evolving interests in psychoneuroimmunology and family systems theory are just two prominent examples of this integrative effort. As with each of these evolving (and embryonic) systems, the observations, judgments, and conclusions must remain tentative. By their very nature, holistic, integrative models take speculative leaps as they try to describe, explain, and predict complex interrelationships among many variables. The task is formidable and never conclusive, yet it is critical to our understanding of ourselves within our environmental systems.

In studying the manner in which each of these ABC components influences each other or how each component functions in relation to the other components, these models have all stressed a functional behavioral analysis (FBA) as their assessment tool. The FBA is simply another way of saying that we are looking at the A-B-C's of our experience. Where I diverge somewhat from previous presentations of the A-B-C model is in my composition and complexity. Many A-B-C models either view the behavior component strictly as operant behavior (Churchman, 1979; Hanson, 1995; Pert, 1987; Prigogine, 1984) or, in one approach (Ellis, 1984), view the B component as self-talk and cognitive in nature.

The integrative models offered by Cormier and Cormier (1991) and Hutchins and Cole (1992) are cogent efforts to integrate environment/mind/body/behavior. These models attempt to describe the interrelationship and covariation between environmental conditions, behavior, and consequences (Cormier & Cormier, 1991; Goldiamond, 1965; Hutchins & Cole, 1992; Mischel, 1971; O'Leary & Wilson, 1975). In the spirit of this integrative rapprochement, Albert Ellis (1993) added the word "behavior" to his rational-emotive approach to therapy to emphasize the reciprocal relationship between thought, action, and emotion.

Likewise, I have drawn from these models and used them as points of departure from the A-B-C model presented in this book. This integration is a daunting task that, far from being the definitive effort, serves as a slightly wider lens in our evolutionary struggle to make sense of the human experience.

Even with the goal of inclusion in building a comprehensive structure such as the A-B-C model, the effort cannot avoid exclusion and deemphasis. Certain cognitive and/or behavioral positions espoused by Skinner, Rogers, Ellis, Bandura, and others are explicitly addressed in the model, whereas other theoretical positions (e.g., Adler, Glasser, Perls) are only implicitly acknowledged. Still other theories seem to be totally excluded, although laudable efforts have been made (e.g., Wachtel, 1977) to encompass their basic tenets within a cognitive–behavioral framework.

An additional choice of omission in presenting this A-B-C model is in the area of severe psychopathology and organic dysfunction. The A-B-C model posits dysfunction as comprising extremes along a continuum of learning or as qualitatively unique pathology. Disorders such as irrational beliefs (à la Ellis) and learned helplessness (à la Seligman) are extreme forms of learned behavior that can readily be explained within an A-B-C framework, but psychoses and cognitive–physical dysfunction caused by organic anomalies (e.g., injury, disease, substance abuse, fetal alcohol syndrome) represent a qualitatively different dimension. This latter category of pathology is certainly acknowledged and addressed in this book (especially where psychosomatic disorder is addressed in Chapter 5 and organically impaired cognition is discussed in Chapter 6), although the primary focus of my description and application of the A-B-C model is based on normal behavior. A secondary focus of this model will be on problems of learning and living that are typical of the human experience.

## Orientation of the Model

**W**henever an attempt is made to understand the human experience, certain assumptions need to be explicated about the approach taken. Any theory must make choices about the perspective followed in viewing people in their many environments. The following represent some of the ways (and thus choices) I could have constructed my understanding about what it means to be human:

**1.** I might choose to view the individual as separate, autonomous, and independent of social or environmental influences. This orientation of studying the individual as the fundamental unit of analysis assumes that intrapsychic dynamics, predominantly genetic in nature, operate to create our personality style or characteristics. The traditional psychodynamic model of Sigmund Freud would characterize this individual personality theory in explaining the human experience. This model posits that personality is an innate developmental unfolding that can result in mental health or mental illness, the latter condition caused by faulty development and residing within the individual as neurotic or psychotic psychopathology. I choose not to adopt this orientation.

**2.** If I concluded that the individual can only be studied and understood within the context of his or her environment, I am applying a cybernetic cast to my theory. A first-order cybernetic model of the human experience tries to explain how the person and external environment interact to influence each other. These therapeutic models (Bowen, 1978; Fish, Weakland, & Segal, 1982; Satir, 1972) shift the focus of study from the psychodynamics of the individual to the patterns of interaction between people within their many external environments. The flow of information (i.e., feedback) that serves as the precursor and consequence of our interactions with others provides the framework for the "person in context" unit of study, a framework referred to as a *system* (Watzlawick, 1990).

From this cybernetic or systems perspective, people are now understood only within the context of their specific external environment. Reality for these people now draws its source from the information that the individuals receive (and perceive) from the external environment. In other words, there is a true reality that exists within each of our many external environments, waiting to be discovered and acted on by us. Problems, mental illness, or dysfunction now results from faulty systems (e.g., "The family is all screwed up.") that have created the conditions for the individual's failure or unhappiness.

The A-B-C model views the human experience from an integrative, systemic perspective, emphasizing the cybernetic characteristics of a fluid, dynamic, individual–external environment interaction. Where the A-B-C model departs from a first-order cybernetic theory is in the actual construction of reality. This shift in the construction of reality requires me to consider a third approach to understanding the human experience: the constructivist approach.

**3.** A postmodern (Gergen, 1991; Hoffman, 1993; Von Glassersfeld, 1984) approach to the human experience proposes that we each construct our own reality through our use of symbols and language. The representations and linguistic structures provided by our language actually frame the meaning and substance of our reality. Using our cognitive structures and processes, we construct representational categories (schemata) in our brain that give meaning and purpose to our experience. We then use these schemata for knowing and understanding our ongoing experiences, thus continually creating new and more complex schemata to understand and interact with the world. Through constant interaction with our many external environments, we construct the covert world (i.e., attributions, expectations, stories, etc.) that define our reality.

The theoretical framework in which I have constructed my A-B-C model is very consistent with this constructivist orientation to the nature of reality. As you will see, although the components of the A-B-C model differ in their source, they converge in our covert representation of our reality as we continually construct the A-B-C's of our experience.

## Organization of the Book

This book is divided into twelve chapters that present a thorough exposition of the A-B-C model. Each chapter will address a different component of the A-B-C model. The greatest challenge in writing this text was in presenting an integrative, holistic, and synergistic model within the linear, reductionist structure imposed by any written text. While the single visual gestalt of Figure 1: The A-B-C Model illustrates the interrelationship of the various components of the model, the cogent, lucid explanation of each component requires a sequential presentation. Consequently, I chose to present the components of the A-B-C's in the order in which I have used the model for diagnostic purposes. After a general introduction and orientation to the A-B-C model in Chapter 1, I present the most salient aspect of our A-B-C's in Chapter 2: Our Operant Behavior. In Chapters 3 and 4 I move to an investigation of the consequences of our behavior, with particular emphasis on the contingency relationship of our actions (and inaction) to our external environment. It is from this behavior-consequence interaction that we begin to see the synergistic nature of the A-B-C model. Chapter 3 looks at those *desirable* consequences that motivate us to action while Chapter 4 presents those *undesirable* consequences that cause us so much pain, grief, and disappointment. The environmental context of our thoughts, feelings, and actions is explored in Chapter 5: Antecedents. As the antecedent factors are considered within the dynamic of our behavior and its consequences we come to appreciate the influence of our physical and social environment upon every aspect of our being. This complex world of people, places, sounds, colors, textures, images, smells, sensations, and temperatures forms the context of our life, and as antecedents, informs our behavior and the consequences that result.

As important as our purposeful actions (i.e., operant behavior) are to our human experience, we are biological beings and could not exist without a physiology that is generally involuntary. Rather than attempt to encompass all of human biology as it relates to the A-B-C model, I have narrowed the focus of my discussion to respondents and our autonomic nervous system. Thus, Chapter 6 provides an overview of our autonomic nervous system and its relationship to our thoughts, actions, and external environment. With the inclusion of our central nervous system in our understanding of the A-B-C's, we will shift our attention to covert behavior and devote the remaining chapters, 7–12, to cognition and the covert world that exists in our head. It is within this covert world that all of our A-B-C's finally come together to form our experience of understanding and purpose. The covert component of the A-B-C model serves as the point of convergence for all that we know, experience, and remember about our A-B-C's. Within the subjective, cognitive realities of our thought we give form and meaning to our antecedents, behavior and consequences. Thus, in Chapters 7–12 we can begin to understand and appreciate the integrative quality of the A-B-C model. Because of the superordinate position of thought (i.e., our covert behavior) in influencing every other component of the A-B-C model, it was pedagogically and experientially appropriate that I address cognition last. Correspondingly, the mechanisms with which we process, understand, plan, and execute our actions (based on the A-B-C's of our mind) are extraordinarily complex and warrant extensive explanation.

Consequently, I devote the entire second half of this book to the cognitive aspect of the cognitive-behavioral model. After an introduction to the nature of thought and cognition in Chapter 7, I move to a discussion of innate covert structures and processes in Chapter 8. These basic mechanisms that prescribe *how* we think provide the framework for studying the context (or *what*) of our thinking in Chapter 9. In Chapter 10 I explore those aspects of our A-B-C's that we personalize as characterizing *us*. This universe of covert a-b-c's that we associate with *us* provides our personal identity and ultimately our concept of *self*. The mechanisms through which we place value and render judgements about this self (or our many selves) direct our attention in Chapter 11. The ultimate integration and yet most intimate experience of our A-B-C's occurs with our experiences of emotion. Thus, the inclusion of emotion into the model provides a natural culmination to my presentation of the A-B-C's of our experience. It illustrates the essential quality of the A-B-C model: placing the most personal and idiosyncratic nature of our own reality within a holistic, universal framework of understanding.

Although I have tried to present this model in a clear, cogent manner, the use of technical terms, jargon, and nomenclature is unavoidable. I have designed the text to be user-friendly by employing many practical examples, cartoons illustrating many of the concepts, and a summary highlighting the major points of each chapter. I have also tried to maintain a relaxed, casual, almost conversational writing style.

One additional comment needs to be directed to readers in the helping professions and anyone else interested in the clinical implications and applications of the A-B-C model. I have used common, everyday descriptions, examples, and cartoons in presenting the theory and minimized clinical/therapeutic references, descriptions, and illustrations. This is based on my firm belief that the principles and dynamics drawn from the A-B-C model must apply to all of us if they truly have validity and utility. I strongly believe that the more personal we look, the more universal we find.

If the principles don't apply equally at the local mall, a classroom, your family room, and a counselor's office, then I question their validity. Thus, the more personal I can make my presentation of the model, and the more personalized you can apply it to yourself, the easier it is to understand and appreciate what the model offers you. And ultimately, the easier and more natural it will be for you to apply it to purposeful change. The clinical applications of the A-B-C model are the focus of the companion text which is now in preparation.

Finally, a word about the cartoons. As an inveterate visual processor and learner, I am constantly using pictures to make sense of the world. The left hemisphere of my brain has been in hiding for years. Consequently, I firmly believe that a picture does say 1000 words, and a cartoon can illustrate a principle of behavior better than any words I could use. So, I have employed lots of cartoons to illustrate many of the concepts, principles, and strategies presented in this book. I have captioned the cartoons with the basic messages within the text and often refer to them in the text. Beyond a good hearty laugh, I hope that these cartoons illuminate the essential meanings for you as they do for me.

**Figure 1** *The A-B-C (Cognitive–Behavioral) Model*

| (A) Antecedent | | (B) Behavior | | (C) Consequence |
|---|---|---|---|---|
| | **Covert** | **Overt** | **Overt** | |
| | **Cognitive (Thinking)** | **Respondent (Physical)** | **Operant (Acting)** | |
| Stimulus or setting event. External environments that set the occasion for behavior (thinking, acting, feeling) to occur.<br><br>$S^{Dee}$ = Green light. A cue that a particular behavior will result in a desirable consequence.<br><br>$S^{Delta}$ = Red light. A cue that a particular behavior will result in an undesirable consequence. | Subjective environment. The process and content of our thinking. Our interpretation of A-B-C as a-b-c.<br><br>Includes:<br>Attributions<br>Expectations<br>Self-concept<br>Self-esteem<br>Beliefs<br>Attitudes<br>Prejudices<br>Self-talk<br>Locus of control<br>Images<br>Fantasies<br>Intrinsic consequences | Reflexive<br>Autonomic<br>Involuntary<br>Biochemical<br>Physiological changes occurring within our body. | Voluntary behavior that we choose to do or not to do.<br><br>Can be: Excess = Behavior done too often or at wrong time.<br><br>Deficit = Behavior done too infrequently or not when needed. | Events (external) that occur during and/or after a particular covert and/or operant behavior. Events can be:<br><br>A. Desirable:<br><br>1. Positive Reinforcement present desirable = C+<br><br>2. Negative Reinforcement remove undesirable = C̶−̶<br><br>B. Undesirable:<br><br>1. Punishment present undesirable, aversive = C−<br><br>2. Extinction remove desirable = C̶+̶ |

**Emotions**

Subjective labels used to describe a specific state of being. Labels reflect the composite of our covert, respondent, and operant behavior within a specific context of antecedents and consequences.

# Chapter 2

~~~~~~~~~~~~~~

# Operant
# Behavior

~~~~~~~~~~~~~~

## Orienting Ourselves

**B**ehavior, or the act of doing some action, represents four interdependent components within our A-B-C model: mind, body, action, and emotion. These components of the model are shown in Figure 2.

In this chapter, we will look at just one of the categories of behavior, action/operant
behavior, as the place to begin our journey through the A-B-C model. Subsequent chapters will direct us through the consequence, antecedent, covert/mind component and
culminate with the respondent/physiological aspects of our experience. But for now, let
us look at overt/operant behavior, the behavior of purposeful action. (See Figure 3.)

## Why Start with Overt Behavior?

**T**he four parts of the behavior, or B, component of the model are: (a) thinking behavior, or cognition; (b) operant behavior, or acting behavior that is voluntary;
(c) physiological and biochemical responses that are generally involuntary; and (d)
emotions, or the feelings and affect experienced in a behavioral episode. Which of
these four parts draws our initial focus depends on the part of most immediate concern. Often, the person begins the analysis with a feeling word in the form of an adjec-
tive that labels the emotion experienced in the situation. One characterizes oneself as
anxious, depressed, scared, angry, confused, jealous, or any of the array of emotional
labels that we have learned to associate with the human experience. As important as
the emotional labels are, they can only be understood within the context of the entire
A-B-C model. But where do we begin?

In the many instances that I have done A-B-C analyses or have presented the
model to students, teachers, counselees, parents, and others over the years, I have
started at various points in the model. Sometimes I start with the A component and
identify the external environment or antecedent stimuli that seem to set the stage for
behavior. I typically start here when it is easiest for the person to identify where and
when a particular situation occurs. This is often a difficult starting place, however,

**Figure 2** *Behavior*

| (B) Behavior | | |
| --- | --- | --- |
| **Covert** | **Overt** | **Overt** |
| **Cognitive (Thinking)** | **Respondent (Physical)** | **Operant (Acting)** |
| Subjective environment. The process and content of our thinking. Our interpretation of A-B-C as a-b-c. | Reflexive<br>Autonomic<br>Involuntary<br>Biochemical<br>Physiological changes occurring within our body. | Voluntary behavior that we choose to do or not to do.<br>Can be: Excess = Behavior done too often or at wrong time.<br>Deficit = Behavior done too infrequently or not when needed. |
| Includes: Attributions<br>Expectations<br>Self-concept<br>Self-esteem<br>Beliefs<br>Attitudes<br>Prejudices<br>Self-talk<br>Locus of control<br>Images<br>Fantasies<br>Intrinsic consequences | | |

TECHNICAL COLLEGE OF THE LOWCOUNTRY
LEARNING RESOURCES CENTER
POST OFFICE BOX 1288
BEAUFORT, SOUTH CAROLINA 29901-1288

**Figure 3** *Operant Behavior*

| Overt |
| --- |
| **Operant (Acting)** |
| Voluntary behavior that we choose to do or not to do. |
| Can be: Excess = Behavior done too often or at wrong time. |
| Deficit = Behavior done too infrequently or not when needed. |

because we are so preoccupied with our thoughts and actions that we are oblivious to the external environment. Viewed chronologically, the A component does occur first in a behavioral episode or chain of behaviors, and it seems logical to start there (i.e., A—B—C), but I have found that the component that we are most aware of and that we have the easiest access to is the B component, our behavior.

On occasion, the consequences of behavior can be so significant or traumatic that I initiate my analysis with the C component. Consequences that elicit strong emotions like joy, pain, fear, anger, and so forth are keenly experienced and need to be addressed first. As quickly as possible, I connect those consequences to the thinking, feeling, and acting behavior (B component) associated with and contributing to them.

Rarely do individuals begin an A-B-C analysis by talking about their thinking or cognition during an experience. They seldom say, "And here's what I was thinking about when," and then describe the episode. Much more of their awareness and memory of the experience are on other parts and components of the A-B-C's. As important as our thinking or cognition is in any particular experience, it often gets lost as quickly as the situation changes. Consequently, the thinking part is not the best starting place in an A-B-C analysis.

Unless experiencing a severe physiological response to a situation, people do not typically start an A-B-C analysis with a description of their physical state. However, people experiencing pain, injury, and psychosomatic and stress-related physical disorders may want to begin by describing symptoms. In such instances, this is an excellent place to begin. Over the course of hundreds of A-B-C analyses, I have found it easiest to begin with a thorough description of the overt acting (what I call operant) behavior. This describes what the person does and, consequently, is easiest to observe, characterize, and validate. And so we will start our study by looking at operant behavior.

## Operant Behavior Defined

As you can see from Figure 3, operant behavior represents all those behaviors that we choose to do. We choose to do them because we hope (or we have learned to expect) that they will produce a desirable consequence or effect on the environment. By doing operants, we operate on our environment with purpose and objectives. Whenever we create a thought or perform some action to create a consequence (some desirable effect), we are doing an operant behavior. We choose to do operants because of the effect that we hope they will have.

Since operants are voluntary, or at least we exercise choice in doing them, they are typically controlled by our skeletal, or voluntary, muscles. A basic characteristic of operant behavior is that it can be observed (and thus validated) by others and be objectively measured in some way. Because we actually do operant behavior, we (and others) can observe it happening, and we can measure the extent to which it occurs. When we describe behavior strength later in this chapter, we will look at the variety of approaches for measuring and quantifying behavior. For now, it is helpful to know that we can measure operant behavior by counting its frequency, recording how long it is done, or observing its intensity. Of course, we can also measure the consequence, product, or effect of doing any operant behavior.

Thus, operant behaviors have three basic characteristics: (a) they are voluntary, (b) they are performed to bring about certain consequences, and (c) they can be observed and measured or quantified.

A fourth characteristic of operants needs to be mentioned here. Since operants are performed to create desired consequences and since consequences typically occur only when we actually do the operant behavior that precedes the consequences, we say that a *contingency relationship* exists between the operant behavior and its achieved consequence. A contingency relationship is an if–then relationship. If the operant behavior is performed, then the consequence results.

This contingency relationship between behavior and consequence implies cause and effect. And in most cases, there is a cause-and-effect relationship between the behavior and the consequence that follows. We learn not to do the operant unless there is a high probability of getting the desired consequence. Conversely, the consequence has a slim chance of occurring unless the operant behavior has occurred. We only raise our hand in class when there is a good chance of being called on (and if we know the answer and want the teacher to recognize our brilliance). The consequence of a great bargain prompts our operants of shopping, but the probability of an undesirable consequence (theft and/or physical injury) is enough to deter us from shopping in a dark, unknown, and crime-ridden part of town. The contingency is clear, and one action increases the probability of the other. The actual contingency between an operant and a consequence is based on probability and is stored in our covert behavior, which we will discuss later.

Fortunately, most of our actions throughout the day are operants. We set the alarm to wake up on time, execute a whole series of operants in the kitchen to enjoy breakfast (as well as meet the physiological need of low blood sugar created during the night), quickly take the trash out as we hear the truck ambling toward us, perhaps kiss the family (lots of consequences there), stop for gas as the needle hovers near E, lock the car door, leave the report on the boss' desk, and proceed with the multitude of operants that we hope will get us through the day successfully.

The more successful we are with our operants, the more frequently we choose to do them. Many of our operants were learned long ago, perhaps as children, when we tried out a behavior (our early attempts at risk taking) and it resulted in something that we really wanted. Or we played a little safer, watched others try a behavior, and observed

**For Better or For Worse®**                              **by Lynn Johnston**

We begin doing operant behaviors practically at birth. (© 1991 Lynn Johnston Productions Inc./ Distributed by Universal Press Syndicate, Inc.)

what the consequences were for them. If they got the consequences that we might have wanted for ourselves, we were more inclined to try the behavior ourselves. This learning of behavior and its consequences through observation has been referred to as vicarious learning (Bandura, Ross & Ross, 1963). Much of our operant behavior has been acquired not through the pain of trial and error, but rather by watching the behavioral contingencies that others experience. We observe a sibling or classmate play hooky, get caught and be severely punished, so we decide that that operant is not for us. On the other hand, when a sibling earns an "A" on a report card and receives lots of praise and special treatment, we decide that those operants—hopefully study, class participation, and lots of hard work—are ones that we want to adopt for ourselves. Whether by direct experience or by observing others (i.e., vicarious learning) we learn contingencies and then choose to perform those operants that have shown to have the contingencies that are in our best interest. Successful operants become permanent fixtures within our repertoire; they become habitual and almost impervious to change.

The notion of knowing contingencies and then exercising choices that will provide us with the best possible consequences is critical to effective coping and self-management, which will be addressed extensively in this book.

Operant behaviors begin to enter our repertoire of learned behavior practically at birth. To meet its basic physiological needs (i.e., those needs for survival that we call *primary positive reinforcement*), the neonate will grasp, suck, phonate, and selectively attend to stimuli to be fed, touched, and cared for. These operants are biologically programmed into the infant's earliest repertoire (i.e., pool of choices) of behavior, but they are continuously refined and developed through direct and vicarious learning.

### Operants and Respondents

Before proceeding further in our discussion of operant behavior, it is important to distinguish operant behavior from respondent behavior. Although both operants and respondents are overt and can be observed and measured, respondent behavior is involuntary and reflexive. Where operants are emitted (i.e., performed) to achieve specific consequences, respondents are elicited (i.e., stimulated or provoked) by stimuli that directly precede them.

The word *respondent* refers to the fact that these are behaviors that occur in response to specific antecedent events (or stimuli). We do not choose to do respondents as we might choose to do an operant to achieve some consequence. Instead, respondents automatically occur following the presence of very specific stimuli. Smoke causes our eyes to water, coldness stimulates a pyliolithic erection (i.e., goose bumps), a loud noise stimulates a startle response in infants, coffee stimulates certain parts of the central nervous system, and in a broader and more pervasive demonstration, certain foods and environmental toxins provoke severe allergic respondents. Respondents are autonomic, involuntary, and represent the action of our autonomic nervous system and those organs controlled by our visceral muscles. We will discuss these respondent physiological and biochemical behaviors in much more depth when we address the physical component of our A-B-C model.

Of immediate relevance to our discussion of the developmental nature of operants is that our largest repertoire of behaviors as infants falls under the category of respondents. We are born with a multitude of reflexes (e.g., Babinski's, tonic neck, patellar, etc.) and our autonomic nervous system that eludes our control but enhances our chances for survival. Over the course of maturation, many of those early reflexes are genetically programmed out of our array of responses and are replaced by operant behaviors (e.g., asking for milk or simply getting it ourselves) that are better suited to our development in a complex world.

### Building a Repertoire of Operants

Each of us possesses an ever changing and constantly increasing repertoire of operant behaviors that serves our needs. Our repertoire of operant behaviors—broad or narrow, complex or simple, effective or ineffective—represents our range of choices for meeting needs and responding to the world. The larger the pool, the broader the range of operants we possess, the more choices we have, and the more opportunities to experience success.

The scope and complexity of our operant behaviors are based on a multitude of factors: innate intelligence, capacity to learn, enrichment of the environment in which we grew up, acceptance and support of our social (predominately family) environment for risk taking and experimentation, and our physical makeup. A sterile, punitive environment inhibits the learning of operant behaviors, whereas a flexible, stimulating, and accepting environment nurtures the broadest array of operant behaviors.

If we define freedom as the opportunity to choose what to do among the greatest number of alternatives, then the greater our repertoire of operant behaviors, the greater our freedom. I often find that troubled or dysfunctional people have much too narrow a repertoire of operant behaviors for their environment. They lack the behavior choices necessary to obtain the consequences they desire.

## Covert Operants

**O**perant behaviors are very deliberate actions taken on our environment. Consequently, many of our operants represent conscious (covert behavior) choices that are the product of deliberate mental activity. Throughout this book, my use of the term *conscious* refers to covert behavior that is deliberate and exists within our awareness. As I watch TV, I may be conscious of a character's dress or the lousy reception. when the telephone rings, I am conscious that I better pick it up by the third ring or my answering machine takes over. I am conscious of my speed when a police car enters my rear view mirror.

Most of our conscious thoughts (covert behavior) instruct the appropriateness of an operant. The covert behavior, "Uh-oh! A cop! Better slow down!" instructs me to do the operant behavior of slamming my foot on the brake pedal. Thus, the operant behavior is a deliberate, voluntary action based on choices generated within the conscious awareness (covert behavior).

Fortunately, many of our covert and/or overt behaviors are not conscious, but are instead unconscious, or what Bandura (1969) has termed *automatic*. They are automatic behaviors in that they are habitual actions that we have learned, usually through repetition, without having to think about them. These habits, rituals, and routines were once performed consciously, but have become automatic over time enabling us to respond efficiently and spontaneously in most usual situations. Novel, complex, or threatening situations do, however, prompt us to rely upon conscious covert and/or operant behavior.

## Learning Operants: Directly and Indirectly

### Experiential Learning: We Know What We Experience

Most of our operant behaviors were learned either directly or vicariously. Direct learning experiences occurred in one of two ways. The first, and often most painful, way was through a trial-and-error process in which we tried out a behavior, experienced the consequences, and learned the contingency (A-B-C relationship). Sometimes this learning was harsh and left considerable scar tissue in the form of pain, regret, fear, and anger in its wake. When we were lucky enough to have a nurturing environment, we learned through a controlled progression of successful experiences. The contingencies for positive consequences and success were programmed for us by others. We will talk a lot about this process of purposeful learning through success later in the book.

Learning operant behavior through actual experiences and receiving its various consequences are the quickest and most enduring ways to acquire a repertoire of behavior. The principle of "learning by doing" has been empirically validated consistently since first applied by John Dewey as the foundation of education. The strength, endurance, and speed of learning are a direct function of the contingency that we actually experience. The A-B-C's that I directly experience are what I know of my past, present, and future. If my assertive, risk-taking behavior brings me power, control, and the consequences I desire, I will perform those behaviors consistently. Conversely, if I am ignored or experience pain as a consequence of asserting myself, I will cease my risk taking fairly rapidly.

### Observational Learning: We Learn from the Success and Failure of Others

Operants not learned experientially were probably learned vicariously. In this process, often referred to as *observational learning,* we learned what operant to do (or not to do) by observing others experience the contingency. Through watching others, we learned not only the A (when and where) and the B (how to perform the behavior), but also whether we wanted to execute the behavior depending on the C (consequences experienced by the model performing the behavior). In observational learning, we see the A-B-C contingency being experienced by others, and then we store this memory within our covert repertoire of behavioral expectations. If we desire the contingency for ourselves, we may execute this behavior when the antecedent signals the appropriate time and place. Observational learning can also teach us not to do certain behaviors when we witness an undesirable contingency.

Although not as powerful as experiential learning, many of our operant and covert behaviors are acquired and maintained in the safety of observational learning. The power and pervasive influence of observational learning are evident in the effect that television, movies, and literature maintain on the scenarios we choose for ourselves. Children and adolescents consumed by their acquisition of new behavior choices are most vulnerable to the vicissitudes of observational learning.

### Vicarious Learning: Choosing As an Act of Trust

A more indirect form of vicarious learning occurs when the model/teacher simply tells us about the behavior and its contingency without actually performing it, leaving us with the information necessary to execute the behavior. This process of vicarious learning, while certainly less risky, is much slower and fraught with errors.

Rules, regulations, sanctions, and instructions represent the broad category of messages we receive from others (external environment) conveying the enforcement of specific contingencies. Driving faster than the posted speed limit may result in a speeding ticket; prompt payment of your taxes will result in an early refund; cigarette smoking will cause serious illness; the early bird catches the worm; Mr. Todd, the algebra teacher, issues a detention slip to anyone late for class. The validity of these caveats may range from absolute to nonexistent. The accuracy and value of their message reflect the reliability of their source and the degree to which we are willing to exercise our trust (and risk) in their professed contingency. Without directly experiencing or observing the A-B-C's of these contingencies, their compliance becomes an act of faith or an exercise in creative risk taking. In either case, the instructive value of vicarious (indirect) learning is tenuous and of dubious help in acquiring a reliable cadre of effective operant behavior.

Although experiential learning wields the strongest influence, observational learning offers advantages of safety and efficiency. The safety comes from choosing a known contingency, and the efficiency derives from the plethora of models (video, audio, written, live—parents, teachers, peers) available to show us the A-B-C's of an experience before we make our choices.

In summary, a primary advantage of observational learning is the opportunity to observe the behavior being performed properly (without the negative consequences for poor performance) and the chance to master the behavior before we might be required to perform it. Effective problem solving, coping, and assertive behaviors are some categories of operant behavior that are best learned before we actually use them. Observational learning is the most efficient and painless method of acquiring this repertoire of operants.

Many operant behaviors exist in our repertoire that are seldom actually performed. Some behaviors (e.g., splicing a wire, caulking a window, resolving a social conflict, or solving a problem creatively) may infrequently occur simply because the opportunity (the antecedent in our model) seldom arises. These operants may quickly fade from memory or may remain extant indefinitely. The longevity of our operant behavior depends on the conditions (or intensity) under which it was learned as well as the nature of the reinforcement contingencies that exist when the behavior does occur. The frequency of positive consequences has a significant influence on the retention of our operant behavior. We will discuss the influence of schedules of reinforcement on behavior when we address the consequence component of our A-B-C model.

### Operants: To Do or Not to Do

Just because we do not perform a behavior does not mean that it is not in our repertoire or that we cannot do it. We can know what to do and how to do many behaviors that we do not perform for a variety of reasons. Most of those reasons revolve around our discrimination of the stimulus condition (i.e., antecedent) surrounding those behaviors as well as the consequences that we anticipate (i.e., covert expectations) for performing the behaviors. In these instances, we can increase the occurrences of a desired behavior by altering those antecedents and related consequences.

Conversely, we may never perform a behavior because we are incapable. This failure of commission may be due to never having learned how to do the behavior or to physical incapability. Thus, the antecedent and consequence conditions are irrelevant. We cannot do this behavior under any circumstances. I cannot play a piano, speak Portuguese, repair a broken water pipe, perform heart surgery, or throw a baseball 90 mph. People who lack the physical capability to perform certain behaviors probably never availed themselves of the opportunity to learn.

For whatever reason, I cannot do certain things now, and changing the antecedents and consequences will not help very much. In fact, setting up reinforcement contingencies for doing them will probably only frustrate me. In such instances, where the behaviors are not in our repertoire, the process of change must begin with learning the behavior or accepting our physical limitations. If a new behavior is within my physical capability but has never been learned, the same principles that apply to behavior change will apply to the building of that new operant.

## Behavior Strength

One important dimension of looking at the various operant behaviors in our repertoire pertains to the particular strength of each behavior. This is the probability of a behavior occurring at a particular time. Some of our operants (e.g., talking, chewing gum, eating, etc.) might be strong most of our waking hours, but others (e.g., cursing, eating dessert, etc.) might be weak most of the time and strong only in rare instances. How can we assess the strength of a behavior? Let's take a look.

Behavior strength can be described and measured in three ways: (a) frequency, (b) duration, and (c) intensity. Some behaviors can accurately be measured in all three ways, but the characteristics of most behaviors lend themselves to one measurement approach. Here is an outline of each approach.

*Frequency of Behavior* The frequency of a behavior is the number of times that the behavior occurs over a specified period of time. Frequency strength can be assessed simply by counting each occurrence. For counting to be accurate, however, each occurrence must have a clear, distinct beginning and end, and the duration of each behavior occurrence should be about the same. Here are some examples of behaviors whose strength can best be measured by a frequency count and a comparison list of those not suitable to counting as the measure of strength:

| A. *Good Examples of Frequency* | B. *Poor Examples of Frequency* |
| --- | --- |
| Miles walked | Telephone talking |
| Pages written | Daydreaming |
| Bills paid | Social conversation |
| Angry comments | Hanging out with kids |
| Drinks consumed | Shopping |
| Compliments given | Attending meetings |
| Cigarettes smoked | Sleeping |

Notice that all of the behaviors in column A have a distinct beginning and end, are fairly similar in the time required to do each one on different occasions, and can be easily counted. Also, the aggregate count of each behavior will accurately reflect any increase or decrease over time. If I paid one compliment yesterday and seven today, I have increased the strength of that behavior.

**Duration of Behavior** Behaviors that vary a lot in the amount of time devoted to doing them are best reflected by duration strength. Notice the behaviors in column B. For each behavior, it is the time devoted to doing them that best measures their strength. Frequency tells us nothing about their strength. If I talked on the telephone once yesterday and five times today, has the strength of that behavior increased? Suppose I told you that yesterday's telephone conversation lasted for 3 h, while each conversation today lasted about 1 min. Yes, the duration of this behavior better reflects its strength, as with each behavior in column B.

**Intensity** A third and much more subjective way of describing the strength of a behavior is in its intensity. I typically equate intensity with the degree of affect, emotion, and energy accompanying a behavior. This level of enthusiasm or emotion with which the behavior is performed is very difficult to quantify; yet, it may be the best reflection of a behavior's strength. In social interaction, recreational activity, general demeanor in work and play, or wherever emotional involvement is valued, the intensity of the behavior is an important measure of its strength. I can hang out and be present with my kids, or I can really hang out and be emotionally involved with them. The duration and frequency of this behavior pale to its intensity.

Assessing the strength of a behavior is an important part of operationally defining behavior when we put the A-B-C's together. The process of integrating all of the components and parts of the A-B-C model into a complete diagnostic picture is referred to as a functional behavioral analysis (FBA). We are, in fact, doing an FBA whenever we systematically gather data about our A-B-C's.

## Problem Operants: Behaviors of Real Concern

**B**efore leaving our discussion of operant behavior, we need to introduce the topic of problem behavior. Much of our unhappiness, dysfunction, failure, pain, and dissatisfaction in life centers on operant behaviors that do not work. All of the operants (both covert/thinking and overt/acting) that get in our way and prevent us from experiencing happiness and success are behaviors of real concern, or BORCs, because that is exactly what they mean to us. Each BORC that we do (or fail to do) poses a problem or concern. It can be behavior that we do too much or at the wrong time or place (e.g., smoking, eating, fighting, ruminating, catastrophizing) or it can be behavior that we do not do enough or at the right time or place (e.g., paying bills, asserting oneself, generating positive covert self-references, setting the alarm clock). In the former case, we are concerned about excessive behaviors, or what we call *excess BORCs*; in the latter case, the problem revolves around deficits in our behavior, a class of low-frequency behaviors that we call *deficit BORCs*. *Excess BORCs* get us in trouble because we do them too frequently or at the wrong time and place. Thus they are problematic acts of commission. In contrast, *deficit BORCs* are operants that we fail to do when called upon, and thus are acts of omission. Whether *excess* or *deficit*, however, the defining characteristic is that it causes us to experience undesirable consequences. Let us explore this further.

Whether the locus of concern centers on excess BORCs, on deficit BORCs, or on both types occurring simultaneously, what makes these operants a concern—what makes them truly BORCs—are the consequences that follow. The consequences of BORCs are unpleasant, aversive, or even painful, and essentially undesirable. These unpleasant consequences may immediately follow those behaviors, or they may occur long after the BORC has occurred. Procrastination (e.g., watching TV) is usually a BORC even though the immediate consequence is desirable. In fact, we usually procrastinate because the immediate consequence is desirable. It is the long-term consequence of procrastination that causes problems for us and thus causes procrastination to become a BORC. The more undesirable these consequences are, the more problematic the behaviors that precede them and the more these behaviors become BORCs. In other words, operant behaviors become BORCs when the consequences for doing them (or not doing them in the case of deficit BORCs) are undesirable. Thus, BORCs are idiosyncratic in that they can only be recognized and assessed by each of us based on our behavior and how we experience the consequences that follow.

My excess BORC of drinking coffee in the evening may be strictly my excess BORC because it results in sleepless, unpleasant nights and groggy, irritable mornings. This same behavior may not be a BORC for you simply because it creates no unpleasant consequences. I know and experience (and sometimes curse) my BORCs. Although yours may be very different, you know and experience (and maybe even curse) yours as well. We will continue our discussion of BORCs throughout this book because the alleviation of BORC is the primary objective in applying the A-B-C model for purposeful behavior change.

So often when reflecting on our unhappiness we focus on the consequences (e.g., reactions of others, responses from our environment) that we dislike, but fail to notice our behavior (i.e., BORCs) that affect these consequences. We blame others, the world, the stupid boss, my crazy brother, that damn VCR, traffic (i.e., all the A's and C's of our A-B-C model) without realizing our contribution. Our study of BORCs within the context of the A-B-C model will cause us to keep the focus on us: our behavior, our BORCs, our A-B-C's.

My BORCs cannot be someone's lousy attitude, the letter carrier's incompetence, or the nasty teacher. They can only be my behaviors (excess and/or deficit) and their undesirable consequences. If conditions in the environment are unpleasant, the A-B-C model directs me to aspects of my behavior that may contribute to this unpleasantness (or my contribution to its resolution). My BORCs are mine, yours are yours, and the A-B-C model helps each of us with our own. This is the essence of self-management, self-control, responsibility, and opportunity.

## Chapter Summary

1. The A-B-C model represents the relationships among antecedents, behaviors, and consequences.

2. The behavior component comprises four parts: thinking, or cognition; operant, or acting, behavior; respondent, or physiological, responses; and emotions.

3. Operant behaviors are voluntary actions performed to create certain desirable consequences. This B-C relationship is called a contingency.

4. Operant behaviors are learned throughout life and tend to perpetuate and even increase when they are successful.

5. We learn operants through direct experience or indirectly through vicarious learning and the modeling of others who appear to behave successfully.

6. The strength of an operant behavior reflects the probability that it will actually be performed. This strength can be measured in terms of frequency, duration, and intensity.

7. Operants can be within our awareness and consciously performed, or they can be automatic, habitual, and out of our awareness, but still accessible to awareness.

8. The acronym BORC stands for behavior of real concern and represents problem behaviors because their consequences are undesirable.

9. Excess BORCs are problems of commission in that their performance causes undesirable consequences. These are behaviors that we do too much or at the wrong time or place.

10. Deficit BORCs are problems of omission in that their absence causes undesirable consequences. These behaviors never occur or do not occur at the right time or place.

**Figure 1** *The A-B-C (Cognitive–Behavioral) Model*

| (A) Antecedent | | (B) Behavior | | (C) Consequence |
|---|---|---|---|---|
| | Covert | Overt | Overt | |
| | Cognitive (Thinking) | Respondent (Physical) | Operant (Acting) | |
| Stimulus or setting event. External environments that set the occasion for behavior (thinking, acting, feeling) to occur.<br><br>$S^{Dee}$ = Green light. A cue that a particular behavior will result in a desirable consequence.<br><br>$S^{Delta}$ = Red light. A cue that a particular behavior will result in an undesirable consequence. | Subjective environment. The process and content of our thinking. Our interpretation of A-B-C as a-b-c.<br><br>Includes:<br>Attributions<br>Expectations<br>Self-concept<br>Self-esteem<br>Beliefs<br>Attitudes<br>Prejudices<br>Self-talk<br>Locus of control<br>Images<br>Fantasies<br>Intrinsic consequences | Reflexive<br>Autonomic<br>Involuntary<br>Biochemical<br>Physiological changes occurring within our body. | Voluntary behavior that we choose to do or not to do.<br><br>Can be: Excess = Behavior done too often or at wrong time.<br><br>Deficit = Behavior done too infrequently or not when needed. | Events (external) that occur during and/or after a particular covert and/or operant behavior. Events can be:<br><br>A. Desirable:<br>1. Positive Reinforcement present desirable = C+<br>2. Negative Reinforcement remove undesirable = C⊄<br>B. Undesirable:<br>1. Punishment present undesirable, aversive = C–<br>2. Extinction remove desirable = C⊄ |
| **Emotions** | | | | |

Subjective labels used to describe a specific state of being. Labels reflect the composite of our covert, respondent, and operant behavior within a specific context of antecedents and consequences.

## Chapter 3

# Desirable Consequences: What We Hope, Expect, and Create

## Orienting Ourselves

**A**ll operant behavior is purposeful. This is a fundamental contention of the A-B-C model. If we can accept this premise, the next logical question surrounds the nature of that purpose. How is that purpose determined? Who determines our purpose? How is that purpose achieved? Are some purposes better than others? What do we know about the purposes that humans strive to achieve? The key to unlocking these questions is the consequence component of our A-B-C model and, most specifically, the relationship between consequences and the operant behaviors that precipitate them. An analysis of this B-C contingency relationship provides the agenda for this chapter. But first, we will look at the C component of the A-B-C model.

We find some consequences highly desirable and attainable under our own control. Consequences that meet these criteria have a strong motivational effect on our operant behavior. These desirable consequences will draw our attention in this chapter. We begin by reviewing the nature of contingencies, which are the if–then relationships that define so much of our experience.

## Contingencies

**I**n Chapter 2, I said that one characteristic of an operant behavior is that it exists in a contingency relationship with a consequence or consequences. This contingency occurs when an if–then relationship operates between the behavior and the consequence. If I pump gas in my car, then it (generally) runs for 2 weeks. If I want my trash picked up, then I have to put it out. If I want my wife to consider a plan that I conjure up for the holidays, then I need to show consideration for a plan that she might have. If I want to perceive myself as a helpful person (a self-valuing covert behavior), then I need to behave helpfully toward others (this is an example of intrinsic positive reinforcement). In each of these examples, a consequence is dependent on doing a behavior, and I perform the operant behavior because my covert expectation holds a high probability that my desired consequence will result.

**Figure 4** *Consequences*

---

### (C) Consequence

---

Events (external) that occur during and/or after a particular covert and/or operant behavior. Events can be:

A. Desirable:

1. Positive Reinforcement present desirable = C+

2. Negative Reinforcement remove undesirable = C̶-̶

B. Undesirable:

1. Punishment present undesirable, aversive = C−

2. Extinction remove desirable = C̶+̶

---

We all have a multitude of operant behaviors in our repertoire. Any one of them could be performed under the right antecedent conditions. Whether we learned those operants through vicarious learning (i.e., observation), by small increments of practice, or simply by spontaneous (or impulsive) risk taking, we learned how, when, and where to behave. The actual performance of any of those in our repertoire depends on the contingency that we expect to occur when we do the behavior. In other words, I may know exactly how, when, and where to behave a certain way, but the expected contingency may predict some undesirable consequence, so I choose not to do the behavior.

Conversely, I may believe (expect) that people like humor and will laugh heartily at a joke (and admire the witty joke teller) so I keep telling jokes that are inappropriate and even bungle a few punch lines. The expected contingency maintains my feeble attempts at joke telling. The determining factor in actually performing the behavior is the expected contingency. If I think my behavior will lead to a desirable consequence, I will probably do it.

Likewise, even if I believe that I can do a particular behavior, an undesirable contingency will inhibit my attempt. I may know the answer to a question in class, but expect an interrogation from the teacher or castigating stares from my classmates, so I decline to answer. There is considerable research to demonstrate that much learning occurs without it actually being performed or displayed because the perceived contingency discourages the learner.

## The Contingency As Covert Behavior

**M**y use of the term *perceived* derives from the importance that our thinking (i.e., covert behavior) plays in our understanding of the B-C contingencies. Let me elaborate on this critical qualification of behavioral contingencies. Until the covert, or cognitive, component of the A-B-C model was considered in the late 1960s, many behavioral scientists believed that operant behavior was strictly under the control of external consequences (i.e., the observable contingency). A rat ran the maze because it wanted the cheese. Getting the cheese was contingent on successfully running the maze. If the teacher provided ample positive reinforcement to a student for participating in class, the student would immediately respond to the contingency and participate even more. If the right contingency was established, it was believed, the behavior most certainly would follow. The thinking (i.e., covert behavior) of the behaver was not particularly relevant; in fact, thinking or cognition (i.e., all that stuff that went on between your ears) was viewed by some as a "black box," unworthy of serious investigation or control.

Unfortunately, this glaring omission of the covert component of the A-B-C model rendered us partially blind to the real human experience and the locus of motivation. Working with negligible cortical processes, the rat probably succumbed to the external contingency (until it got satiated on cheese or was more tired than hungry that day), but praised students may choose not to participate because they do not trust the contingency. Their covert expectation might be that "the teacher will just demand more if I participate, so why bother?" Or students might simply discount the external contingency set up by the teacher because "teachers have never recognized me before when I tried to participate, so why try now?" In either case, it is the students' covert expectation of the B-C contingency that governs their decision to behave (or take the risk). We will have a lot more to say about the influence of covert behavior in Chapter 6. For now, as I describe various types of external contingencies, it is enough to be aware that the covert expectation of the behaver is the ultimate motivation to behave or not to behave.

As described in Chapter 2, the strength of a behavior represents the probability of its occurrence (as measured in frequency, duration, or intensity). And if we conclude that the probability is based on our covert expectation of achieving our desired consequence, then the strength of a behavior derives from the power of the contingency in motivating the person to act or not to act. Again, it is the (covert) expected contingency that motivates us to actually behave.

## Immediate Versus Distant Consequences

Besides the if–then dimension of the contingency, the temporal spread between the B and the C significantly influences the strength of the behavior. Generally speaking, the more immediately the consequence follows the behavior, the more influence the consequence has on the behavior. The longer the delay between B and C, the less influence the C retains, and the lower the probability of doing the behavior. Well! This last point is certainly no surprise. Children live by the credo of "immediate gratification." And every problem from avoidance and procrastination to the most severe forms of substance abuse (e.g., drugs, alcohol, and tobacco) can attest to the power of immediate consequences over longer-term consequences. On the other hand, some C+'s are to be savered now.

As you will discover shortly when I discuss the different kinds of consequences, most behaviors result in multiple consequences. Although the most immediate consequence draws our attention and motivates our behavior, each behavior that we perform has a ripple effect in our environment and in our future. I may choose to watch *Casablanca* for the 12th time because it is so nostalgic (plus, it helps me avoid thinking about repairing the leaking pipe under my sink or the medical forms that I have to fill out for my son's dental work), but I'll pay later. The immediate consequence of pleasure (C+) and the avoidance of discomfort (X−) are enough to seduce me to watch Sam "play it again." The eventual consequence of a flooded kitchen or the loss of our dental insurance reimbursement are somewhat in the future and easy to remove from my covert expectations. Besides, those unpleasant consequences in the remote future might never even occur. And anyway, I can deal with those problems when I really have to. As Scarlet proclaimed, "I'll deal with that tomorrow." Pass the popcorn, please!

### Payoffs and Secondary Gain

Sometimes a delayed or very long-term consequence can be so powerful—its reinforcement value so profound—that it motivates behavior even in the face of immediate displeasure. When we observe the immediate contingency of a behavior leading to an undesirable consequence (a C− or X+), we wonder what is going on. The power of immediate gratification (reinforcement) is so strong and so apparent in our explanation of behavior that instances of delayed gratification are often novel and perplexing. Of course, there are those obvious examples of delayed gratification when a person works, struggles, and may even suffer to get ahead, to save up enough for that glorious vacation, to get into that favored university, or even just to avoid the hassle of doing taxes at the last minute. In each instance, the motivating consequence is somewhere in the distant future. In spite of the delay, its value outweighs any immediate discomfort that we might endure to achieve it. We often equate this form of delayed gratification with maturity, a characteristic of self-management that we will address extensively in later chapters.

The consequences that we strive for and that we sometimes purposely program into our lives to motivate our behavior can be thought of as "payoffs." Essentially, a payoff represents a desired outcome that I obtained through some purposeful action. As you will see shortly, payoffs can be the receipt of something I want (i.e., getting a C+) or the removal of something I do not want (i.e., avoiding or escaping a C−). As with any consequence, payoffs can be immediate or delayed. Payoffs can also be very explicit and obvious to everyone, as when I turn up the furnace to warm the house, instruct my young daughter to wear her bike helmet to avoid injury, or place a new ribbon in my printer for more legible documents. Every time we do something for a purpose (i.e., a consequence), that consequence becomes a payoff.

Fortunately, most payoffs are clear and obvious to the behaver and observer alike. Their A-B-C's are easy to understand. Sometimes, however, the payoff is not particularly apparent. We see the behavior, but cannot identify the consequence that is motivating it. In fact, the B may seem to be resulting only in C−'s or X+'s, as is often the case with behavior we label as self-destructive or masochistic.

Sarah is an obese individual who eats constantly, never exercises, and seems to be destroying herself; Frank is the class clown who constantly exhibits disruptive behavior that incurs the wrath of teachers, classmates, and parents; and Lenny is the disorganized, forgetful, and irresponsible salesman who just can't seem to get it together. All exemplify perplexing behavior with obscure payoffs. In instances such as these, even though the purpose of the behavior is so obscure, a payoff can be found if we search hard enough. The obscure payoff that is unknown to the observer and unknown (or unacknowledged) to the behaver is referred to as the *secondary gain* for performing that behavior. The concept of secondary gain as the hidden or unrevealed payoff is exceptionally helpful in understanding those seemingly inexplicable behaviors.

Sarah's obesity and resultant immobility may allow her to abstain from threatening social situations, sexual relationships, and the responsibility of employment. The class clown derives considerable attention for his disruptive antics and, in the process, forces his contentious parents to conciliate and postpone their divorce, at least until they "straighten that kid out." And everybody rallies around the irresponsible, topsy-turvy salesman, helping him out, and basically, rescuing him from himself. In taking care of him, they place minimal demands on his time because they know that "he's just not up to it."

So what motivates Sarah, Frank, and Lenny to perpetuate their dysfunctional behavior? Secondary gain. Are our three protagonists aware of the secondary gain that motivates their behavior? Probably, at some level. If we accept my initial premise that all behavior is purposeful, then at some point all three of these folks choose to pursue their behavior for the secondary gain derived from it. Does their behavior make sense? Yes. The challenge is in discovering the consequence for a behavior that seems totally purposeless, or even injurious, to the behaver.

We could ascertain the strength of their behavior and the value of its payoff by the tenacious manner in which they maintain that behavior. Resistance to change is a strong measure of the impact of secondary gain on the behavior preceding it. Let us direct our attention to the specific categories of consequences.

## Categories of Consequences

As the C component of our A-B-C model indicates, there are four categories of consequences, each manifesting a different contingency. A convenient way of depicting these four contingencies is in a $2 \times 2$ consequence matrix. The two dimensions of the matrix are: (a) the action that is taken on the consequence (present or remove) and (b) the effect that this action has on the preceding behavior (increase or decrease). I will present the matrix (Figure 5) and then describe each of the four cells.

## Desirable Consequences

Under the top dimension of the consequence matrix that presents the Effect on Behavior, there are two cells under Increase. These two cells (1 and 2) are labeled Positive Reinforcement and Negative Reinforcement, respectively. Further study within each of the two increase cells reveals that, although both consequences strengthen the behavior that precedes them, the action taken on the consequence is quite different. Because both consequences strengthen behavior, each has the word *reinforcement* in its label. The first word of each label characterizes the action taken on the consequence causing a strengthening of the behavior. In cell 1, the first word is *positive* indicating that something is being presented or that the behavior is receiving something. In the case of positive reinforcement, what is received is desirable. Consequently, when I refer to the process of positive reinforcement, I use the shorthand C+.

**Figure 5** *Consequence Matrix*

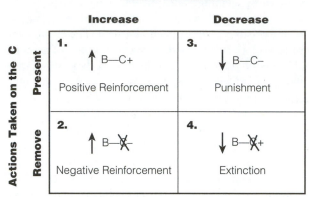

The word *negative* appears in cell 2, signifying that something is being removed (escaped) or prevented from happening (avoided). With negative reinforcement, something unpleasant is being removed, thus resulting in a desirable consequence. Since a negative is being removed, I use the symbol "⊗–" when signifying negative reinforcement.

The consequences appearing in cells 3 and 4 are both undesirable and have the effect of decreasing or weakening the behavior preceding them. Before talking about these undesirable categories, let us set our sights on the desirable consequences. We will start by looking at positive reinforcement.

## Positive Reinforcement

Technically speaking, positive reinforcement occurs when an action, object, or event is presented to a person for performing an operant behavior, and the person chooses to do that operant again to receive that consequence. This definition implies a few important assumptions. First, since the person is choosing to repeat the operant, the consequence must be desirable (i.e., have some value) to the person. Second, the presentation of the desirable consequence must be contingent on performance of the operant behavior. And third, according to some random or fixed schedule or reinforcement, the desired consequence must be presented following performance of the operant. The particular desirable C+ serving as a consequence is referred to as the *positive reinforcer*, while the actual process of executing the B–C+ contingency is called *positive reinforcement*.

Practically speaking, positive reinforcement is the joyful experience of life. It is through the process of positive reinforcement that most of our (pleasurable) learning occurs, and it provides the motivational charge that propels us through the day. Upon awaking in the morning, the expectation of frequent and valued C+'s throughout the day is a motivating and even an exhilarating experience. The expectation of a day devoid of C+'s can create sadness, depression, and lethargy. In many ways, positive reinforcers reflect our values and comprise the priorities that give direction and meaning to our lives.

Previously, I referred to the strength of an operant, which is the probability of its occurring. When I talk about the power of a consequence to motivate us, I use the term *value*. A high valued C+ is much prized and is a strong motivator for our operant behavior. Highly valued C+'s produce strong operants. As we discuss the kinds of C+'s, you will see that they vary greatly in their value; primary C+'s have the greatest value and some secondary C+'s only marginally influence us.

At this point, you may be thinking, "I don't need C+'s from my environment to motivate me. And much of the pleasure, satisfaction, and joy that I derive from life comes from within, without C+'s following my behavior." I concur with your thinking completely. I do many behaviors that do not seem to produce external C+'s. Without the expectation of praise, comment, monetary gain, privilege, or any other environmental effect, I clean, study, perform chores, read mystery novels, and help others. And I derive great joy and satisfaction from performing tasks, engaging others, or simply contemplating life without the need of external (C+) feedback. So how does the A-B-C model explain this phenomenon that seems to contradict the B–C+ contingency?

The answer lies in our covert. It is true that many of the C+'s that motivate us derive from our external environment. Being paid for a completed job, getting a refund at the store by asserting ourself, seeing the TV go on when we use the remote, or receiving some acknowledgment for a courtesy are all operants maintained by external C+'s. But through a process of learning and maturation, we acquire the covert capacity to reinforce ourselves positively. We also learn to engage in behaviors that feel good, that are pleasant and satisfying, simply through the process of doing them. Those C+'s that we give to ourselves (through our covert self-talk) and those behaviors that are pleasurable "just in the doing" come from within us and thus represent intrinsic reinforcement.

The phenomenon of intrinsic reinforcement explains a large part of the satisfaction (and motivation) that we experience in life. It is especially germane to altruistic behavior and to folks who seem to march to the beat of their own drummer. Whereas extrinsic reinforcement pertains to behaviors that are strengthened and perpetuated by C+'s emanating from the external environment (i.e., everything outside of ourselves), intrinsic reinforcement comes from within our mind. Extrinsic reinforcement was paramount in building our repertoire of operant behaviors throughout our childhood, but as we mature into adulthood, intrinsic reinforcers sustain an ever larger proportion of our operants.

When we discuss the development of intrinsic reinforcement later in this chapter, you will see that many of our intrinsic C+'s had their origin in external reinforcers. My introduction of intrinsic reinforcement so early in this chapter stems from its importance in explaining so much about behavior. Although the following material addresses the contingencies operating from extrinsic consequences, I hope that the existence and importance of intrinsic reinforcement have been suitably acknowledged.

At the extrinsic level, positive reinforcers can occur at a few different levels.

*Primary Positive Reinforcement*  Primary C+'s are our most basic reinforcers. Without them we could not exist. To survive as individuals, we must have food, water, oxygen, tactile stimulation (for neurological development), and adequate body heat. We are born with these biological needs and they continue throughout our life. From the moment of birth, the pursuit of these primary C+'s take precedence, except when each need is temporarily sated. None of these needs for primary C+'s were learned. Each was biologically programmed into our repertoire for survival.

From the broader perspective of our survival as a species, it has been suggested that sexual orgasm be classified as a primary reinforcer. There is certainly no question that male sexual orgasm is necessary for our survival as a species, and its consideration as a primary reinforcer meets the condition of being biological and unlearned. As a primary C+, sexual orgasm is also instrumental in the establishment of secondary reinforcers (to be discussed shortly) and serves as the motivational force for much of our operant behavior. It certainly seems to be the paramount preoccupation of adolescents.

Fortunately, we were born with the array of operant and respondent behaviors required to obtain most of these critical C+'s. We could grasp, suck, bite, swallow, breathe (a respondent) in our struggle for some, and when all else failed, we could cry. Of course, we depended largely on a nurturing environment to provide these C+'s. When the external environment fails us, we are incapable of thriving or even surviving. Over the course of our infancy and early childhood, we acquire (learn) an increasingly complex repertoire of operants in our continuous pursuit of these primary C+'s. Instead of grasping, we learn to hold; from sucking, we learn to sip and chew; from shivering, we learn to pull up a blanket; and in place of crying, we learn to verbalize our needs (or we combine our crying with our verbalization into that most effective strategy known as whining).

Certain biochemical actions within the body, especially areas of the central nervous system, stimulate a sensation of euphoria and well-being and thus may qualify as primary reinforcers. I mention these physiological C+'s here only because of their physical nature and thus their capacity to function as primary reinforcers. Later in this chapter, I will subsume these physiological changes as the product and essential ingredient of a class of activity reinforcers associated with self-arousal and stimulation. Increased secretion of certain neurotransmitters such as dopamine and endorphin (the body's natural pain suppressant) produce pleasurable physical sensations. These pleasurable sensations can be stimulated naturally by operants such as vigorous physical activity (as in the runner's high) or artificially by the operants involved in drug consumption. The rush experienced by the consumption of opiate drugs is as strong and positively reinforcing as the high of the thrill seeker putting life on the line to climb a mountain, risk everything to win at the casino, or risk death on the highway.

There are elements of all addictive behavior to suggest that the physiological (biochemical) changes produced by these addictive operants have positively reinforcing qualities that maintain the addiction indefinitely. The vast range of self-stimulatory behavior pursued so intrepidly by humans—and most of the animal kingdom—illustrates the creativity and endurance of primary reinforcement. Activities (operants) that purposefully induce these physiological changes will be discussed again later in this chapter.

## Secondary (Conditioned) Reinforcers

At the same time that we are learning operants to acquire these primary C+'s, we are also learning to associate particular environmental experiences with those C+'s we value so highly. Environmental events to people, places, objects, and anything at all that is connected with the primary C+'s. A mother's facial pattern, smell, and voice quickly become associated with those primary C+'s crucial to the infant. Before long, those connections to primary C+'s extend to other "significant caregivers" such as the sound of mom or dad in the kitchen preparing a bottle, the favorite blanket that provides much needed warmth, and the teddy bear that is so stimulating to the touch. The infant rapidly learns to associate (or discriminate) the presence of these objects, people, sounds, smells, and images with acquiring those all important C+'s.

Through this association learning, the infant begins to value these associated events almost as much as their primary C+ companions. I have used the term "almost" because the connection between the primary C+ and its associated event, object, or person can be tenuous. The reinforcement value of the associated event is conditional on its continued association with the primary C+. We refer to these associated conditional reinforcers as *conditioned reinforcers*. Because of their learned association with the primary reinforcers, we can also refer to them as *secondary reinforcers*. To the extent that the infant experiences love for that which provides for his or her primary C+'s, we could also say that the infant experiences a conditioned love toward those secondary C+'s. These early secondary reinforcers have been referred to as "love objects," and they play a significant role in our development of trust, security, intimacy, and in our capacity to love.

Just as infants act on the environment to acquire primary C+'s, they begin to display operants intended to achieve secondary C+'s. Because other people (often referred to as significant others) are often associated with the acquisition of primary C+'s, the broad spectrum of social interaction becomes a secondary reinforcer. The mere presence of others (aunts, uncle, neighbors, even siblings—when they were not providing C–'s) becomes a powerful C+. And the young child quickly learns a myriad of social operants to capitalize on these secondary reinforcers and their concomitant primary C+'s. Perfection of communicable language, delayed gratification, assertiveness, and even showing off quickly enter the operant repertoire of the young child. Thus, the phenomenon of learning evolves.

A very critical difference between primary and secondary reinforcers relates to the universality of each. Primary reinforcers by their very immutability apply to everyone. We all must have air, water, food, and so forth to exist; consequently, these primary C+'s motivate everyone. They retain their high value throughout our lives. I know of no exceptions.

Secondary reinforcers, on the other hand, have no universality. Their value is solely dependent on their association with primary C+'s. Because secondary reinforcers are learned as opposed to biologically programmed into us, they reflect our own unique environment, culture, and learning experiences. We could say that secondary C+'s are idiosyncratic in that they comprise different people, objects, things, and events for each of us. Your teddy bear, favorite song, walking shoes, recreational sport, car, or an

C+'s are individualistic. Thank heavens! (© Tribune Media Services, Inc. All Rights Reserved. Reprinted with permission.)

evening with Uncle Frank may all possess very high secondary reinforcement value for you but have little motivational (C+) value for me. Likewise, I might drive 500 m to buy a Mike Schmidt rookie baseball card, but you might not bother to pick one up off of the street. To some students, the opportunity to feed the fish or clap the erasers holds inordinate (for me anyway) value; they perform monumental tasks to get it. But for other students, these privileges hold no value; in fact, they might perceive them as punishments (C–). However, the same students that shun the fish and erasers might work hours for the opportunity to take the ball out at recess.

So if secondary C+'s are so individualistic, how can we know what they are? Easy. Ask the behavers. Or better yet, observe them and notice the consequences that they seem to pursue with considerable energy and diligence (i.e., operant strength). You know what your valued secondary reinforcers are—what you work hard for. I could learn what they are by asking you or by frequently watching what you do. The idiosyncratic nature of secondary reinforcers is crucial to our understanding of human motivation and must be a foremost consideration in building contingencies for purposeful behavior change.

There is a universe of secondary reinforcers permeating our environment, just waiting to energize and motivate us. To better study them, we can classify them into four categories: social, material, activity, and token. Let us look at each separately.

*Social Reinforcers*  As the term implies, social reinforcers are affirmations received from others. We typically think of social reinforcers as verbal in nature and packaged in the form of praise, compliments, acknowledgments, answers in the affirmative, and other verbal messages that we want to hear. A "wonderful job!" or "you look marvelous!" can motivate lots of operants. Written affirmations (letters, notes, etc.) also fall within this verbal category. Although grades, stars, checks, phone calls, and notes home are technically considered token reinforcers, their social affirmation and the social manner in which they are given might easily classify them as both token and social reinforcers.

Equally influential, yet much subtler, are the nonverbal social reinforcers we look for (consciously or automatically) from others. The face is a cornucopia of social communication. How often has a conversation been maintained (reinforced) by attentive eye contact, only to be discontinued abruptly by the diversion of your listener's eyes? Through social learning, we have become masters at detecting approval or disapproval in the facial expression of others. We look to a smile, widening of the eyes, and lifting of the head as one leans toward us to tell us that our listener approves, cares about what we are doing or saying, and wishes us to continue.

Physical gestures comprise another broad category of potential social reinforcers. The more obvious examples are hugging and kissing, but physical proximity, posture, and touch can all send C+ messages. The literature is voluminous in exposing the variety and surreptitiousness of social reinforcers around the world. If you agree, just smile!

*Material Reinforcers* Sometimes referred to as tangible reinforcers because of their physical nature, material reinforcers are those objects, things, and possessions that we covet so dearly. From the broadest expanse of real estate to the smallest computer chip, material reinforcers motivate our activity. This is especially true for our commercial, or vocational, operants. The indictment of being a "materialistic society" simply amplifies the pervasiveness of this contingency. Unlike token reinforcers, which derive their value from what they can be traded for (we will discuss these shortly), material reinforcers have utility and purpose in themselves.

Whatever physical possession you value represents a material reinforcer. Clothing, automobiles, houses, stereos, computers, and designer sneakers are the more conspicuous material C+'s, but some people really do value wool underwear, and almost everything has become a collectible. My house is filled with material reinforcers, some resulting from arduous operants and others acquired quite easily (or simply by being in the right place at the right time). The material C+'s that I seem to value most are consequences of work and effort.

*Activity Reinforcers* Participation in a pleasurable, relaxing, or positively stimulating activity can be a highly valued C+. This participation can be passive and observational, as when you watch TV, attend a sporting event, or listen to music, or active, as when you play a sport, dance, read, play an instrument, or take a walk. There are numerous experiences that we covet because of the joy, excitement, and stimulation (or conversely, relaxation) that we derive. When applied to children, we often structure these C+ experiences within specific contingencies and refer to them as "privileges" to be earned. The opportunity to watch TV, draw, look at a magazine, or take an early recess can powerfully motivate children as well as the rest of us. As with all secondary reinforcers, activity reinforcers are individualistic; some like to read nonfiction, while others love a juicy novel. Whereas a Sunday afternoon consuming TV football is the ultimate peak experience for some, it is a waste of time for others. Give them a robust set of tennis or a snooze on the hammock.

In 1965, David Premack discovered that the opportunity to engage in a high-frequency behavior (i.e., any behavior engaged in frequently) can actually serve as a C+ for a behavior that is less enjoyable, and thus occurs at a lower frequency. For example, the opportunity to draw pictures can serve as a C+ for completing math problems for a child who enjoys art. The application of this phenomenon is referred to as the Premack principle, and it has many practical uses for purposeful behavior change.

Another facet of experiences under acting reinforcers is those physical changes that are purposely produced by operant behaviors. These highly elevated forms of physiological arousal can induce biochemical changes in the body (see Chapter 5 for details) that we experience as energizing, sensually stimulating, and even euphoric—approximating an altered state of consciousness. This enhanced arousal can be induced naturally through rigorous exercise (e.g., running), sustained concentration (e.g., a favorite hobby), or disciplined meditation (e.g., yoga, TM). Elevated secretions of endorphins and other neurotransmitters that accompany these naturalistic activities create the state of euphoria we have come to call the "runner's high" or the mediator's "tranquillity." Regardless of the label, you know when you experience it because it feels so good. To those of you who can draw upon these natural highs in your daily life (without them becoming an excessive preoccupation), congratulations. You are truly fortunate.

Just as motivating but considerably more deleterious are those activity C+'s that alter the body's biochemistry artificially. Any foreign substance ingested to induce physiological arousal or relaxation falls into this category. Alcohol, tobacco, caffeine, THC, opiates, and so forth all alter our physical experience in desirable ways (at least at the inception of use), and in so doing, serve as powerful C+'s. Narcotic drugs, alcohol, and the spectrum of mind-altering drugs have been accused of being vehicles of avoidance and escape from pain and unhappiness, but what is overlooked is the powerful sense of pleasure (rush, high, euphoria) that they induce at their inception. (After addiction, their use is motivated more by avoidance and escape from pain rather than receipt of pleasure.)

Some behavior scientists have suggested that human beings are innately programmed to seek natural highs and altered states of consciousness and that these experiences are tantamount to primary reinforcers. Maybe so! But there is no question that a significant part of our society, as well as cultures throughout the world, directs a large proportion of their operants to the pursuit of these activity reinforcers.

**Token Reinforcers** In and of themselves, token reinforcers possess very little value. You cannot eat, wear, drive, or build a house with coins and paper money. What do you do with stars, checks, points, coupons, or tokens if you cannot redeem them for something? If your answer is "nothing," then you realize the direct value of tokens. But what you also appreciate is the indirect value of token reinforcers, which lies in whatever we can trade them for: houses, cars, clothing, activities, vacations, social recognition (Remember Ross Perot in the 1992 presidential election?), privacy, security, excitement, companionship, and so on. In fact, we can probably use token reinforcers (primarily money) to acquire most of the reinforcers that I have previously cited. It is what we can do with them that determines the true value of token C+'s. This is why we hoard, save, slave, gamble, and fight over them so much. Token C+'s are the most flexible and uniformly pervasive of all secondary reinforcers. Most students value grades, stars, merits, trophies, and ribbons, and most adults work for money. This uniform standard of value also explains why token reinforcers are so useful in establishing contingencies for purposeful behavior change.

One last point needs to be made before leaving the topic of positive reinforcers. In more instances than not, operant behaviors lead to multiple consequences, which can occur simultaneously or in tandem. Diligent study behavior by a student can result in an A grade (token), lots of praise from teacher and parents (social), enabling the student to attend a Phillies baseball game with mom and dad (activity, I think), and money (token) to purchase a thick, warm Phillies sweatshirt (material). Which of these reinforcers possesses the greatest C+ value is hard to say. The crucial factor is that the student chooses to perform the operants necessary to acquire them, and the environment supports his or her covert expectation for success.

## Negative Reinforcement

Have you ever avoided eating certain foods because they made you sick in the past? How about refrigerating certain foods that spoil rapidly? Do you turn off a lamp before changing the bulb? Did you learn to carry your gloves on days when the temperature falls below freezing? How do you react to certain streets or intersections that become jammed with traffic during rush hour? Did you learn an alternate route? Do you ever find yourself fabricating little white lies to avoid certain social encounters that you experienced as dreadful in the past? If any of these life encounters sounds familiar, you have clearly experienced the phenomenon of *negative reinforcement*.

In each of these examples, you performed a particular operant behavior to avoid or escape from some form of punishment (C–). If this operant was successful, you quickly learned to perform that same behavior the next time you faced (or covertly expected) that punishment. Through this process you learn lots of ways to avoid punishment in the future. You refrigerate foods, turn off light switches, wear warm clothing, navigate circuitous routes around traffic, and fabricate stories and rationalizations for the purpose of avoiding or escaping something unpleasant. And you continue to perform these operant behaviors as long as they work. By work, I mean that they result in the desired consequences, which are not consequences of receiving positive reinforcement, but consequences of removing something punishing or aversive. These avoidance and escape behaviors may never result in acquiring positive reinforcement but they do not need to. They are perpetuated by their success in avoiding or escaping some C–. The removal of punishment (i.e., pain or discomfort) is purposeful and motivating, and thus becomes our second category of desirable consequence.

Negative reinforcement appears in cell 2 of the consequence matrix as ↑ B–$\cancel{C}$–. It can be defined as the removal of punishment resulting in an increase in the behavior that caused that removal to occur. As you can see from cell 2, the B occurs or even increases (i.e., is built or reinforced) because it causes a punisher (i.e., something negative) to be removed. Consequently, we call the process negative (referring to consequences being removed) reinforcement (referring to the effect that this removal has on the behavior preceding it). Because negative reinforcement involves the removal of punishment (i.e., $\cancel{C}$–'s), your understanding of its meaning and process requires some knowledge of the nature of punishment. Punishment is an undesirable consequence, depicted in cell 3 of the consequence matrix as the presentation of a C–, and I will discuss it in much greater depth in the next chapter. You may want to familiarize yourself with the section on punishment (pp. 47–51) before you proceed with this discussion on negative reinforcement.

### Learning from Negative Reinforcement

From our earliest years of life, we experienced pain, hurt, injury, embarrassment, humiliation, and even acute fright—all of which serve as C–'s. Each of these C–'s was a potential learning experience; the more immediate and severe the C–, the quicker we learned. If we were spanked for melting crayons on the heater vent, we stopped that behavior real fast. After scalding our tender feet, we learned to check the bathwater temperature before stepping in. We even learned to detect if mom was in a bad mood so as not to incur her wrath with our "creative" behavior. Many of these learning experiences taught us what not to do, because to do them invariably resulted in our getting a C–.

But just as we learned to inhibit behavior that resulted in punishment, we also learned to exhibit behavior because of its success in avoiding or escaping C–'s. In discussing what we learn from negative reinforcement, it is important to include the inhibition of behavior (behavior that I call excess BORCs) along with the performance or exhibition of behavior (behavior that I call deficit BORCs). Melting crayons on the heater vent is an excess BORC in need of inhibition or elimination. Checking the temperature of the bathwater is a deficit BORC in need of increased performance (i.e., antecedent).

Much of our early learning from C–'s was painful. Since we did not intuitively know about all the C–'s in our environment, we often experienced the C– as we became aware of it. In other words, we were in it before we knew to expect it and possibly avoid it. Whether we call this trial-and-error learning or just learning from our mistakes, it was a lousy way to learn. Life seemed like a continual struggle with a crisis occurring every time we found ourselves immersed in another C–. A fight on the playground, a scolding in the principal's office, a lecture from dad, a spanking, an injury (physical or emotional), or even an altercation with the law were all experiences (C–'s) that we seemed to "just find ourselves in."

### Escape Behavior

Confronted with the experience of C–'s, the first behaviors we might have learned were escape. By apologizing, creative rationalizing, shutting our mouth, begging, making amends, outright lying, or just bolting out the door, we attempted our escape from the C–. We learned from our successes and failures, with success breeding repetition and failure prompting alternative escape strategies. Thus, we can define *escape behavior* as operant behavior that we choose to do to remove a C– that we are currently experiencing. Escape behavior that is negatively reinforcing will probably occur the next time we actually experience the C–.

### Avoidance Behavior

Even if it is effective, the problem with escape behavior is that we still have to experience the C– before we escape. If all we learn and have to rely on for coping is escape behavior, our lives will be truly miserable. Wouldn't life be much easier if we could somehow prevent those C–'s from occurring in the first place? You bet! The key is in anticipating the C–'s in our path before they happen and then taking the necessary precautions to prevent them from happening. These anticipatory operant behaviors designed to prevent C–'s before they actually occur are called *avoidance behaviors*. Folks who have *learned* and can rely on a large repertoire of avoidance behaviors are *generally* a lot happier and more effective in life than those who continually have to fall back on escape as their coping strategy. Let me explain why I highlighted the words learned and generally in reference to avoidance behavior.

Sometimes we learn to avoid C–'s through vicarious, or observational, learning. If we are fortunate, a danger may be revealed to us by someone else, and they may even show us how to avoid it. Other times, we learn about potential C–'s by observing others' experiences and successfully avoiding them. For example, we do not have to suffer the devastation wrought by certain drugs to appreciate their C– value or even to avoid them. We have models and examples all around us if we are willing to look. Those are the fortunate few who have encountered an environment replete with lessons of what to avoid and how to do it before experiencing the pain of a C–. For most of us, we had to learn from direct experience. And that direct experience was escape. Fortunately, as we learned, we spent less time escaping and more time avoiding.

If the C– that we escaped from or had to endure until it ended (e.g., severe corporal punishment, social castigation, physical abuse, or serious injury) was immediate and severe, we learned to prevent it from happening again. That learning included the context (When? Where? How? Who was the punisher? i.e., the antecedents) in which that punishment occurred, the behavior that caused or contributed to the C–, and the actions (avoidance behaviors) that would keep it from recurring.

Perhaps the most crucial learning for avoidance was the context, or antecedent conditions, preceding the actual C–. Discrimination of the environment for signals that a C– is on the horizon is the first step in avoidance and effective coping. Our external environment is full of blatant and subtle signals to be alert to potential C–'s. That empty seat on the bus next to the school bully, the teacher's grimace, a parent's scowl, the attractive brochure for merchandise that you "may have already won," and the empty glass and encouragement of a few "friends" to have just one more drink for the road are all inviting behaviors that lead to punishing consequences. Each of these conditions (antecedents) is a seduction to act as well as a crucial signal that certain actions will lead to predictable C–'s. Strategies for accurately reading the A's for predicting and avoiding probable C–'s will be our focus in Chapter 5.

Relative to escape behavior, avoidance behavior is typically more successful, adaptive, and also much less anxiety provoking. This is especially true when the C– being avoided is immediate, consistent, and severe. If my boss is truly an angry, hostile, aggressive creep just waiting to attack and demean anyone within reach, my avoidance behaviors of totally distancing myself from this person are adaptive and successful. On the other hand, if the boss is not like this at all and the C–'s that I expect are based on fictions (i.e., the rumor mill, a misunderstanding) rather than facts, then my avoidance behaviors are dysfunctional and will only make matters worse.

Escape is based on actually experiencing the C–, whereas avoidance is based on the covert expectation that a C– will probably occur. If we read the environment correctly, and if that probability is truly correct, our avoidance is appropriate and successful. But if we do not read the environment correctly and the expected C– is not really there, then our avoidance is inappropriate and potentially destructive.

Furthermore, avoidance behavior of imagined C–'s (i.e., C–'s that are not there and thus do not occur) is always negatively reinforced and, consequently, is repeated indefinitely. If I constantly avoid my boss, I do not experience the C–'s that I expect. My covert expectation tells me that I avoided punishment by completely staying away from the boss. This avoidance behavior increases at work as long as I think it is resulting in ⊠–, even though the C–is not really there. The trouble is I do not know that the C– is not really there. Why? Because my avoidance behavior is preventing me from actually experiencing that, instead of being a creep, my boss is really a soft-hearted teddy bear who wants to be loved like the rest of us.

This inappropriate and inaccurate avoidance behavior is the basis for some bizarre and dysfunctional activity that we often label as *phobic* or *neurotic*. We will address this problem behavior more extensively when we discuss BORCs later in the book.

Avoidance behavior that has no current basis in fact is *fictional avoidance behavior*. Behavior that does, in fact, avoid a C– that is really present is *factual avoidance behavior*. Sometimes, factual avoidance behavior, because of its strong negative reinforcement, continues long after the C– has ceased to exist. Withdrawing and hiding our feelings in the presence of an abusive and rejecting parent may have been truly adaptive at one time, perhaps way back in early childhood when we had no other way to cope. But those avoidance behaviors are unnecessary and destructive when employed much later in life. A loving spouse, nurturing friend, or even repentant parent may pose little threat of the C– that we so tenaciously (and successfully) avoided. But we do not allow ourselves to risk that chance. Consequently, factual avoidance behavior becomes fictional avoidance behavior, and everyone loses.

If you expect (in your mind/covert) punishment or a C– to occur, your body physically prepares itself to cope. As extensively discussed in Chapter 6 on respondent behavior, this coping takes the form of fight or flight and necessitates the body's arousal and physiological mobilization. The physical arousal (e.g., muscle contraction; increased alertness, heart rate, respiration; etc.), what I call anxiety, is highly adaptive to effective coping, but it takes a severe toll on our health when intensified or prolonged. When we accurately detect (discriminate) from our environment that a C– is forthcoming, our covert planning combined with our heightened arousal (anxiety) enable us to successfully execute our factual avoidance behavior. Once the probability of the C– subsides, the crisis abates, and our body relaxes. We have adaptively coped. The criterion for our success is the elimination of the C–.

The problem with fictional avoidance behavior is that it is pervasive, maladaptive, and not subject to valid criteria of success. Fictional avoidance behavior is stimulated by the imaginary C–'s that we create and perpetuate on our mind (covert): "The bridge will collapse!" "I know that I will suffocate in an elevator!" "This food will poison me!" "People hate me and will try to hurt me!" "Germs are everywhere and will cause illness and death!" Each of these fictions (beliefs and self-talk) projects a terrible C– to be avoided with total dedication. The presence of the anticipated C– automatically calls the body into action. Mobilization and thus anxiety increase precipitously. And we zealously, almost ritualistically, perform our fictional avoidance behavior.

Since the C– is not externally real (it is internally or subjectively real only in our mind), we cannot use its elimination as the criterion for success. Consequently, we are forced to use the performance of the fictional avoidance behavior itself as the criterion for success. Scrubbing every inch of the house, staying in the bedroom day after day, walking 20 flights of stairs, and eating the same food become ends in themselves. Their justification (negative reinforcement) is the experience of doing them.

Simply by doing the avoidance behavior, we remove the C– (at least in our mind) and reduce our anxiety. This elimination of the imagined C– and the reduction of our anxiety serve to negatively reinforce our fictional avoidance behavior and, hence, perpetuate its use. Since the expected C– is self-created, it becomes more frequent and pervasive in our thoughts, and its concomitant anxiety forms an ever larger part of our everyday experience. Our ruminations about the potential C– become obsessions as the avoidance behavior in response to them becomes a compulsion.

Whereas fictional avoidance behavior has no valid (objective) rationale, and thus solely perpetuates our belief that the C– has been avoided, factual avoidance behavior is supported by an accurate discrimination of the ABC contingencies. Factual avoidance behavior reflects adaptive coping when the real C–'s are anticipated, avoided, or minimized. In Chapter 4, we will study the influences of other kinds of undesirable consequences on our thoughts and actions.

## Chapter Summary

**1.** Operant behavior exists in a contingency relationship in which the consequence is dependent on performing the behavior.

**2.** It is our covert expectation of the B–C relationship that directly governs our operant behavior.

**3.** Although many consequences can follow and influence behavior, it is the immediate consequence that has the greatest influence.

**4.** Secondary gain refers to payoffs (C+'s or C̶–'s) that maintain behavior that seems self-defeating and without purpose.

**5.** Positive reinforcers (C+'s) are pleasurable and desirable consequences that reinforce the behavior that precedes them.

**6.** Extrinsic reinforcement pertains to those behaviors that are strengthened and perpetuated by C+'s emanating from the external environment. Reinforcement that is self-generated (i.e., in our covert) is called intrinsic reinforcement.

**7.** Reinforcers that maintain our biological/physiological needs are called primary reinforcers.

**8.** Any consequence that a person desires and acts to acquire is a positive reinforcer. Positive reinforcers are idiosyncratic to the particular needs and desires of the behaver.

**9.** Secondary reinforcers are conditioned through their association with primary reinforcers and acquire their reinforcement value through learning.

10. Praise, compliments, and verbal and nonverbal affirmations are valued social reinforcers that motivate many people.

11. Activity reinforcers such as hobbies, interests, exercise, and work provide intrinsic enjoyment and satisfaction simply in their doing.

12. The most frequently occurring positive reinforcers exist in the form of money, stars, checks, tokens, grades, and all the other consequences whose value is based on the material, activity, and social or primary reinforcers that they can obtain.

13. Negative reinforcement is the removal of punishment (C–) resulting in an increase in the behavior that caused the removal to occur.

14. Escape behavior is what we do to remove a C– that is currently being experienced. If successful, escape behavior is negatively reinforced.

15. When we covertly expect a C– to occur and then act to prevent its occurrence, we are performing avoidance behavior, which is another form of negative reinforcement.

16. Successful avoidance behavior is based on our ability to discriminate the antecedents for signals that the C– is imminent.

17. Factual avoidance behavior is based on the prevention of real C–'s, whereas fictional avoidance behavior is designed to prevent nonexistent C–'s.

**Figure 1** *The A-B-C (Cognitive–Behavioral) Model*

| (A) Antecedent | Covert | (B) Behavior | Overt | (C) Consequence |
|---|---|---|---|---|
| | **Covert** | **Overt** | **Overt** | |
| | **Cognitive (Thinking)** | **Respondent (Physical)** | **Operant (Acting)** | |
| Stimulus or setting event. External environments that set the occasion for behavior (thinking, acting, feeling) to occur. $S^{Dee}$ = Green light. A cue that a particular behavior will result in a desirable consequence. $S^{Delta}$ = Red light. A cue that a particular behavior will result in an undesirable consequence. | Subjective environment. The process and content of our thinking. Our interpretation of A-B-C as a-b-c. Includes: Attributions Expectations Self-concept Self-esteem Beliefs Attitudes Prejudices Self-talk Locus of control Images Fantasies Intrinsic consequences | Reflexive Autonomic Involuntary Biochemical Physiological changes occurring within our body. | Voluntary behavior that we choose to do or not to do. Can be: Excess = Behavior done too often or at wrong time. Deficit = Behavior done too infrequently or not when needed. | Events (external) that occur during and/or after a particular covert and/or operant behavior. Events can be: A. Desirable: 1. Positive Reinforcement present desirable = C+ 2. Negative Reinforcement remove undesirable = C̶ B. Undesirable: 1. Punishment present undesirable, aversive = C− 2. Extinction remove desirable = C̶ |
| | | **Emotions** | | |

Subjective labels used to describe a specific state of being. Labels reflect the composite of our covert, respondent, and operant behavior within a specific context of antecedents and consequences.

# Chapter 4

<hr>

# Undesirable Consequences: Contingencies We Dislike

<hr>

## Orienting Ourselves

In Chapter 3, we looked at the motivational effects of consequences that we desired. Whether experienced extrinsically or intrinsically, highly valued C+'s influence the choices in operant behavior that we make. Likewise, our capacity to avoid or escape aversive consequences (C–s) teaches us a large repertoire of coping behaviors that can help us fend off the slings and arrows of life. Motivationally, negative reinforcement can be just as powerful as positive reinforcement, but the relief of negative reinforcement never approaches the satisfaction of earned C+'s.

Unfortunately, not all of our actions or inactions lead to desirable consequences. More often than we would like, our actions result in consequences that we find undesirable. At times, we encounter punishment, embarrassment, and even pain as a result of some operant of omission or commission. At other times, we find that our behavior no longer achieves the positive reinforcers that we had come to expect. Our goal seems unattainable and we experience a loss of motivation and may even choose to give up on that particular behavior. In both instances, we encountered undesirable consequences and the deleterious effect of receiving C–'s or losing C+'s as a result of our actions. These principles of punishment and extinction receive our attention in this chapter. Figure 4 reviews the consequence component of our model.

Now that we have covered consequences that strengthen or increase behavior, we are ready to shift to consequences that have the opposite effect. Although punishment and extinction both weaken, inhibit, or eliminate behavior, they have many differences ranging from the action taken on the consequence to the specific effect that each consequence has on the behavior preceding it. We will start with punishment and then move to our second undesirable consequence, extinction. With completion of our study of extinction, we will have covered each of the four categories of consequences. We will then be able to look at the effects of various presentations of consequences on our operant behavior. These schedules of reinforcement have a dramatic effect on our actions. But first we examine undesirable consequences.

**Figure 4** *Consequences*

---

### (C) Consequence

---

Events (external) that occur during and/or after a particular covert and/or operant behavior. Events can be:

A. Desirable:

1. Positive Reinforcement present desirable = C+

2. Negative Reinforcement remove undesirable = C̶-̶

B. Undesirable:

1. Punishment present undesirable, aversive = C–

2. Extinction remove desirable = C̶+̶

---

## Punishment

Let us return to the consequence matrix on page 32. Cell 3 presents the contingency in which something is presented to the behaver, and the effect is to decrease the behavior that precedes it. The contingency looks like this: ↓ B—C–. The consequence is represented by the letter C, and the – stands for negative, aversive, or unpleasant, which is how the consequence is experienced.

Punishment, or C–, occurs when we receive an object, event, or reaction that we do not desire. We experience the C– as negative enough to change our behavior so that we do not experience that same C– again. Let's suppose I decide to eat chicken that I discover deep down in my freezer and carrying an expiration date about 6 months old. If I get moderately sick 3 h after eating it, I will probably not eat it again. If I get severely sick, with all of the symptoms of salmonella, I may throw out the entire contents of my freezer. I doubt that I would throw out the freezer, but maybe! The point is that punishment affects behavior, and the more immediate and severe the punishment, the greater its effect on behavior. We will look at this effect after we discuss the characteristics of punishment.

### Characteristics of Punishment

Just as positive reinforcement can be extrinsic or intrinsic, so can punishment. In other words, punishment can occur from our external environment (other people, objects, events) or it can be self-imposed in the form of intrinsic punishment. If my teacher criticizes me for turning in a sloppy, disorganized term paper and if her comments hurt me, then her criticism is extrinsic punishment of my "term-paper behavior." Likewise, I may experience the entire term-paper task as arduous and unpleasant (i.e., intrinsically punishing). I might even add more intrinsic punishment to the task by berating myself for doing such a lousy job. Self-talk such as "That stunk, Wally! You can do better than that" serves as intrinsic punishment. Some of us are masters at self-punishment.

A second key characteristic of punishment is its subjectivity. Punishment is presented to you, and you experience it as aversive, and modify your behavior to not experience that consequence again. Hearing her name called in class might humiliate and embarrass Sue to the extent that she will never draw attention to herself again (at least not in that class). Hearing her name called by the teacher is a powerful C–. Helen, on the other hand, might love to hear her name announced in class for any reason at all. Rather than being a C–, hearing her name in public might be a valued C+, prompting her to behave in all sorts of attention-seeking ways. A teacher of these two students who is unaware of the idiosyncratic effects of public/social recognition is liable to punish Sue for diligent work and positively reinforce Helen for fooling around and disturbing her classmates. Just as with positive reinforcement, punishment is in the eyes (and ears) of the beholder or behaver.

As mentioned previously, punishment is most effective in inhibiting, weakening, or eliminating behavior if it is immediate and intense. Immediate refers to the temporal latency between the behavior and the C–. The shorter the latency, the greater the impact on behavior. If I smoke a cigarette and immediately start coughing and experiencing chest pains and shortness of breath, I might reconsider the next cigarette. Unfortunately, the C–'s produced by cigarettes appear long after the behavior is completed and the damage is done. Many of our BORCs (e.g., substance abuse, recklessness, and self-indulgence) do not incur C–'s until well into the future. It is the short-term or immediate consequences of C+ or ⊠– (remember secondary gain?) that maintain these behaviors.

Immediacy vis-à-vis long-term consequences is especially pertinent to criminal behavior and our criminal justice system. If criminal justice imposes C–'s (as well as the removal of C+'s) for criminal behavior, what is the covert expectation of a mugger, burglar, embezzler, or even a murderer? In all probability, the C– occurs long after the crime, if it occurs at all. And when it does occur, the association, or A–B–C contingency, has lost its meaning and impact. Immediacy must be a key to effective, purposeful punishment.

The intensity of punishment refers to its severity or discomfort as experienced by the behaver. If you ever inserted an electric plug into an outlet while standing in water, you fortunately lived to learn from it and will never do that again. It is not uncommon for the survivors of a serious automobile accident never to enter an automobile again. Some immediate and severely intense C–'s can be so traumatic as to cause "one-trial learning." You only had to experience the C– once (as a serious injury, embarrassment, humiliation) to learn when (A) and how (B) to avoid the C– in the future.

As I said in discussing negative reinforcement, the experience of immediate and especially severe C–'s can induce factual avoidance behavior that quickly evolves into the fictional avoidance behavior of phobias and anxiety disorders. Punishment of extreme severity and immediacy can certainly inhibit and even eliminate behavior; in some exceptional circumstances, it may be indicated, but its overall effect is deleterious. I will discuss the "down side" of punishment after looking at its different levels.

Similar to positive reinforcement, punishment can also occur at different levels. These levels parallel those of positive reinforcement.

### Primary Punishment

Any consequence that is physically painful, injurious, or otherwise physically debilitating would *probably* be experienced as a punisher. I stress "probably" because the final determination of whether a consequence is, in fact and effect, really a punisher is solely in the experience of the behaver. For some folks, physical abuse in the form of slapping, spanking, whipping, lacerating, and even burning is experienced as pleasurable, or at least offers sufficient secondary gain to offset any of its negative effects. Masochistic behavior such as self-inflicted and other invited physical "abuse" is not punishment. Conversely, mild stimulation such as tickling, stroking, bright sunlight, normal noise, and even touch is experienced by some people as C–'s. The only way to really know is to ask and/or observe.

We all have certain foods that we find aversive to the taste, smell, or digestion. While some find chocolate highly toxic, others thrive on it. Whatever causes a physiological aversion, and an unpleasant experience, is a primary punisher. The example of primary punishment that most of us are familiar with (for some, too familiar) is corporal punishment (corporal meaning "of the body"). Fortunately, the legal, ethical, and even efficacy considerations of this purposely applied consequence have rendered it obsolete in most of the civilized world.

### Secondary Punishment

The more frequently experienced and purposely applied form of punishment occurs in overt disapproval from others. The manifestations of social disapproval range from a scowl and rolling of the eyes to blatant name calling and verbal abuse. Sarcasm, putdowns, epithets, and criticism are all forms of verbal secondary punishment. Nonverbal secondary punishers are legion and range from disapproving facial gestures to the emotive waving of the middle finger.

Contrary to the adage "Sticks and stones will break my bones, but names will never hurt me!" secondary social punishers do hurt. Their injury resides in our covert, where we experience it as embarrassment, humiliation, guilt, and ultimately shame. Secondary punishers from others cast doubt on our sense of worth, value, efficacy, and acceptance. We do, of course, have choices as to how we process this punishing feedback in our covert. We can discount and invalidate its accuracy, discarding it to the trash heap of "mean, stupid, or ignorant others." In this case, the feedback does not qualify as punishment. Or we can ascribe meaning and credibility to the punishing feedback. We then use the feedback to build and reinforce our own feelings of inadequacy and worthlessness (i.e., our covert standard of acceptability, which I will discuss in Chapter 10). Other people's pronouncements of our stupidity, incompetence, insensitivity, ad nauseum are directly translated in our covert to something like, "Yes, you're right. I could have told you so!"

Depending on how immediate, specific (descriptive), relevant, and potentially corrective the social punishment presented by others and received by us (the behavers) is, we can respond in adaptive or destructive ways. Although we will discuss cognitive/covert change mechanisms extensively in Chapter 11, suffice it to say here that feedback from others is experienced as punishing when we accept it as valid and use it to question our competence, worth, and adequacy. Even our questioning shakes our confidence and forms the basis of our embarrassment, humiliation, guilt, and shame. If that foundation of confidence in our competence, worth, and efficacy is not strong (and has not been validated through extrinsic and intrinsic C+'s), secondary/social punishment has devastating effects. Not only does it cause many of our operant behaviors to weaken and decline, but the covert expectation of and credibility ascribed to social C–'s engender all of the stress reactions described in Chapter 5. Yes, names do hurt.

## Effect of Punishment on Behavior

As should be clear from our discussion so far, behavior that results in punishment, especially if immediate and intense, does not continue. It weakens, inhibits, or totally stops. Let us look at each of these effects.

"Whether a behavior weakens, inhibits, or totally stops, it is under some form of antecedent stimulus control. We learn to covertly expect C–'s by observing our environment and assessing the context (i.e., when, where, by whom, under what conditions) in which C–'s have the highest probability of occurring. This process of stimulus discrimination, which is the focus of our next chapter, is critical to coping with punishment effectively.

When the blatant and subtle messages from our external environment tell us that a C– is near, we covertly recognize its probability (i.e., primary appraisal), covertly assess how best to cope with it (i.e., secondary appraisal), mobilize our physical resources for effective coping (i.e., the fight-or-flight alarm stage of the general adaptation syndrome), and then do whatever operant behavior seems appropriate. If the perceived C– is not particularly immediate or intense, we may continue to perform the punishable behavior less frequently, with less emotional intensity, and certainly less obtrusively. Although we continue, the behavior has been weakened.

On the other hand, if the C– is clearly imminent and aversive enough to avoid, we totally stop the behavior only as long as the A tells us that the C– is highly probable. The discontinuance, or inhibition, of the "punishable" behavior is stimulus bound (i.e., based on the presence of the "A–red light") and returns to full strength as soon as the A signals that the coast is clear.

A particularly immediate, intense, and unpredictable C– causes the preceding behavior to totally stop. Because of the punishment's unpredictability, the behaver cannot discriminate the context (i.e., A) of its occurrence. Consequently, no occasion or antecedent is safe to perform the behavior. The behavior is discontinued and over time is dropped from the behaver's repertoire.

A brief example of each effect might clarify your understanding of these dynamics. I am strolling through a department store with my wife, who is doing some shopping. My favorite TV show is about to begin, so I run to the electronics department. All of the TVs are boxed and unassembled, so I open a box, place a TV on the shelf, plug it in, turn it on, and watch my show. While I am watching, the manager rushes over to me. Here is what could happen:

> The manager might glare at me and rearrange merchandise in my immediate vicinity, all the while keeping an eye on me. I turn down the volume but continue watching unobtrusively. My behavior has weakened.

> The manager castigates me for my intrusive, aggressive, and reckless behavior, at which point I immediately turn off the TV and retreat to another part of the store. In an instant, the manager is summoned to the opposite end of the store

by a customer. I return to the scene of the crime, turn on the TV, and continue to watch as long as I can see the manager at the other end. Each time he gets within hearing distance of the TV, I turn the TV off and retreat to another part of the store, only to return when he is safely at a distance. My TV watching has been inhibited by his presence and the probability of his social punishment.

The manager screams loudly and announces my stupidity and impudence before a throng of shoppers. He is enraged and appears ready to sock me in the nose. He explains that I am responsible for any malfunction of the TV. He storms off and I quickly lose sight of him as he turns down an aisle. His reaction was intensely punishing, and I have no idea when he might return. I turn off the TV and leave quickly, never to do that again. My impulsive behavior has totally stopped.

Before we leave the subject of punishment, one important characteristic needs emphasis. Punishment, as a learned contingency, teaches the behaver what not to do, but it seldom teaches what to do. Under punishment, the punishable behavior is either weakened, inhibited, or stopped, but no operant behavior is learned in its place. Of course, avoidance or escape behavior is learned, but that avoidance is typically to weaken, inhibit, or stop the behavior in question. For weakened or inhibited behavior, any additional learning that occurs is either lying or deception. And what is learned in most instances of punishment is fear and anger toward the punisher and an underlying anxiety about the expected C–.

## Extinction

**E**xtinction refers to the dynamics in which a behavior is extinguished (weakened or stopped) when the expected positive reinforcer (C+) no longer occurs. We do not extinguish the behaver, although some parents and teachers might experience fleeting thoughts of doing so. In fact, extinction is very different from punishment.

Extinction is often confused with punishment because they seem to have the same effect of reducing or eliminating behavior. But this attenuation effect on behavior is about the only similarity between them. A quick review of cell 4 of the consequence matrix (page 32) reveals the most important difference between the two decreasing consequences. The contingency for extinction appears as ↓ B–$\cancel{C}$+. Notice that in extinction, a C+ is actually taken away or in some way prevented from following a particular behavior. When this happens, the particular behavior weakens or stops completely, but unlike under punishment. Let us look more closely at extinction.

### Characteristics of Extinction

As with all of these B–C contingencies that we have been studying, extinction is a natural, common effect of change. Just as there are numerous C+'s that motivate us to behave, changes in our environment as well as changes within ourselves eliminate or diminish the occurrence and value of those C+'s, causing us to change our behavior. Here are some examples:

## FOR BETTER OR FOR WORSE

Punishment and extinction have one thing in common: They both hurt. (© 1992 Lynn Johnston Productions Inc./Distributed by Universal Press Syndicate, Inc.)

You have maintained a close relationship with your neighbor for many years. Whenever you call or stop by her house, she welcomes you with enthusiastic conversation (a valued C+ for you). And when you meet in public, you are demonstrably pleased to see each other. Then suddenly, your neighbor takes a new job and moves away. You call a few times, leave messages on her answering machine, even write her a letter, but each effort to restore the friendship is met with silence. After a while, you stop calling and writing. Your social behavior toward her has been extinguished.

As a lover of classical music, you consistently tune into your local public radio station. Tuning in each morning has become a habit; you just assume that the C+ of their Bach, Beethoven, and Mozart selections will always be there. Suddenly one morning, after a disappointing fund-raiser by the station, you are informed that classical music has been replaced by news and talk show entertainment. Now, this new format is tolerable (i.e., it is not a C–), but the loss of your beloved classics is devastating. You emotionally appeal to the station to reconsider, but to no avail. A few days later, you change to another station. Your habit of turning to your old station has been extinguished—and so might your financial contribution.

Over the past few years, you have been using your bank's automatic teller machine (ATM) for all of your banking transactions. One day, the ATM is out of order and you're forced to go elsewhere. Two days later, the same thing happens. You try the next day and are successful. Your following visit finds that your card is rejected, yet it works elsewhere! Your next two visits find the ATM out of order, and you try once more, but this time, the ATM is out of money. This becomes your final visit. Your behavior of visiting that ATM has been extinguished.

You have a big yard with beautiful grass in the front of your house. Come football season, the neighborhood children decide to use your beautifully manicured lawn for a playing field. You are very upset and angry but hesitant to chase them off (punishment for their playing) for fear that they will retaliate and vandalize your property. So, you decide to use extinction. You tell the kids that you want to convert your lawn into a garden and that their playing on the lawn will "till it just right." You pay each kid 25 cents for tilling your lawn by playing football.

On three successive occasions, you pay them for their "gardening service." But just before their next game, you tell them that you're broke and can't afford to pay them anymore. Disappointed, they walk away in search of another field. They refuse to play in your yard if you do not pay them. This is an example of purposeful extinction.

These four examples contain all of the common characteristics of extinction. In each, a C+ that had been experienced (and thus became a covert expectation) was removed. The neighbor's attention, classical music, a successful transaction with the ATM (C+ = $), and the 25 cents were experienced as C+'s, became expectations, and then ceased. And as they ceased, so did the motivation to communicate with the neighbor, tune into the public radio station, use the ATM, and perform gardening services by playing football.

You may have noticed in the examples that the persistence of behavior under extinction differs greatly. This difference in the speed in which behavior is extinguished, or the persistence of behavior when the C+ is finally removed, is based on the past experience that the behavior has had with the B–C+ contingency. The frequency with which the behavior has resulted in the C+ is its *schedule of reinforcement*, which we will discuss at the end of this chapter. Behavior that is just getting established, or that has always resulted in the expected C+ (i.e., schedule of continuous reinforcement) as with the kids losing their 25 cents, tends to extinguish the quickest once the C+ is removed. This is probably because the covert expectation for the C+ has not been established as a high probability.

Conversely, behavior that has not been positively reinforced every time, but frequently enough to establish a strong covert expectation of getting the C+, may persist long after the C+ has been permanently removed. This periodic C+ is referred to as *intermittent reinforcement* and is a very powerful schedule for sustaining behavior. Anyone who has sat for hours pumping coins into a slot machine or calling for more cards can attest to its motivational power. The persistence in visiting the ATM illustrates this. The ATM worked just often enough to sustain a covert expectation that it might work again. If the C+ never occurs, the behavior eventually stops altogether. But that eventuality is a function of our reinforcement history for that particular behavior.

Another characteristic of extinction that also depends on the behavior's reinforcement history (or schedule of reinforcement) is its effect on behavior. Intermittent C+'s increase the persistence of behavior. On the other hand, continuous C+'s preceding extinction cause more rapid extinction, but an initial increase in behavior frequency and intensity (emotional response) before the behavior actually stops. The classical music example illustrates this. You consistently received the music you desired until it abruptly stopped. Your first response was to emotionally increase your efforts to reestablish the C+. When that failed, your behavior quickly extinguished.

If a vending machine has always worked for you and then suddenly your change doesn't produce the coffee, what do you do? You initially pour more change in and possible bang or kick the machine. If no coffee pours out, you stop pouring in. When a child has consistently gotten the attention of a parent and that attention is withdrawn (and the child is ignored), what happens? The child works even harder at getting attention, motivated by the covert expectation that "I got it before, so I just have to work a little harder to get it again." If the C+ was initially for misbehavior, then it is the misbehavior that increases under extinction.

For those attempting to use extinction purposely to decrease or eliminate behavior, it is crucial to remember the distinctions between extinction and punishment. Extinction does not involve presenting something aversive or unpleasant. To ignore a child's disruptive behavior (when that child wants attention) is extinction; to reprimand or yell is not extinction. The reprimand or yell might be punishment, or it could be experienced as positive reinforcement.

One purposeful application of extinction occurs when a disruptive child is removed from the scene of the disruption and placed in a neutral (nonreinforcing) setting. This strategy is called "time-out." As an application of extinction, time-out works when the disruptive scene from which the child is removed possesses C+ value for that child (i.e., the child wants to be there), the process of removing the child is neither a C+ nor a C–, and the neutral, or time-out, setting does not possess C+'s or C–'s. We will talk more about the covert aspects of extinction strategies in Chapters 9 and 10.

## A Word About Depression

Severe problems can result from excessive C–'s and deficient C+'s. We have already discussed (and will do so extensively in Chapter 6) how the covert expectation for C–'s constitutes fear and stimulates the physiological response of anxiety. In its more extreme and pervasive occurrences, extinction creates a problem of a different kind: depression. There is strong evidence that some forms of depression have an organic or biochemical etiology. Bipolar disorder as well as certain affective disorders stem from hormonal and other biochemical imbalances. It is also clear that even mild forms of mood disorders (dysthymia) and reactive depression correlate with biochemical disturbances, if not as the cause, certainly as a physiological effect.

My purpose in drawing attention to this debilitating complex of syndromes is to suggest that extinction is the primary culprit in most depression. This is especially true when the absence or removal of highly valued C+'s from the external environment is processed by the behaver as the covert expectation for the absence or loss of C+'s. Such a covert expectation for ⊠+ could be the sudden loss of that C+, as in the reactive depression brought about by the loss of a loved one, dislocation from reinforcing friends, family, and culture, or even a severe financial loss necessitating a more austere lifestyle. Or the depression could be more pervasive and not tied to any particular loss, but covertly experienced as a constant belief (covert expectation) that the world—even life itself—is devoid of C+'s. This consuming belief that no environmental person, event, experience, or consequence offers the remote probability of a C+ constitutes the fundamental ingredient in chronic depression.

Robert Hedaya (1996) reports a number of studies of brain activity in bipolar and major depressive patients that reveal diminished electrical activity in the brain's pleasure centers (i.e., accumbens nucleus and associated frontal cortex). Disregulation of dopamine and serotonin neurotransmitters in these areas seems to account for this inability to experience the pleasure of any C+. When the depression has a strong organic component (either as the cause or the effect), the pleasurable experience of C+'s is severely diminished (i.e., extinguished) by the brain's inability to process the sensation of pleasure. In less severe forms of depression, anhedonia (the inability to experience pleasure) has also been associated with biochemical disregulation (Ashton, 1992).

Whether reactive or chronic, the essential dynamic is extinction, and the effect is to weaken, inhibit, and even stop the vast array of operants that could obtain the C+'s that we all value and need in our lives. We will continue this discussion of depression in Chapter 7.

## Intrinsic Consequences

Earlier, I introduced the concept of intrinsic consequences in reference to self-imposed positive reinforcers. Although I have presented these four categories of consequences as illustrating externally, or extrinsically, produced consequences, each category can be generated and sustained with our covert (mind). Just as I can positively reinforce myself for something I have done (or did not do), I can also punish myself. All of those negative self-references—"I am stupid." "What a lousy job." "I look silly." "I can't do this." "What a poor parent I am." And so on—are forms of intrinsic punishment. I can also experience intrinsic extinction by failing to positively reinforce myself for actions that once received substantial self-praise. If we accept that intrinsic positive reinforcement (sometimes in the absence of extrinsic C+'s) builds and maintains operant behavior, it seems reasonable to assume that the termination of this intrinsic C+ has the opposite effect. What do you think?

In many instances, intrinsic consequences actually follow the performance of an operant behavior. Were I ever to bowl 200 (or even put two strikes together), I might praise myself for "still having it!" and label my feelings as proud or energized. My covert C+ follows my performance and increases the probability of doing that operant (bowling) in the future. Sometimes, however, the projected/expected consequence is in anticipation of the B–C contingency and actually occurs before the operant. In fact, expected consequences of C– and ⊠+ may actually prevent the operant behavior from ever occurring. If I expect to fail at bowling and cringe at the prospect of making a fool of myself (C–'s for me), I might decline an offer to bowl and suggest a movie instead.

We can punish or extinguish (weaken, inhibit, or stop) our operant behavior by generating the expectation for C–'s or ⊠+'s. This attenuation of operant behavior may be very adaptive when the C– is empirically valid. To covertly expect injury (C–) when darting through speeding traffic helps me mediate my impulsive and reckless behavior. But I can also generate the covert expectation for C–'s that have no external reality. I could weaken, inhibit, or stop my social initiating behavior by telling myself that "I'm a loser." "I will fail." "People will think I am weird." "I'll be rejected." "I'll be ignored." "They'll make fun of me!" Each of these covert expectations is either a C– ("They'll make fun of me!") or a ⊠+ ("I'll be ignored."). The first statement ("I am a loser.") is a self-reference that probably provides the basis for the other C–/⊠+ expectations. In any case, whether intrinsic punishment or extinction, the effect is to weaken, inhibit, or stop behavior and to perpetuate anxiety, depression, and unhappiness.

## Schedules of Reinforcement

**A** few times throughout this chapter, I referred to schedules of reinforcement. This term has relevance because it characterizes the rate or frequency with which C+'s actually follow the operants that produce them. Schedules of reinforcement do pertain to the B–C+ contingency relationship, and the phenomenon of extinction is a predictable consequence of some of these schedules. Thus, an understanding of extinction will greatly enhance your understanding of why certain schedules leave us unmotivated and pessimistic toward future C+'s.

In our natural environment, the rate and frequency with which we experience C+'s following our operant behavior differ tremendously. In some rare instances, every time we do a behavior, we receive the desired C+. Doing factory piecework or working on commission might represent this kind of schedule. The C+ occurs after a specific "B" (i.e., assembling the part or making the sale) has occurred. Sometimes we have to do a lot of B's before getting the C+, like doing math problems or washing dishes. At other times we never know when the C+ is coming, but we know it follows some B. As different as the schedules of C+ are, each has a distinct effect on our behavior. And if you are particularly concerned about purposeful behavior change, you need to consider the schedule of reinforcement.

Essentially, we can base our delivery of C+'s on the number or frequency of B's performed (the *ratio* dimension), or on the period of time after which the behavior must be performed (the *interval* dimension). For each dimension, we can base our presentation of the C+'s on a fixed and consistent (between C+ presentations) schedule or on a variable and inconsistent (performance of B's before each presentation of the C+) schedule. Consequently, we have two dimensions with two schedules each, comprising a total of four schedules of reinforcements: (a) fixed ratio, (b) variable ratio, (c) fixed interval, and (d) variable interval. Figure 6 shows the pattern of behavioral response that you can expect under each of these schedules.

### Ratio Dimension

The C+ is made contingent on the number or frequency of behaviors emitted between the delivery of each C+.

**Fixed Ratio (FR)** The reinforcement is made contingent on the completion of fixed or the same number of behaviors. For example, an FR-1 schedule means that every behavior is followed by a C+ and is called a "continuous reinforcement schedule." An FR-5 indicates that five performances of a behavior are required before delivery of the C+. Some of the characteristics of FR schedules are:

**1.** If the ratio is small at the beginning, the rate of responding is large. The quickest way to start a behavior is to use an FR-1 (continuous) schedule. When I start a new behavior, I want to get the C+ as soon as possible.

**2.** If the ratio is too large, I have to work too hard to get the C+, and so I slow down or even stop. Very high fixed ratios discourage the behaver from trying. This is called *ratio strain* and occurs, for example, when the teacher requires 10 workbook pages completed

**Figure 6** *Schedules of Reinforcement Profile*

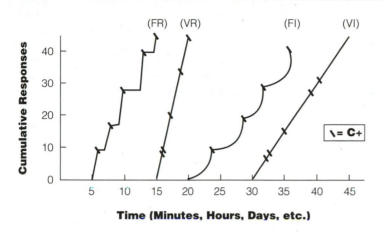

perfectly before the student can take recess. When parent tells a child with a D+ average in school that he or she can go roller skating after bringing home a report card with all A's, that's ratio strain. It creates frustration and surrender with little effort.

**3.** In FR schedules, behavers quickly identify the ratio of behavior required for the C+. As the ratio gets higher, they tend to stop for a while after obtaining the C+ because the C+ temporarily loses its value (due to satiation) and they need a breather before starting the behaviors again. They also have learned that the next few behaviors will not result in a C+. This period of inactivity following receipt of the C+ is called the *postreinforcement pause*. You can readily see it as the flat, horizontal line after each C+ in Figure 6. After the postreinforcement pause, the rate of responding increases abruptly until the next C+.

***Variable Ratio (VR)*** The reinforcement is made contingent on the number of behaviors emitted since the last C+, and the actual number of behaviors required for each C+ differs around a specified mean. For example, a VR-5 schedule might mean that the C+ comes after four behaviors and then after six, five, seven, three, five, one, and nine for a total of eight B-C+ trials. The average of these numbers is five, thus a VR-5. The best example of this very common schedule is gambling. The payoffs (C+'s) on slot machines vary. Sometimes it takes ten coins, the next time it may require only two, and the next seven, and then four, and so on. You have a blast pumping money in and telling yourself, "This is the one. This is the lucky silver dollar."

As you might surmise, VR schedules are very powerful in keeping behavior going for a long time. Although FR-1 schedules are best at starting behavior, VR schedules are best at prolonging it, as its profile in Figure 6 shows. Some of the characteristics of VR schedules are:

1. They produce a very high and steady rate of behavior.

2. They are very resistant to extinction. Because the exact mean and schedule for C+'s are so difficult o discern, the behaver never knows which B will produce the C+ and is therefore motivated to keep trying. Some people with certain behaviors that have been maintained on a VR schedule actually continue the behavior long after the C+ has totally disappeared. Investing in stocks, drilling for oil, and searching for loose change between furniture cushions are just a few examples. Harold Stassen successfully ran for governor of Minnesota more than 40 years ago and never gave up. Although election victories are on a fixed interval (2–4 year) schedule, Stassen's persistence suggests some reinforcement on a VR schedule.

## Interval Dimension

The C+ is made contingent on the first behavior after a specified period of time. Whatever the behaver does during the interval of time is irrelevant in getting the C+. The behavior must be done after the time interval has elapsed. Under interval schedules, we try to discriminate time more than behavior because the only B that gets the C+ is the one following a certain period of time. Consequently, as we identify the time interval, we tend to do very little behavior until the very end of it. Does this sound familiar? How would you characterize your academic/study behavior during a particular term or semester? If you answered "procrastination," then welcome aboard. Procrastination is the product of interval schedules, especially fixed interval schedules. Here's why.

**Fixed Interval (FI)**   The C+ is made contingent on the emission of a B after a fixed and consistent period of time. The number after the letters represents the time interval between C+'s. An FI-16 might represent 16 weeks, the duration of a typical semester. Let's take the example of a FI-1, where the 1 represents a period of 1 hour. No C+ would occur for 1 hour. Then, as soon as the hour expired, the next B would result in the C+. After the C+ was presented, the next hour would begin.

Under FI schedules, our main task is to identify the time interval between C+'s. In other words, we discriminate the antecedent that tells us when the C+ can be expected and when we will not get the C+ regardless of what we do. Once we discriminate the time interval, we wait until the end and then behave. This gradual learning of the time interval and then responding at the end is referred to as the *scallop effect*, shown in the FI profile in Figure 6. Notice that as discrimination of the time interval improves, the behavior occurs progressively closer to the end, with hardly any behavior during the interval. School curricula that rely on grades (C+'s?) distributed only after the end of a time period (e.g., term, semester) tend to show the scallop effect. Here are some other characteristics:

1. The overall rate of behavior is low.

2. The slow, steady decline in behavior during the interval represents extinction. If you know the C+ will not occur, why do the B?

*Variable Interval (VI)* Reinforcement under this schedule is made contingent on the first B after a period of time that varies around a specified mean. Whereas the mean or average for VR schedules reflects behaviors, the mean under VI schedules represents the average of time intervals. This schedule is not as common as the others in the natural environment, but it does occur whenever you have to perform some behavior during an unspecified (and unpredictable) period of time before you can get the C+. A naturalistic example is fishing, with catching a fish as the C+ (I specify this because the C+ for fishing is often other than catching a fish). You never know when a fish will strike, but you need to have your line in the water to find out. Some other characteristics of VI schedules are:

**1.** They produce a sustained but low rate of behavior, as revealed in Figure 6.

**2.** The larger the interval mean, the lower the rate of behavior that results.

**3.** These schedules are very resistant to extinction. Because you never know just when the C+ will occur, you always retain the covert expectation that this time might be lucky. This characteristic of VI schedules has kept me fishing for years, and a frequent customer at my local fish market.

## Noncontingent Consequences and Superstitious Behavior

Throughout this chapter, I have discussed consequences that were contingent on performing a behavior. I would like to close the chapter by suggesting that not all C+'s are received contingently, just as not all C−'s are removed contingent on our behavior. There is a category of behaviors that we perform because we think (covertly expect) that they will produce certain C+'s and C−'s, but in fact, the consequences are unrelated and independent of the behavior. "Superstitious behavior" refers to behavior that is performed to produce either a C+ or a C− when the B–C contingency does not really exist.

Most of us possess some superstitious behaviors. We use our lucky pen on test day, wear a special shirt to an important interview, throw salt over our shoulder, perform some tasks only at special times (e.g., Horowitz's 4 P.M. performances), always exit a building by the same door that was entered, never walk under a ladder, wear napkins on our head and perform exotic movements to improve our luck at gambling, ad infinitum. All of these behaviors are performed in the hope (and expectation) that they will bring us luck and increase our chances of getting the C+/C− we desire.

Athletes are particularly adroit at superstitious behaviors. Certain meals before a game (e.g., Wade Boggs's famous chicken), clothing (e.g., the stench of continuously worn socks during a winning streak), preparation rituals, and the presence or absence of certain objects or individuals at a game are only a few of the superstitious behaviors performed in sports. Kids model professional athletes and adopt their superstitions for themselves as if they really work. Ironically, these noncontingent B's often do work for both the model and his or her young protégés. Let me explain.

When viewed with strict objectivity, superstitious behaviors do not cause our performance to improve on a test any more than inverting our hat improves our team's hitting. But what these behaviors can do is influence our covert expectations in ways that indirectly increase our chances for the C+/⊠–. When we introduce our covert behavior (i.e., expectations, attributions, beliefs) into the dynamic of our superstitions, we find that they do work. Whether we call it the placebo effect, psyching ourselves, magic, or just the power of faith, our covert expectations in the efficacy and workability of our superstitious behavior build our confidence, reduce our anxiety, and sustain our commitment to succeed—all of which produce an improved performance and a better chance at really achieving the consequences we desire. Spitting three times and tapping home plate twice with the bat does not cause my son to get a hit. But the act of doing them increases his self-confidence, reduces his anxiety, and improves his concentration, and all of these do improve his hitting. The same effect can be said about most of our superstitious behaviors. We retain them for a purpose, and they often work simply because we expect them to. I will discuss these covert dynamics of placebo and self-fulfilling prophecy in later chapters.

## Chapter Summary

1. Two categories of undesirable consequences are punishment (the presentation of C–) and extinction (the removal of C+). Both consequences cause behavior to weaken, inhibit, or stop.

2. Punishment can be both extrinsic and intrinsic, and it is particularly effective in reducing behavior when it is intense and immediate.

3. Corporal punishment is a primary punishment when it causes physical pain, injury, or discomfort. It can be effective, but it usually is not. It produces considerable avoidance, anxiety, and typically only teaches what not to do.

4. Secondary punishers include social disapproval, criticism, sarcasm, and verbal abuse. They do not hurt physically, but they sure hurt covertly (emotionally).

5. Extinction occurs when an expected C+ is withdrawn or otherwise prevented from occurring. Depending on our history of reinforcement with this C+, we may increase our behavior before decreasing or stopping it. Time-out is a common use of the principle of extinction.

6. The sudden loss of a highly valued C+ can create a form of reactive depression. The covert expectation of life devoid of C+'s can create chronic depression and a severe diminution of behavior.

7. Just as we can positively reinforce ourselves, we can punish ourselves and deprive ourselves of C+'s. These intrinsic consequences can affect our operant behavior in spite of any consequences provided by our environment.

8. A fixed ratio-1 (FR-1) schedule of reinforcement indicates that every behavior results in a C+. This is also called a continuous reinforcement schedule.

9. As fixed ratios increase in size, the postreinforcement pause becomes more prominent.

10. The variable ratio schedule of reinforcement is the most powerful in maintaining persistence of behavior. Gambling operates under this schedule.

**11.** Fixed interval schedules of reinforcement are the most prone to creating procrastination because the behaver knows that the behavior is not reinforced until the end of the interval. This is called the scallop effect.

**12.** A fisher knows that he or she needs a baited hook in the water to catch a fish. *When* a fish decides to bite is quite variable in time. Consequently, a fisher would most likely appreciate a variable interval schedule of reinforcement.

**13.** Although superstitious behavior is directly noncontingent on the B–C relationship, insofar as it increases our covert expectations for desirable consequences, it indirectly affects the B–C contingency.

**Figure 1** *The A-B-C (Cognitive–Behavioral) Model*

| (A) Antecedent | | (B) Behavior | | | (C) Consequence |
|---|---|---|---|---|---|
| | Covert | Overt | Overt | | |
| | Cognitive (Thinking) | Respondent (Physical) | Operant (Acting) | | |
| Stimulus or setting event. External environments that set the occasion for behavior (thinking, acting, feeling) to occur. $S^{Dee}$ = Green light. A cue that a particular behavior will result in a desirable consequence. $S^{Delta}$ = Red light. A cue that a particular behavior will result in an undesirable consequence. | Subjective environment. The process and content of our thinking. Our interpretation of A-B-C as a-b-c. Includes: Attributions Expectations Self-concept Self-esteem Beliefs Attitudes Prejudices Self-talk Locus of control Images Fantasies Intrinsic consequences | Reflexive Autonomic Involuntary Biochemical Physiological changes occurring within our body. | Voluntary behavior that we choose to do or not to do. Can be: Excess = Behavior done too often or at wrong time. Deficit = Behavior done too infrequently or not when needed. | | Events (external) that occur during and/or after a particular covert and/or operant behavior. Events can be: A. Desirable: 1. Positive Reinforcement present desirable = C+ 2. Negative Reinforcement remove undesirable = C̶ B. Undesirable: 1. Punishment present undesirable, aversive = C– 2. Extinction remove desirable = C̶ |

**Emotions**

Subjective labels used to describe a specific state of being. Labels reflect the composite of our covert, respondent, and operant behavior within a specific context of antecedents and consequences.

# Chapter 5

<hr>

# Antecedents:
# Our External Environment

<hr>

## Orienting Ourselves

**W**e started our discussion with a look at operant behavior, which we found was voluntary actions designed to produce desirable consequences. The exploration of those consequences was our focus in Chapter 3. In chapter 4, we directed our attention to undesirable consequences and described the contingency relationship between behavior and its various consequences. We found that this relationship follows certain principles and patterns depending on the schedule experienced in receiving positive reinforcers (C+'s).

We are now ready to put the B–C contingency into an environmental context that defines the when and where of our thinking and acting behavior. To truly understand the nature and purpose of our behavior, we need to analyze the external conditions under which it occurs. Since these conditions precede our behavior, we will refer to them as *antecedent stimuli*, or *antecedents* for short. Throughout this book, I use the shorthand A in referring to the antecedent component of our A-B-C model.

After we discuss the interrelationship that antecedents have with operant behavior and consequences, we will shift our attention to our involuntary or respondent behavior in Chapter 6. Through an analysis of the environmental, cognitive, emotional, and behavioral elements of "stress," Chapter 6 will demonstrate the A-B-C model as an integrative system. The structures and processes through which we actually perceive and understand our A-B-C's and, ultimately, construct our own subjective reality will be explored in the remainder of our chapters. It is truly in our covert world that all of the elements of our A-B-C model converge to give meaning, comprehension, and purpose to our lives.

But first, we must provide an environmental context for our behavior and its consequences. A good place to begin is with a review of the antecedent component (Figure 7).

## Antecedent Stimuli As Setting Events

**A**ll thoughts and actions occur within an environmental context. If you have a question, you raise your hand *in class*, (in all except mine, where shouting out is the norm) or if you are *on the street* or *in a store*, you approach someone and excuse the

**Figure 7** *Antecedents*

### (A) Antecedent

Stimulus or setting event. External environments that set the occasion for behavior (thinking, acting, feeling) to occur.

$S^{Dee}$ = Green light. A cue that a particular behavior will result in a desirable consequence.

$S^{Delta}$ = Red light. A cue that a particular behavior will result in an undesirable consequence.

interruption. If you are *home*, you probably yell it out. Each of the places in italics is an environmental/external context for different behaviors. And each environmental context signals information about the behavior that has the best chance of receiving either a desirable or undesirable consequence. Through the information that it imparts, each environmental context serves as the "setting event" for a particular behavior. Being in a classroom with an important question serves as the setting event for the behavior of raising your hand if you expect to be called up in a cordial way and receive an acceptable answer. In this way, being in a classroom and needing information are antecedent conditions that stimulate the behavior of hand raising. Consequently, I will refer to the environmental context for a specific behavior as the antecedent stimulus for that behavior and, thus, the A component of our A-B-C model.

In my hand-raising example, I have identified two antecedents for hand raising (and two for not hand raising, i.e., on the street and at home). The two antecedents are: (a) being in a classroom and (b) experiencing a need. The classroom environment represents an external antecedent because it exists within your external environment. "Being in the classroom" refers to a physical environment that sets the occasion for behavior to occur. It represents the where of our external antecedents and comprises everything and everyone present in that environment. The seating arrangement, location of the teacher and chalkboards, and condition of the desks all define the where of our antecedents. And so do the people present. The receptiveness of this particular teacher to answering questions as well as the receptiveness of the entire class to tolerating questions significantly determine whether this classroom is an antecedent for hand raising. We have all been in classes where the presence or absence of certain people either invites or inhibits hand raising.

The activity that is occurring around you is an additional stimulus that can set the occasion for behavior. What is happening in your external environment contributes important information about the appropriateness or inappropriateness of certain behaviors. If everyone around you is laughing and joking (and experiencing desirable consequences), it sends a far different message than if everyone is solemnly or anxiously reading notes or following a lecture. I will talk more about this antecedent control dynamic when I discuss norms later in this chapter.

An additional antecedent that stimulates hand raising is your need for information. Any need that exists within us, such as a physiological need for water or a need for information, can serve as an antecedent. I will refer to these as *internal antecedents* because of their internal locus. There are many covertly initiated antecedents that influence our overt behavior. These covert (or in the mind) antecedents, much like

internally identified needs, are self-initiated and not contingent on any external antecedents. We can generate thoughts and recognize internal needs independently of
our external environment. And these internal antecedents can set the occasion for a
multitude of overt behaviors.

So now we have identified two antecedents for hand raising: an internal need and a
place called a classroom. But just knowing the where and the need are still not enough
to stimulate us to raise our hand. Do you always raise your hand when you have a question in class? If your answer is "no," then when don't you raise your hand? Would you
raise your hand if the class period were about to end and your classmates were poised
for the mad dash out the door? Probably not. And the reason is because the timing
would not be right. Moreover, you could expect C–'s/⊠+'s from your classmates (and
perhaps even from your teacher) for asking a good question at the wrong time.

Time is critical because it tells us when a particular behavior will result in certain
consequences. It is just as crucial a setting event as where and the need. You might get
away with yelling out your question at home in midafternoon or early evening, but try
it at 3 A.M. and you can surely expect a C– or ⊠+.

We will come back to our hand-raising example many times in this chapter because
it illustrates how antecedents set the occasion for, or "call up," very specific thoughts
and actions through the information they communicate to the behaver. This information can be viewed as messages that say:

| Under These Antecedent Conditions: | Certain Behaviors Will Result in | Desirable Consequences C+/⊠– |
|---|---|---|
| What | | |
| When | | |
| Where | Certain Behaviors | Undesirable |
| Need | Will Result in | Consequences C–/⊠+ |

Do you recognize this message? It includes the essential information that we need
about the A-B-C's of any particular experience. Every second of every day in every external environment (antecedent), you are bombarded with messages that essentially
follow this same refrain:

Certain B's Will Result in Desirable C's

Under These A's

Certain B's Will Result in Undesirable C's

Since you are now reading this book, we'll assume that your antecedents are telling
you that this is the time and the place to do this behavior (i.e., reading or looking at
the cartoons). Let's see if you can identify exactly what these antecedents are and what
messages they are sending you. Just stop for a moment and apply this to your immediate experience of reading. After you read this brief paragraph and the following four

questions, put your book down and identify the internal and external antecedents that exist for you right now. Here are some questions to guide you in your analysis of immediate antecedents:

1. What are your antecedents now?

   External:   Where are you?

   What is happening around you?

   When is this occurring?

   Internal:   What needs are you aware of now that support your reading?

   Are there any needs that might be interfering with your reading?

2. What messages do these antecedents tell you about the appropriateness of your behavior (reading) now? In other words, in what ways are your antecedents setting the occasion for you to be reading or anything else that you might be doing?

3. What consequences (immediate and long-term) can you expect from reading now?

4. What do your antecedents tell you about behavior that would be inappropriate now? What behaviors would you not do now because the immediate or long-term consequences would be C–'s or ⊠+'s?

Now put your book down and give it a try for about 5 min, but don't forget to come back.

Welcome back! Could you identify some of the ways that your antecedents are influencing your behavior? Don't be concerned if you didn't identify all of the subtle antecedents that influence how, when, and where you behave. Inconspicuous aspects of our external environment can take on powerful antecedent stimulus control. The furniture that you are sitting (or lying) on, the lighting, room temperature and humidity, ambient sound (e.g., music, drone of a computer, talking, traffic), proximity to mealtime, the television schedule (the soaps are strong A's), and even the comfort of your clothing can set the occasion for you to read this book or do something else. The importance of this exercise is that you begin to recognize some antecedents in your life and start to appreciate the role of antecedents in the A-B-C model.

Good stimulus control involves building in green lights for the B–C contingencies that we like. (© Tribune Media Services, Inc. All Rights Reserved. Reprinted with Permission.)

## Stimulus Control

This antecedent analysis exercise gave you the opportunity to think about your immediate environment, how it influences your behavior, and the consequences of that behavior. Sometimes it is especially important to use the data from your antecedents for making decisions about your behavior. But not all antecedents are processed or used in a conscious way. As mentioned in Chapter 2, our covert behaviors (thoughts) and overt behaviors (actions) are often automatic, and we behave without consciously thinking about the antecedents that are influencing that behavior. The antecedent(s) exists and signals us to behave, but we are unaware of the process.

Unlike respondent behavior that is truly reflexive, automatic behaviors can be brought under conscious (covert) control; they have just become habitual and automatic over time. This is especially true when we are performing routine tasks or habitual behaviors that always occur under the same A-B-C conditions and have a long history of receiving the same C+'s or ⊠–'s. Washing dishes, turnpike driving, jogging, watching TV, eating dinner, and brushing your teeth are some of the many automatic behaviors in our repertoire. But even these automatic behaviors are under stimulus control. You don't brush your teeth when you enter your car for a long trip across country, nor do you start jogging when the call for "dinner!" is heard, though it may not be a bad idea. You may not even be (consciously) aware of the antecedents that are signaling these behaviors to action. If you ever wondered whether you brushed your teeth, turned off the iron, or left lunch money out for the kids, then you know exactly what I mean.

Most of the time, the automatic behaviors under stimulus control are quite functional, enabling us to perform routine tasks efficiently and freeing our covert for other thoughts. When automatic behaviors get us into trouble, stimulus control can be very destructive and very perplexing. Abuse of drugs, alcohol, and food, extreme forms of avoidance behavior, and aggressive/antisocial responses can sometimes be so habitual as to become automatic behaviors under stimulus control. The first step in remediating these automatic BORCs and regaining control over them is usually to consciously identify the antecedents that are controlling them, much as we did in our previous exercise. We'll return to this topic throughout this chapter.

## Stimulus Discrimination: Reading Your Antecedent Traffic Lights

Every external environment that you encounter contains numerous antecedents for your behavior. Even in our simple example of hand raising, there were at least three different antecedents that formed the signal that it was okay to raise your hand because a desirable consequence would probably result. The actual processing and interpretation of these messages occur in your mind (covert behavior). Although I will cover these covert processes in much greater detail in later chapters, suffice it to say here that the information value of the messages imparted by the antecedents is only realized through your covert (mental) processing of them. When you consciously size up your environment and assess the accurate messages from your antecedents to determine the various B–C contingencies before you, you are engaging in the cognitive process of *stimulus discrimination*. That is, you are trying to determine what the environment (antecedents) is telling you about your various behavioral choices.

Just as antecedents represent such macroscopic categories as when (time), where (place), what (objects, persons, or events), and need, the physiological and cognitive processing of these antecedents into meaningful information—the process of perception—involves the microscopic range of human sensory modalities. We live in many external environments rich in sounds, smells, tastes, tactile sensations, colors, and images. Our survival and optimal enrichment within these environments require us to extract, or discriminate, recognizable sounds, images, tastes, and so forth from this cacophony of environmental stew. Each bit of environmental information is absorbed by our sensory receptors, converted into biochemical impulses that are filtered through our central nervous system, and electrochemically recognized within the vast information-processing plant of our cerebral cortex.

Much of this biochemical information is not brought to conscious awareness, even though we continue to discriminate and respond to its molecular message. Automatic and habitual behaviors still retain the dynamics of stimulus discrimination. We have all experienced déjà vu, when a certain feeling or thought is aroused by a stimulus (antecedent) that we process below our threshold of awareness. A theater performance provokes our experience of a long forgotten romance; a screen door slamming on a warm summer day takes us back to happy times with grandparents; and the image of a large, dark shadow evokes childhood fears experienced when we found ourselves lost in a strange neighborhood. Our powers of stimulus discrimination operate on all that we have experienced in the past, need to know in the present, and will find helpful in the future. It may be that what we attribute to intuition is actually past A–B–C contingencies that are long since forgotten yet still within our long-term memory, and thus subject to stimulus control.

At a conscious level, information processing as covert behavior also necessitates stimulus discrimination at a microscopic level. From our earliest neonatal discriminations of our mother's smell or facial image, we used and refined our sensory apparatus to survive and thrive in the world. Instances of ineffective and inaccurate stimulus discrimination could result from poor learning or our own impaired physiology. This latter disability can stem from any physiological and biochemical defect that interferes with our senses or the cognitive processing of information derived from these senses. More apparent are the discrimination problems resulting from defective hearing and vision. Less visible yet equally disabling are the subtle biochemical imbalances within the frontal lobe of cerebral cortex experienced by sufferers of attention deficit hyperactivity disorder. Attention problems exacerbate appropriate stimulus discrimination and contribute significantly to the impulsive and aggressive behavior exhibited by children and adults with this disorder. Impulsivity, a primary characteristic of children with ADHD, describes children who act before they think. Whereas deferred thinking includes reflection on when and where to do a certain behavior, premature action is based on little or no stimulus discrimination. Children with ADHD may perform their best behavior—but at the wrong time or in the wrong place. This example illustrates that the cognitive process of stimulus discrimination, as with all covert and overt behavior, is a function of biological and environmental variables.

Stimulus discrimination is a natural, conscious process that occurs constantly as we interact with our many environments. Our awareness and discrimination of these external and internal environments reveal what we need to know to succeed within them. In so doing, perhaps the most valuable information that we obtain from our analysis of these antecedents reveals our behavioral choices and the various consequences that we can expect from each choice. Fortunately, most situations we encounter provide antecedents that accurately display this critical information. Our hand-raising example included enough antecedents that combined to send the message that hand raising was appropriate because the consequences were relatively desirable to the behaver. A prompt, cordial response from the teacher, acceptance by the class, and an accurate answer were highly probable consequences of hand raising. Assuming that these consequences were either C+'s (i.e., attention, recognition) or X–'s (i.e., escaping confusion or avoiding a mistake on an exam) for the hand raiser, the antecedents provided sufficient information for making a behavioral choice.

The choice to raise our hand was made because we (covertly) expected either a positively or negatively reinforcing consequence. However, the information that provided the data base for building this expectation and the subsequent choice to do the behavior came from the antecedents. The when, where, what, and need information from the antecedents signaled the reinforcing B–C+/X– contingency, and so we raised our hand. In other words, the antecedents functioned as a "green light" for the performance of hand raising because of their association with the reinforcing consequences. Thus, we can say that these particular antecedents were a green light (i.e., A–green) for that particular behavior. The technical term for green-light antecedents is *discriminative stimuli*, or $S^{Dee}$ for short. The $S^{Dee}$'s are antecedents that signal that certain behavior will result in C+'s or X–'s.

## Antecedents: Green Lights

**A**ntecedents that signal or set the occasion for behavior to occur are analogous to green traffic lights. Just as green traffic lights do not control your car but signal you to proceed on your journey, antecedents–green signal you to go ahead with your behavior because the consequence will probably be reinforcing. In most environments and situations, the external antecedents function as green lights for certain behaviors. Our task is to discriminate, or read, the antecedents to figure out what the messages are.

Our most common, routine, everyday environments provide antecedents that we can rely on for clear, consistent messages. That's why we perform so many automatic behaviors in those situations. From the moment you awake in the morning (and the noise of the alarm is an antecedent–green light for reaching over and turning it off), you are constantly confronted with antecedents that signal or set the occasion for your behavior. If you brush your teeth first, then the bathroom provides numerous A–green lights for the complex behavior involved in brushing your teeth. The presence of the toothpaste tube serves as an A–green light for opening it, and the open tube and toothbrush in your hand serve as an A–green light for squeezing the toothpaste onto the brush, which serves as the A–green light for placing it in your mouth and brushing, and completion of your ritual of actually brushing serves as an A–green light for rinsing your mouth, and so on throughout your day. If, by chance, you found the tube to be empty, it, along with other antecedents (e.g., the time, presence of other family members, etc.) would serve as A–green lights for other behaviors, such as screaming for help or perusing your medicine cabinet.

Most of the time, our stimulus discrimination is easy, automatic, and successful. The process becomes more challenging in more novel situations and environments, when we are not always sure what the antecedents are telling us. Because of our uncertainty, we don't know whether to proceed with confidence (that the consequences will be C+/☒–), with caution, or not at all.

Our traffic light analogy sheds more light on this dilemma. Traffic lights are not always green. Sometimes they are red. Other times they are yellow. And sometimes they don't work at all (and they seem to be white), in which case we often become immobilized, unsure, and threatened by any movement. Just as traffic lights give multiple (and even conflicting) signals, antecedents provide more than just green lights. Discriminating the reds, greens, yellows, and whites of our antecedents is one of the most pervasive challenges that we face in realizing the desired consequences in life.

## Antecedents: Red Lights

The antecedents in our hand-raising example provided ample green lights for raising our hand. These antecedents told us what not to do because the consequences would be undesirable (C–/☒+). The classroom situation did not signal us to sing, eat, perform jumping jacks, urinate, or do any of a universe of behaviors that would have been deemed inappropriate. The performance of any of these behaviors would surely have resulted in C–'s or ☒+'s—thus, their "inappropriate" characterization. Again, what announced the inappropriateness of these behaviors was the information revealed by the antecedents. Along with serving a green light function, signaling the "go ahead" for a particular behavior, these antecedents also signaled a red light for other behaviors.

These same classroom antecedents might also have signaled "Caution: Proceed with care." The appropriateness of typing lecture notes into a laptop computer or calling out your question at a moment of silence may be unknown. You are not sure what the consequences are, so you inhibit your behavior, try to assess the contingency by observing others, or take the risk and try it. Trial-and-error learning is often our only resource when faced with yellow and white antecedents.

Antecedent–red lights are much easier to interpret than yellow and white because their message is clearer: A certain behavior (by commission or omission) will result in an undesirable consequence (C–/☒+). These messages signaled by our external environment are processed in our covert and translated into covert expectations of what will happen when certain behaviors are performed or not performed. As I mentioned earlier, the same antecedents that provide green lights for certain behaviors also provide red lights for other behaviors. The technical term for red-light antecedents is *stimulus delta*, or S$^{\text{Delta}}$ for short. The S$^{\text{Delta}}$'s are antecedents that signal that certain behavior will result in C–'s or the loss of C+'s. Figure 8 gives some examples.

**Figure 8** *Antecedent Messages: Green, Red, and Yellow*

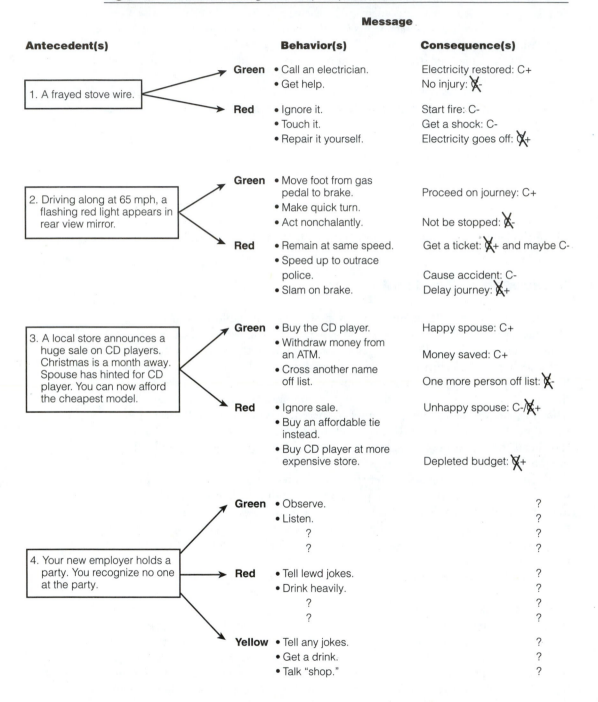

A number of characteristics of antecedents are illustrated in these examples. I will highlight a few:

**1.** Each antecedent condition represented a time, place, situation/event, and a person—that is, when, where, what, and who. The important message of each antecedent reflected any combination of these factors.

**2.** Each antecedent communicated green lights for some behaviors and red lights for others.

**3.** The green lights signaled behaviors that resulted in desirable consequences—C+'s and/or ⊠–'s.

**4.** Notice the effect that red lights had on behavior. In every instance, the red light signaled the occurrence of a C–/⊠+ if a particular behavior occurred or continued. The frayed wire signaled the probability of a C– (shock) if touched. The red light signaled us to stop or refrain from starting certain behaviors—touching wire, driving faster, going to another store—to prevent undesirable consequences. The green light part of each antecedent stimulated our covert to identify behaviors that we could do to avoid/escape a C– or to avoid losing a C+. This is why we say that the red light messages of antecedents stop or prevent behavior, whereas the green light messages turn behavior on. In terms of what we actually learn from these messages, green lights teach us what to do, while red lights teach us what not to do. This contrasting effect is significant when we are purposely programming for learning. When the only messages that we receive from our antecedents/environments are red lights, we restrict our action and curtail the development of a broad, reinforcing repertoire of behaviors. "Do" teaches so much more than "Don't."

**5.** Each antecedent condition could also have provided yellow (caution) and white (?) light information, but the first three examples provided such distinct green and red lights, I left yellow and white out.

**6.** Each antecedent condition provided information that could be used for decision making and purposeful action. The process of differentiating green from red light messages is called stimulus discrimination.

**7.** Stimulus discrimination offered information about different contingencies, and this provided the basis for choice. How we exercise or ignore those choices affects the consequences we experience and the learning that we acquire for our next encounter with that antecedent.

**8.** In antecedents where the green and red light messages were clear, familiar, and unambiguous, the choices were much easier. The more unique or novel the situation, as in example 4, the more difficult it is to decipher the green, red, yellow, and white light messages. In example 4, the behaver wasn't sure how to behave at the party, thus the profusion of question marks.

## Stimulus Discrimination: The Process

**N**one of us were born instinctively knowing all of the green, red, yellow, and white messages existing in our external antecedents, but we were born with the instinct to learn through the process of stimulus discrimination. From infancy on, we observe and study our environment for clues that tell us when, where, who, and under what conditions certain actions will meet our needs. Our green light for crying quickly became mom's absence (plus some internal antecedent conditions), while her presence might be a green light for smiling, phonating, and grasping. This early stimulus discrimination, perhaps our first, propelled us on a path of continual attempts to read our environment.

In the early years, this path thrusts us into frequent ambiguity. Everything new and unexperienced presents us with the challenge of learning what is appropriate, best, and the right thing to do. A new gang of kids encountered on the playground, a new (or substitute) teacher, taking the school bus, and dinner in a restaurant all represent antecedents with their own unique messages for us to figure out. Forced with this risky task, we probably took the safest route and learned by observation. We picked up cues from watching others behave or, better yet, had an older sibling, parent, teacher, or experienced elder tell us what our antecedents meant.

Sometimes if we were not sure what was appropriate, we took a risk and just did it. If we were right, we stored that information in our covert and proceeded to take even more risks. After all, even risk taking can be increased through positive and negative reinforcement. Over time, our antecedents became progressively more familiar, consistent, and comfortable. Our antecedents' predictability became a source of security and safety that even helped us define our own identity. We just knew how to be sixth graders, how to ride a bus, how to eat in a restaurant, and how to be best friends with our gang. This security enabled us to take risks gradually within a parameter of safety. Novel antecedents were not too threatening because a mistake only produced minor C–'s and ⊠+'s. Our environment saw to that.

It was only when we faced highly ambiguous or continually changing antecedents that we experienced confusion, caution, anxiety, and even depression. A move to a new neighborhood, separation from old friends, upheaval in the family, and even promotion to a new school can create antecedent ambiguity. If you ever encountered any of these experiences, you can probably remember your discomfort and the conscientious effort required to discriminate the new green and red lights. You may have been the assertive, confident leader in the old environment, but reverted to a shy, cautious, observant follower in the new one. That is, you needed to get a "fix" on the new antecedents and regain your sense of self-control in knowing the what, when, and where to do certain behaviors to achieve C+'s and ⊠–'s. Whether we call it culture shock (Toffler, 1984), learned helplessness (Maier & Seligman, 1976), or simply homesickness, disruptions in our environment redefine the messages of our antecedents and undermine our ability to make effective stimulus discriminations.

### *Norms As Social Antecedents*

As we interact with and experience our various external environments, we learn the messages that are consistently and reliably conveyed by the most prominent antecedents.

We learn that we never chew gum in Mr. Frank's class, we always wear jeans and a T-shirt to our Tuesday bowling match, we eat dinner around 6 P.M., and never, never walk with our parents when we visit the local mall. Each of these four separate (discriminated) environments represents specific A's that communicate very precise A-B-C contingencies. The contingencies might be communicated subtly and implicitly, as in the edict that gum chewing in Mr. Frank's class results in detention; these A-B-Cs are announced publicly and enforced consistently. Other contingencies, such as wearing jeans and a T-shirt while bowling, are revealed implicitly (usually through observational learning), yet are just as certain and rigorously enforced.

Whether implicitly or explicitly revealed, these most prominent and consistently enforced A-B-C contingencies represent the *norms* of each of our many environments (i.e., antecedents). As norms, these socially established and maintained contingencies explicate and stabilize our expectations of appropriate and inappropriate, acceptable and unacceptable, covert and overt behaviors. The social group (neighbors, classmates, team, colleagues, gang, etc.) operating within these environments establish and/or maintain these norms with conviction and zeal, often embracing them as the cherished values of "our" group. Our acceptance in the group becomes contingent on our compliance with these established norms.

One violates a norm by ignoring or resisting a sanctioned A-B-C contingency at great peril. Consequently, we devote much of our conscious attention to identifying (i.e., discriminating) the nature of these different norms. Stimulus discrimination represents our attempt to discriminate the A-B-C contingencies we can expect within each environment. In familiar surroundings, with family and friends, the norms are well established and the discrimination is automatic—we come to dinner at 6 out of habit. Conversely, in novel and unfamiliar (especially threatening) environments, our knowledge of the norms may be sparse and untested, causing us to consciously and cautiously observe, learn, and possibly test the contingency if risk taking has been reinforced in our past.

The existence and influence of norms are constantly brought to our attention because norms represent society's (and thus, our covert) expectations for what will probably happen if we behave in certain ways in certain situations. When explicitly described and consistently enforced, norms provide a sense of security and stability in our lives. The tyranny of norms rest in the manner in which they restrict freedom of choice and repress experimentation with the vast array of contingencies open to the human experience. Consider the norms operating in your own environments: family, church, school, job, and so on. In which environments (antecedents) are the norms formal and explicit? Implicit yet rigidly enforced? Flexible and fluid with a plethora of acceptable behavioral choices? Your answers reflect the diversity and power of norms in our daily experience.

Our challenge is not to control all the norms in our environments, nor can we limit these norms to safe and predictable parameters. The unknown affords rich opportunity for growth and invigoration. Our moment-to-moment vigil in responding to the exigencies of our many environments calls for us to appreciate the impact of norms and accurately discriminate their substance. In so doing, we can realize the agenda and values manifest in our various environments and, with knowledge and security, exercise choices leading to maximum success.

## Antecedents: Ambiguity and Contradiction

Difficulty in stimulus discrimination is a major source of stress. When red and green messages are clear, consistent, and unambiguous, we can be most secure in our behavioral choices. We may not like these choices, but at least we know what contingencies to expect. A boy who is placed into time-out (remember, ✗+) every time he tosses expletives at his sister will quickly learn the choices he has based on predictable consequences. His sister (and presence of a parent) become the red light for his lewd comments. If, on the other hand, his sister and/or parent often laugh at his profanities and praise his creativeness in using them (all a C+ to him), then he will be much more unsure as to how (and when) to respond the next time.

This insecurity is even more pronounced when the external environment sends highly inconsistent, ambiguous—and even contradictory—antecedents. A home where the presence of a parent might be a green light for the child's approach behavior (e.g., initiating verbal and/or physical communication) one time and a red light for the same approach behavior another time will leave the child feeling confused, anxious, and out of control. These mixed messages create a double-bind (Bateson, G., et al., 1956) for the child. Another example of this double-bind occurs when parents tell a child that "In this house, arguments are to be settled peacefully," and yet the parents viciously battle with each other constantly. And when reconciliation is attempted by one parent, the other parent exploits it for further attack. How does the child read these messages? The only way for the child to cope in such a confused and dysfunctional (to use the current lexicon) family and maintain some sense of control is to withdraw, deny the threatening reality, and compulsively "play it safe." This "playing it safe" might require the child to compulsively make everything perfect—don't leave anything to chance. If this scenario sounds familiar, it is because it is played out constantly in many homes with an alcoholic parent(s). Children of alcoholic parent(s) devote inordinate time and energy trying to discriminate the green from the red lights, and they recoil from any yellow or white antecedents. They become masters at observing and discriminating the antecedents, as if their life depended on it. And it often does.

## Antecedent Green Lights: Characteristics and Functions

Antecedent green lights can set the occasion for behavior to occur in a variety of ways. They can signal for the behavior to occur, instruct the behaver how to perform the behavior, facilitate environmental conditions that enable the behavior, and potentiate the behavior by influencing its consequences. Let's look at each of these functions in more detail.

### Signals

A primary function of antecedent green lights is to signal the behaver as to the most appropriate time, place, and context to act; that is, when to expect the highest probability of achieving a C+ or ☒– following the behavior. Relative to green lights, signals communicate information that tells us:

**1.** A certain action (i.e., doing or not doing a behavior) will result in positive reinforcement.

**2.** A certain action (i.e., doing or not doing a behavior) will result in negative reinforcement.

This class of antecedents can occur in many forms and manifestations, and all signal that a desired consequence probably follows a particular behavior. Blatant or subtle, visual or auditory, clear or obtuse, familiar or strange, green light signals are a natural, pervasive part of our environment. We might experience them in any of the following categories.

*Cues*  These are time, place, and activity events that signal us to actions.

Water boiling over the rim of a pot tells us to lower the heat.

The sight and sound of the ice cream truck signal to get mom or raid the piggy bank.

The date, weather, and a free weekend set the occasion to till the garden and clean the mower.

Several daily newspapers on an uncut lawn tell us that our neighbor is away and signal us to keep an eye on their house.

A swerving car late on a weekend night signals us to keep a good distance.

The display of time is a ubiquitous signal that governs so much of our behavior. What time is it? Got to go.

*Social Messages*  Interpersonal signals can be verbal or nonverbal (e.g., physical gestures and movements).

The head nods and smiles that say "okay."

The words that give the go ahead: "Yes." "Okay." "Good." "Please." "Do it!"

The stern, grimaced face that says, "Better change your behavior!"

The eye contact that says, "Keep going. I'm listening." Or the diverted eyes that say, "Silence," or a different topic will be reinforced.

The open arms and physical posture that say, "Approach!"

The twirl of the hand that says, "Go ahead," or "Keep going."

The physical proximity that invites greater intimacy.

*Clothing*  Our dress and that of others reveal much about acceptable behavior.

Military uniforms, with their insignias of rank, signal very explicit rituals of authority and respect.

Many occupations maintain the same ritualized codes of dress and the proper response to that dress. The notion of "dress for success" suggests the importance of clothing in influencing your behavior and that of others.

There is a vast body of literature documenting the effect of dress on sexual behavior and gender stereotypes. Sexual advance based solely on clothing is an invalid yet not uncommon use of this category of antecedents.

**Signs** Visual symbols that communicate the appropriateness of specific behaviors are society's most frequent application of signal green lights.

Road signs communicate everything from the speed limit (how to avoid an unpleasant consequence) to the brand of suntan lotion to use.

Commercial advertising tells us where to shop and where to get a bargain.

Your refrigerator door is probably covered with notes that remind you what to do, when, and where. Mine is.

My computer keyboard has a multitude of signs that tell me which keys to press for specific consequences.

A specific label indicating a favored brand of product tells me that C+'s/⊠–'s can be expected from its use.

## Instructions (Tell You How to Do the Behavior)

While signals tell us when and where to do certain behaviors, instructions tell us how to do the behavior. Although both set the occasion for behavior to occur, instructions go beyond signals by informing behavers of what they need to know and do to actually perform the behavior. In so doing, instructions actually teach the behavior as exemplified by the following categories.

**Directions** Information that describes the actual performance of a behavior is a direction.

Many products I buy include a set of printed directions for assembly and use. As a visual learner/processer, I use the picture on the box (or what I think it looks like) and toss the directions away. This sometimes results in C–/⊠+.

Verbal directions are pervasive in education, but can be difficult for many children to follow and process.

Multisensory directions given visually, auditorially, and even kinesthetically are the easiest to process for most people.

Written directions can be delivered in the form of books, sequential outlines, and any form of curriculum materials used for educational purposes.

**Demonstrations** These are graphic illustrations, visual and/or auditory, modeling appropriate (and sometimes inappropriate) behavior.

Live demonstrations connect the model and observer in the most personal way. They also offer the opportunity of model–observer interaction and instantaneous correction of the observer by the model.

Recorded demonstrations such as audio- or videotape, computer disk, or written documentation are inexpensive and easily transportable, but may retain very limited generalization over time and diversity of audience.

For difficult and complex behaviors, the most effective demonstrations are performed by models who share characteristics (e.g., age, gender, grade, ethnicity, etc.) with the observer and acknowledge the difficulty of the behavior demonstrated. In fact, demonstrating the behavior perfectly (referred to as *mastery modeling*) may produce less actual learning then demonstrating the behavior imperfectly with small increments of improvement. This form of *coping modeling*, developed by Kazden (1984), capitalizes on the observer's capacity to identify and thus imitate the model.

*Examples* Many times, we learn a complex behavior through the observation of models performing live or recorded behavior similar but not identical to the learned behavior. Behavioral examples give scope as well as depth to our antecedents. In addition to serving as a demonstration of some performance, examples provide facsimiles of the real thing. A prototype will reveal what the actual item will look like.

*Prompts* Environmental events that assist us at the beginning of a behavior by signaling us to begin or actually guiding our behavior are called prompts.

Much like signals and cues, although more deliberate and explicit, prompts can serve as green lights to begin or maintain a behavior because they signal that a C+ or ⊗– will probably follow.

Prompts can also serve a red light function by signaling not to do a behavior because its performance will result in a C– or ⊗+. A conspicuously parked police car will prompt drivers to slow down, while a "closed" sign in a store window will prompt prospective customers to go elsewhere.

Prompts are often most critical in the learning of new behavior. Prompts may be verbal (e.g., explanations), visual (e.g., modeling), and even physical (e.g., helping one get started with a task). An important feature of most prompts is their temporary employment. Prompts, like reminders and helpers, are designed to start behavior. Once the behavior is established, the prompts are gradually removed or faded out. We will talk much more about the process of fading a little later in this chapter.

*Facilitators* Facilitators create conditions that enable you to perform the behavior. We are often unable to perform a behavior simply because we lack the necessary equipment, tools, space, and other environmental resources. Most home repair tasks require a hammer, pliers, and that marvel of technology, the cordless screwdriver. Without them, even the most sophisticated carpentry skills are useless. Likewise, a large open field is critical for the development and performance of many athletic behaviors. Tennis prowess would certainly not evolve beyond the covert stage without a racket, ball, and surface to play on. Each of these environmental aids provides a critical and timely resource that enables and facilitates a desired behavior.

*Tools* These are the hardware and software resources required to perform a desired behavior.

> Written communication requires anything from the basic technology of a pencil (or stick) to the sophistication of a computer.

> Most sports require elaborate, and often expensive, equipment to perform adequately. Gloves, skis, helmets, and precision bikes—the inventory of sporting goods conglomerates—have become indispensable to the contemporary athlete.

> As the plumber charges $85 for a 12-min repair of our leaky faucet, we quickly realize that as much as we are in awe (and debt) of her skill, we are helping finance those extraordinary tools that enable her to complete the job.

*Aids* As with prompts, we often need aids and crutches to help us learn complex and difficult behaviors. Once the behavior is mastered, these supports can be removed.

> Most of us were fortunate to have a steady hand or pair of training wheels to keep us upright as we struggled to master the bicycle. Oh, how we couldn't wait to get rid of those unsightly and embarrassing training wheels, but blessed be their initial support.

> Flashcards with the answers conveniently on the back are a valuable resource in learning a wide range of skills from arithmetic to vocabulary.

> My daughter learned to type and perform keyboarding skills on a "Muppet" keyboard. This user-friendly device enabled her to perform many keyboard operations with ease and confidence.

> Many disabled individuals become fully functioning and productive through the use of various prosthetic devices. Wheelchairs, computerized and automated speech devices, artificial limbs, signers, and lead dogs are only a few examples of aids that enable behavior to occur.

> A relatively new category of aids that facilitate the performance of behavior comprises the various drugs and medications designed to regulate and enhance behavioral (covert and overt) performance. These medications are used to regulate the body's physiology so that optimal functioning can occur. The most common examples of medicinal aids are stimulants (e.g., Ritalin) for attention deficit–hyperactive disorder (ADHD), clockers (e.g., Clonidine) for Tourette's syndrome, tricyclics and antidepressants (e.g., Tofranil, Prozac) for depression, and sedatives (e.g., Valium) for anxiety reduction. This latter medication eliminates the C– of pain while simultaneously creating the green light antecedent for an array of operant behaviors.

> All of these medicinal aids serve as green lights for functional behavior. I find it helpful to view them as setting the occasion for behavior to occur by physiologically enabling the person to perform. These drugs do not model, instruct, signal, or teach behavior, but they do enable people to use other principles of behavior (the A's and C's of their environment) to learn and then maintain that learned behavior. Ritalin does not teach, signal, or reinforce study skills in an ADHD

diagnosed child, but it does enable a distracted, impulsive, and hyperactive child to attend and focus well enough to learn how to study and then to actually study when required.

Every time we load up on caffeine to improve our concentration (or stay awake), consume that additional alcoholic beverage to relax or muster the courage to confront a stressful event, or even smoke a cigarette to settle ourselves down, we are using antecedents as aids in behaving.

Aids can also be used as red lights for the purpose of disabling certain behavior. Antabuse, a medication taken by some alcoholics, prohibits their body's ability to adequately synthesize alcohol. When alcohol is consumed, Antabuse causes severe (though temporary) sickness. Antabuse in the body sets the occasion for alcohol not to be consumed because of the severe C– that surely follows. Unfortunately, the addictive qualities of alcohol are such that Antabuse is often avoided or the C– is actually endured (remember secondary gain?). Examples of other red light aids include safety latches on cabinets that reduce accessibility of young children, guardrails and other highway barriers, and home circuit breakers and fuses. Can you think of others?

**Space and Facility**  Every behavior requires its own physical space. Adequate space is the prerequisite antecedent facilitator for everything from exercise to the privacy of our most intimate behaviors.

A secure, hard, and spacious floor is a critical aid in tap dancing. I studied tap dancing for 2 yr as a young child, but my budding career came to a screeching halt when my parents installed wall-to-wall carpeting throughout our house. A sad but true story. Could my parents have been using stimulus control?

**Potentiators**  These are antecedents that increase or decrease the probability of doing certain behaviors by changing the value or nature of the consequence expected to follow that behavior. The interaction effect of the various components of the A–B–C contingency is never more evident then when we consider that our (covert) expectation of a given consequence is instrumental in setting the occasion for the precipitating behavior occurring in the future. The value, probability, and accessibility of a C+ has a direct influence on the potential for a given behavior occurring at a particular time and place. Assuming that I am capable of doing a behavior, such as cooking popcorn in my microwave oven, my behavior has the greatest potential for occurring when: the value of the C+ is greatest (i.e., my body craves popcorn); the probability is high that I can do the behavior now (i.e., I have the time, microwave oven, and popcorn now); and the C+ is readily accessible (i.e., the popcorn is "all mine"). Each of these environmental conditions—C+ value, probability, and accessibility—contributes to the antecedent for cooking the popcorn. They set the occasion for the behavior to occur.

Too much of a C+ can cause satiation in that particular C+, thus decreasing its value. No matter how much we enjoy attention, food, and even a superbly played musical selection, continued indiscriminate exposure creates satiation and reduces its motivational value.

As the value of a C+ increases, the greater is its motivational power as a green light antecedent for the behavior required for obtaining that C+. The familiar adage is certainly true that "you can lead a horse to water, but you can't make it drink." It is, however, equally true that you can increase the probability of its drinking if you fed it lots of salty peanuts. An abundance of salty peanuts (the potentiator) increases the value of the water (C+) and results in a significant increase in drinking behavior. Successful bartenders probably discovered this potentiator long ago.

The covert expectation that a B–C+ contingency has a high probability of occurring under a specific antecedent condition enhances the green light power of that antecedent. In this sense, we might say that covert behavior (as expectations) initiates and validates the green light through its capacity to discriminate the existence of that specific antecedent condition. We will elaborate on this principle as we analyze the cybernetic regulation of our A-B-C system in Chapter 9.

Anyone experiencing success in the enterprise of maximizing human effort knows that the control over the access or availability of C+'s is critical to its motivational power to behave. Shared and employee ownership of business production and profits have significantly increased worker productivity and greatly expanded those green lights for diligence, honesty, and profitable work behavior. Conversely, the inaccessibility of the C+ diminishes the green light potential of the antecedent environment. My son will probably not clean his room for TV time if our TV is broken, nor will he vigorously pursue his homework when its completion is unrecognized by his parents or teachers.

## Stimulus Generalization

### Finding Similarities Throughout Our Environment

Throughout this chapter, we have paid considerable attention to the principles that identify the green, red, yellow, and white lights in our external environment—the process of stimulus discrimination. Fortunately, these environments have enough stability, our experiences retain enough similarity, and our memory of these experiences provides enough integrity that we need not be consumed by a constant vigilance of discriminatory contingencies. Every environmental antecedent is not a novel, complex, or threatening experience requiring cautious analysis to ensure safety or success. But when we do confront challenging experiences, we can effectively employ our covert powers of stimulus discrimination and respond appropriately.

Most of our initial learning of operant behavior occurs under very specific antecedent conditions; we first learn to hold the hand of our parents), aggressively take objects from our siblings, or even tell lewd jokes to our best friends. Over time, however, we learn to perform those behaviors under antecedent conditions similar but not identical to the original. We hold the hand of our grandparent, teacher, neighbor, and even crossing guard. Unless our behavior toward these similar yet different antecedents produces a C–/☒+, we continue and even gradually expand these A-B-C experiences.

**Figure 9** *Stimulus Generalization*

| Antecedent–Green Lights | Behavior | Consequence |
|---|---|---|
| Original A1–Green (Parents) | B–1, Hand Holding | C+, Tactile |
| | | ⊗–, Protect |
| A2–Green (Grandparent) | B–2, Same | C–Same |
| A3–Green (Teacher) | B–3, Same | C–Same |
| A4–Green (Neighbor) | B–4, Same | C–Same |
| A5–Green (Crossing Guard) | B–5, Same | C–Same |

This process of expanding the antecedents that elicit the same operant behavior is called *stimulus generalization*. It is the opposite of stimulus discrimination. Our success in experiencing the C+'s and ⊗–'s we desire in life depends on our ability to maintain both forms of antecedent stimulus control. In most cases, the extent of our stimulus generalization is a function of the similarity between new antecedents and the original.

Figure 9 illustrates the natural and critical process of learning that occurs through stimulus generalization, but also suggests the harmful effects that can result from inappropriate generalization (sometimes called overgeneralization). We all need to generalize our physical display of affection toward loved ones in our environment, but some antecedents are inappropriate, dangerous, and off limits, in which case discrimination is called for. This realization is the basis behind many instructional programs for children focusing on self-management (impulse control), assertiveness (the A's for saying "yes" and "no"), and physical safety (good touch–bad touch).

Also gleaned from Figure 9 is the crucial importance of reinforcing consequences (C+ and ⊗–) in the actual learning and execution of stimulus generalization. We generalize our operant behavior to new and different antecedents to the extent that these antecedents portend predictable and valued reinforcers. Once joke telling is punished or ignored, we discriminate those antecedent red lights (classroom, teacher, dinner table, church, etc.) and regulate our behavior accordingly. Joke telling may only occur at school in the presence of a permissive teacher (or that green light for much "testing" behavior—the substitute). If we see Uncle Frank reaping only laughter and approval for his spicy banter at a family reunion, we might just try out a few jokes at the table. If positive (reinforcing) consequences ensue, we might be well on our way to a career in stand-up, or at least an antecedent that maintains those payoffs for such jocular behavior.

An especially abhorrent behavior such as aggression might follow these same dynamics of stimulus generalization. A child who consistently, even if only intermittently, receives reinforcing (C+/⊗–) consequences for aggressive behavior toward siblings is prone to use hitting and grabbing behaviors (the realm of verbal and physical abuse) toward peers, spouse, and an ever-expanding circle of others. I will expand upon this phenomenon of learned aggression shortly. The point I wish to highlight now is that in the myriad occasions in which our learning and generalization of operant behavior to new environments is played out, a key operating principle is the perceived (covert)

contingency between our antecedent (external) environment and expected consequences. We expand our repertoire of behaviors to whenever and wherever we believe
our interests are served.

The salutary effects of stimulus generalization are manifest in the freedom and spontaneity in which we use our repertoire of operant behaviors to negotiate the infinite
array of antecedents in our external environments. Without effective stimulus generalization, our subjective world (covert behavior) would be cautious and constrained,
creating a restricted and even immobilized repertoire of operants. Those unable to
generalize their behavior to novel antecedents tend to narrow the richness and diversity of either environment and eschew functional risk taking, all of which restrict their
freedom of movement and opportunity. Conversely, the adverse effects of poor stimulus generalization are legion. Let me highlight just a few:

**1.** Perhaps the most insidious face of stimulus generalization appears in stereotyping
and prejudice. Stereotyping is a covert stimulus generalization process in which the
thoughts (attributions and expectations) and concomitant feelings about a particular
antecedent (e.g., person, place, object, or event) are generalized to all antecedents
even remotely similar (but still within the same class or concept). For example, some
gastrointestinal illness associated with a tainted taco might "teach" the generalization
that all tacos are poisonous, Mexican food is bad, and all Mexicans must suffer from
this affliction.

Such grossly invalid generalizations can even be learned vicariously. We are all familiar with stereotypes created and perpetuated by our environment (e.g., social groups, institutions, media). Some of these stereotypes may even be accepted without any direct
experience, still internalizing their generalization into our own covert behavior (attributions and expectations). With little experience or in most cases no direct empirical evidence, we come to believe such unfounded stereotypes as Italians are criminal, Jews are
miserly, blacks are shiftless, professors are nerdy, adolescents are rebellious, lawyers are
mercenary, southerners are slow and dense, and so on. Even when the stereotypes are
positive (e.g., Catholics are pious, Germans are efficient, social workers are committed
to others, etc.), they are just as invalid, restricting, and inaccurate.

By their very function, stimulus generalizations as stereotypes become expectations
and judgments about certain B–C contingencies that we can expect from those generalized antecedent conditions before we actually experience those A–B–C contingencies. These prejudgments are the substance of prejudices. The stereotype that girls are
inferior to boys in math supports the prejudice that girls will only fail when placed in
an advanced math class. Adherence to this prejudgment leads to a restriction of math-
ematics learning opportunities for girls, adversely affecting their math testing performance and ultimately perpetuating the original stereotype. Our actions (behavior)
resulting from our prejudices often perpetuate those prejudices and erroneously validate those stereotypes (stimulus generalizations). This self-fulfilling prophecy continues the cycle of error and injury.

**2.** As mentioned previously, aggressive behavior toward siblings is certainly subject to
stimulus generalization, especially if the aggressors experience constant—or even intermittent—C+'s or ⊘'s for their efforts. Although the roots of aggression are still

contested, with impressive evidence for a biochemical etiology (Comings, 1990), there is ample support for a social learning and stimulus generalization factor (Bandura, 1986). Successful aggressive control of a sibling easily creates the covert expectation on the part of the aggressor (as well as the victim) that force will establish the same successful control over C+'s and C✗'s with peers, parents, and ultimately the entire social environment.

We see that some social groups and cultures have established aggression (from discriminate acts of violence to restrictions of basic freedoms) as the social norm. Such cultural norms may also demonstrate stimulus generalization by expanding the antecedents for aggression to include everyone outside of our group—the insidious beliefs in us versus them. This dichotomous covert belief system is rife with prejudices and stereotypes.

**3.** Our discussion of stimulus control (discrimination and generalization) thus far has looked at its effect on operant behavior. Stimulus generalization as applied to respondent behavior follows similar principles but in a more causative fashion. Where the antecedents of operant behavior set the occasion for behavior to occur (as green lights) or not occur (as red lights), the environmental antecedents for respondent behavior actually cause the physiological response, bypassing the intermediary covert (conscious) processing of A–B–C contingencies.

Chapter 6 describes the physiological arousal (general adaptation syndrome) that can result from the presence of noxious antecedents. The antecedents, or stressors, elicit anxiety and collectively mobilize our behavioral resources for fight or flight. Any antecedent stimulus can serve as the initial stressor if its presence is contiguous to the experience of a C–. The more severe the C– and its temporal association with the antecedent, the more rapid and permanent the learning of the A-B-C contingency. Stimulus discrimination in response to stressors is a critically adaptive mechanism for affecting coping and human survival. Even stimulus generalization can be desirable and adaptive when the stressor truly represents a range of similar antecedents. The anxiety and associated coping operants in response to a hot burner on a stove can be just as adaptive in response to a hot iron, smoldering fire, or tropical beach at midsummer.

Stimulus generalization becomes maladaptive when the generalization exceeds the actual antecedent(s) that originally elicited the respondent behavior. For a small child, nearly drowning in a lake will certainly condition a very cautious and overtly fearful response to the antecedents represented by that particular lake. This heightened arousal and cautious operant response (i.e., coping) should generalize to any unfamiliar recreational swimming antecedents (i.e., pools, ponds, oceans, etc.). Adaptive coping becomes maladaptive—destructive and immobilizing—when the antecedents generalize to anything associated with water. This generalization is especially debilitating when the intensity of the original respondent (physiological arousal) remains as acute to each succeeding exposure to all water antecedents. Under these generalizing conditions, anxiety—perpetuated by its concomitant covert behavior of fear—leads to immobilization and extreme forms of avoidance and escape behavior. These are the essential ingredients of a phobia.

*A Concluding Thought About Stimulus Generalization*

Stimulus generalization is so pervasive and such a natural part of our learning that we seldom consider its positive and negative implications. It has even been identified as the basis for certain therapeutic processes. This dynamic is referenced (and used) in counseling as *transference*, the natural process in which the client's covert behavior (thoughts, feelings, expectations, attributions) toward his or her parent (the original antecedent) is generalized to the counselor (the new antecedent). As the nurturing authority figure of the parent, the counselor is able to evoke the dormant and sometimes dysfunctional covert and overt behavior of the client, bringing it under therapeutic scrutiny. A comparable dynamic of generalization, referred to as *countertransference*, occurs with the counselor toward the client.

## Concepts: Discriminating Within Generalizations

**B**efore leaving antecedents and the naturally occurring principles of stimulus control, one additional principle needs some attention: concept learning. This involves the combination of stimulus discrimination between distinct classes or categories of antecedents (and adjoining B-C contingencies) and stimulus generalization within the class of diverse A-B-C manifestations sharing attributes. Concepts represent covert perceptions and understandings of how experiences are similar in nature (i.e., stimulus generalization) and how experiences are distinctly different (i.e., stimulus discrimination). Our covert behavior includes a multitude of concepts that define objects, people, places, events, and even ideas. Lamps, Democrats, cities, holidays, and honesty are examples of concepts in that they are each united by some common property and yet are distinct from other concepts not sharing that property. By property, we mean the characteristic that is similar for each stimulus included in the concept.

Lamps share the property of being devices for producing light from some power source. This concept includes many examples with the same property: heat lamps, lighthouse lamps, hanging lamps, oil lamps, and so on. Lamps are not chairs, holidays, or Democrats (though some profess to be guiding lights), as none of these distinct concepts share this defining property of lamps. From the perspective of the A-B-C model, lamps comprise many antecedents that all have this common defining property and thus form a concept. We can actually form a concept of any or all parts of our A-B-C experience.

We have concepts of objects (e.g., cars, books), persons (e.g., women, African Americans, astronauts), places (e.g., home, school, seashore), and events (e.g., marriage, illness, Easter). All serve as antecedents for behavior and associated consequences (i.e., B-C components).

Generalizations of behaviors that share properties or attributes can also form the basis of concepts. Aggressive, impulsive, shy, friendly (i.e., adjectives we use to characterize and label each other) serve as concepts we use to both discriminate and generalize our experience of behavior.

Concepts of punishment, pleasure, loss, pain, safety, and even happiness represent generalizations of consequences of our actions. Often, we attach judgments of value to the concepts we hold for the consequences of our actions.

Our covert behavior also maintains more complex concepts that include or integrate all of the components of our A-B-C experience. Concepts such as honesty, thrift, integrity, goodness (and badness), responsibility, and freedom each represent a class of actions (behaviors) within their antecedent and consequence context. Any of these complex concepts describe an array of similar behaviors that we do or don't do under certain environmental conditions and are functionally related to specific consequences. Thrift involves behaviors of saving, investing, selling, and bargaining within certain boundaries of opportunity to create consequences of either acquiring or maintaining C+'s or pecuniary gain. Although there are many manifestations of thrift (and related labels, e.g., parsimony, frugality, stinginess), we can readily distinguish it from nonthrift (i.e., extravagance and excess).

A concept such as honesty readily illustrates this discrimination between diverse classes of contingencies and generalization within the variations in which these thematic A-B-C contingencies are displayed. We can generally recognize honesty when experienced by ourselves and witnessed in others. We can precisely describe the character of an honest person, and both identify and describe honest behavior. With even greater aplomb, we can recognize and distinguish when honesty is not being exhibited. Whatever label we use—cheating, lying, deception, falsification, graft—they all carry the common ingredient or property of dishonest action. We believe (and hope) that we can detect evidence of dishonesty in our experience and adjust our behavioral responses accordingly. In fact, our capacity to achieve those C+'s and C✗'s we desire is predicated on our ability to recognize (discriminate) these contrasting classes, or dimensions, of human behavior. Honesty and honest behavior may not always produce our most desired consequences, but a sober, realistic (and honest) assessment of our actions will accurately reveal our presence within or without the class of contingencies we discriminate as honesty.

As covert behavior, concepts form the framework, or classification system, from which we identify, recognize (discriminate and generalize), and ultimately respond to our external and internal environment. When valid and reliable, concepts enable us to function in our world with confidence, spontaneity, assertiveness, and success. Under these conditions, our concepts become "automatic thoughts," enabling us to generalize our actions most appropriately and expediently. Without concepts, our constant attention to stimulus generalization would immobilize us.

## Chapter Summary

1. Antecedents serve as the external environmental setting events for behavior and related consequences.
2. As setting events, antecedents represent or define the where, what, when, and need relative to particular covert and overt behavior.

3. When overt and/or covert behavior only occurs in the presence of specific antecedents, those behaviors are under stimulus control. Unlike respondent behavior, where the physiological response is autonomically controlled by the antecedent, covert and operant behaviors are voluntarily exhibited in the presence of environmental antecedents.

4. Automatic behaviors are simply unconscious habits of thought and action that we acquire through repetitions of A-B-C experiences. Automatic behaviors can be made conscious and deliberate.

5. Our attempt to discriminate what our environment (antecedents) is telling us about the various B-C contingencies we can expect is called stimulus discrimination.

6. Antecedent green lights reveal B-C+/⨉̶ contingencies. Their messages serve as a "go" (or "do") for certain behaviors.

7. Antecedent red lights reveal B-C–/⨉̶+ contingencies. Their messages tell us to "stop" or "avoid" certain behaviors.

8. Our behavior in the presence of antecedent yellow lights becomes cautious because the message from these antecedents is that we may or may not experience a C–/C+ as a result of our actions. Antecedent white lights are more ambiguous because they reveal no information about A-B-C contingencies that we might experience.

9. We experience considerable stress when we cannot figure out (i.e., discriminate) the B-C expectations from the messages (antecedents) in our external environment. New and unfamiliar (or inconsistent) environments cause us to learn the A-B-C contingencies cautiously through vicarious and observational learning.

10. Socially established and maintained A-B-C contingencies represent group norms.

11. Antecedent green lights can have many characteristics and functions ranging from those that tell us when/where to behave (i.e., signals) to those that tell us how to behave (i.e., instructions), and finally to those that actually help us perform the behavior (i.e., facilitators).

12. Potentiators are antecedents that enhance the motivation to do certain behaviors by increasing the value of the consequence following completion of that behavior.

13. Stimulus generalization occurs when our response to antecedents expands to those that are similar but not identical to the original antecedent under stimulus control. Stimulus generalization is thus the opposite of stimulus discrimination.

14. The prejudgments (i.e., prejudices) involved in stereotyping represent the covert stimulus generalization process in which thoughts (i.e., attributions and expectations) and accompanying feelings about a particular antecedent are generalized to all antecedents even remotely similar to the original. Stimulus generalization quickly goes awry when the A-B-C contingency being generalized is no longer empirically valid. Most stereotypes succumb to this fallacy of generalization.

15. A concept represents a combination of stimulus discrimination between distinct classes of antecedents and stimulus generalization within the class of antecedents that share attributes or properties.

**Figure 1** *The A-B-C (Cognitive–Behavioral) Model*

| (A) Antecedent | Covert | (B) Behavior | | (C) Consequence |
|---|---|---|---|---|
| | | Overt | Overt | |
| | Cognitive (Thinking) | Respondent (Physical) | Operant (Acting) | |
| Stimulus or setting event. External environments that set the occasion for behavior (thinking, acting, feeling) to occur.<br><br>$S^{Dee}$ = Green light. A cue that a particular behavior will result in a desirable consequence.<br><br>$S^{Delta}$ = Red light. A cue that a particular behavior will result in an undesirable consequence. | Subjective environment. The process and content of our thinking. Our interpretation of A-B-C as a-b-c.<br><br>Includes:<br>Attributions<br>Expectations<br>Self-concept<br>Self-esteem<br>Beliefs<br>Attitudes<br>Prejudices<br>Self-talk<br>Locus of control<br>Images<br>Fantasies<br>Intrinsic consequences | Reflexive<br>Autonomic<br>Involuntary<br>Biochemical<br>Physiological changes occurring within our body. | Voluntary behavior that we choose to do or not to do.<br><br>Can be: Excess = Behavior done too often or at wrong time.<br><br>Deficit = Behavior done too infrequently or not when needed. | Events (external) that occur during and/or after a particular covert and/or operant behavior. Events can be:<br><br>A. Desirable:<br>1. Positive Reinforcement present desirable = C+<br>2. Negative Reinforcement remove undesirable = C̶<br><br>B. Undesirable:<br>1. Punishment present undesirable, aversive = C–<br>2. Extinction remove desirable = C̶ |

**Emotions**

Subjective labels used to describe a specific state of being. Labels reflect the composite of our covert, respondent, and operant behavior within a specific context of antecedents and consequences.

# Chapter 6

<em>~~~~~~~~</em>

# Respondents:
# Behavior of Our Body

<em>~~~~~~~~</em>

## Orienting Ourselves

**N**ow that we have described operant behavior in relationship to its antecedents and consequences, we are able to turn to our physiological responses to those A-B-C components. This physical component of the model represents the body in our environment/mind/body integration. I refer to our physical responses as *respondents* because they respond to environmental and covert stimuli. In so doing, respondents are generally involuntary, reflexive, and physiological. As you will see, they encompass all of the organ systems, such as our autonomic and central nervous system, endocrine system, and immune system, that regulate our body's continual struggle to survive within its many challenging environments.

I present this component of the A-B-C model last because of its complex interrelationship with all of the other components. As involuntary, reactive, almost reflexive behavior, respondents are at the mercy of our environment, thoughts, and operants. The slightest alterations in our physical and social surroundings and the smallest nuance in our thinking challenge our bodies to adapt. Transcending the role of helpless victim, however, respondents influence our thinking, impair or enable our operant behaviors, and determine our capacity to interact with our environment.

The mutual influence of our body, mind, and environment is critical to understanding this chapter. When our environment is fraught with threat and our covert world is filled with fear and worry, our respondents adapt by mobilizing our physical resources to cope with the threat, meet the need, and rise to the occasion. This process of adaptation will be a central dynamic in our discussion of respondents. I have drawn on a body of literature (Asterita, 1985; Bloom & Lazerson, 1988; Pelletier, 1992; Rice, 1987; Selye, 1976) in describing the body's adaptation to stress and as our best example of respondent behavior. Although this chapter integrates and radically simplifies a complex array of physiological processes (and attendant medical jargon), a more sophisticated exposition of this neurophysiology appears in the references cited. Before we begin, let us take a quick look at the respondent component of our A-B-C model (Figure 10).

**Figure 10** *Respondent Behavior*

| **(B) Behavior** |
| :--- |
| **Overt**<br>**Respondent**<br>**(Physical)** |
| Reflexive<br>Autonomic<br>Involuntary<br>Biochemical<br>Physiological changes occurring within our body. |

## Our Mind/Body System

As noted previously, respondents represent the wide range of reflexive, physiological, and biochemical actions that constantly occur within our body. Most of these actions are autonomic, genetically programmed into our biological makeup, and beyond our awareness and conscious control. Respiration, digestion, homeostatic maintenance of our body temperature, and cell metabolism are just a few bodily functions that maintain us without our conscious effort. Although all of these automatic functions qualify as respondent behaviors, I focus on our neurological and autonomic nervous systems operating interactively with the other A's, B's, and C's of our model.

Previously, I suggested that most of our respondents are involuntary. I said "most" because advances in behavioral medicine (Cousins, 1989; Siegal, 1986) have demonstrated that some of our biochemistry can be controlled through conscious effort (e.g., nutrition, biofeedback, meditation, and many stress management techniques). Later, we will talk about these techniques for purposeful control of respondents, but for now, let us stay with involuntary respondents.

Our understanding of the A-B-C model as an integrated mind/body/environment system requires a review of our body's (i.e., physiological and biochemical) response to the other subsystems. As with all components of the A-B-C model, the relationship between mind (i.e., covert or cognitive factors) and body (i.e., neurological, physiological, immunological, endocrine, and biochemical factors) is interactive, representing an interdependent subsystem within the larger A-B-C system. Each of the parts gives and receives information enabling us (mind and body) to maintain physical homeostasis, defend against injury, and adapt to environmental challenges. These systems must work together for us to survive.

All living organisms are biologically programmed to survive. Our body executes this genetic programming through a constant and predominately automatic sequence of processes that both maintain equilibrium (i.e., homeostasis) and enable adaptation. In homeostasis, our body operates to meet its physiological needs efficiently and effectively, using the minimal amount of resources and energy in the process.

Although our body is superbly suited to maintain this internal state of stability, it faces another more challenging task of ensuring this homeostasis in the face of continual environmental change. Since we live in a constantly changing physical environment,

**ZIGGY**®

© 1985 Universal Press Syndicate

What would happen if every respondent had to be consciously engaged? (Ziggy © 1985 Ziggy and Friends, Inc. Reprinted with permission of Universal Press Syndicate. All rights reserved.)

with its toxins, demands, stimulation, threat—all those irritants we call *stressors*—our body is also programmed to meet the exigencies of the external world. Through biochemical and physiological processes, we mobilize, adjust, and defend in a process called *adaptation*. Adaptation enables us to cope, overcome adversity, and succeed, but it also induces stress, anxiety, and psychosomatic illness. Adaptation as a bodily response to our environment is an excellent demonstration of the mind/body/environment integration and the physical dynamics within the A-B-C model. Let us look at these physical dynamics more closely.

## Change As a Stressor

Any change requires some degree of adaptation by our body. We could even say that all change—for the good (i.e., a birthday, a new job, a letter from an old friend, a vacation) or for the bad (illness, an argument, a broken dishwasher, and all unpleasant experiences)—provokes adaptation and coping. Recent research (Bandura, 1997; Gerin, Litt, Deich, & Pickering, 1996; Schneiderman, McCabe, & Baum, 1992), however, poses two qualifiers to this contention. Both reflect the function of the mind (i.e., covert behavior) as the mediator between the events/changes in the external environment (i.e., antecedent stimuli) and the physiological response (i.e., respondent behavior) of the body.

First, the change or environmental event must be perceived (e.g., brought into covert/conscious awareness) before it elicits a physiological response. If we are unaware of the broken dishwasher or the math test tomorrow, our physiology is unaffected by these events. Second, our thoughts and cognitions are sufficient to stimulate a strong physical adaptation response even if there is no external environmental change or event. Our covert behaviors (i.e., thoughts) are potent targets for adaptation. Many of us are exquisite at perpetuating thoughts of threat and despair within environments that are safe, nurturing, and fully secure, and thus we experience the unnecessary adaptation that these thoughts cause our body to endure.

Before looking at this environment/mind influence on the body, a few terms need to be defined. Throughout this chapter, we will refer to the experience of stress. As used in our A-B-C model, stress is a complex syndrome (sequence of actions and responses) comprising five interrelated parts, or ingredients. These interactive parts include: (1) the external stressor; (2) the cognitive meaning or interpretation given to the stressor—fear, when the stressor signals a C–; (3) the autonomic arousal in preparation for fight or flight (anxiety); (4) the operants performed to cope with the stressor; and (5) the external consequence that we experience (or expect) as pain or displeasure.

A stressor represents any environmental event (antecedent stimulus/red light) or the covert perception of an environmental event (even if the event does not exist externally) signaling (to the individual) that some undesirable consequence will occur. This undesirable consequence could be punishment (remember C–, to receive something unpleasant or aversive) or extinction (remember ⊘+, the removal/loss of something pleasant or desirable). The covert expectation of either of these undesirable consequences causes us to become concerned and physiologically aroused. The covert expectation (real or imagined) of a C– (punishment) is called fear and represents the second ingredient of our stress experience.

## Anxiety

**W**hen our covert expectation is of punishment, our physiological arousal prepares us to avoid, escape, or somehow minimize the effect of this punishment. This arousal or mobilization of our resources to cope with the expected C– has been referred to as the fight-or-flight response (Cannon, 1932). The body's adaptation to the perception of stressors and the expectations of C–'s will be referred to as anxiety in our stress model and can best be understood by looking at Hans Selye's (1976) general adaptation syndrome (GAS).

All creatures are designed for survival, defense, and adaptation. Animals survive in a hostile, dangerous environment through their capacity to fight off attack or flee when warranted; in other words, fight or flight. Their anxiety in the face of these threats is quite adaptive. It enables them to mobilize their strength and attack or run quickly away. This anxiety, or physiological arousal, is automatic and essentially reflexive in response to the perception (expectation) of punishment.

Humans are biologically programmed for the same fight-or-flight response. Perceiving a stressor, we automatically experience physiological arousal (anxiety) that enables us to avoid or escape the expected punishment. This fight-or-flight coping mechanism works exceptionally well for our animal friends. Unfortunately, as Selye found, this coping response does not often work very well. In fact, this primitive reflex of anxiety in preparation for fight or flight fails us in our daily interactions with our social environment and serves as the culprit in many ailments and psychosomatic illnesses plaguing humans today. Let's take a closer look at Selye's GAS and then examine the price we pay for our human fight-or-flight respondent behavior.

We can better understand this environment/mind/body integration and the stages of the GAS by using a common experience. It is one that involves the stressor of being called on by the teacher to summarize very difficult material before the entire class. This experience is one rendition of "public speaking anxiety," and the anxiety reaction can be so acute as to render the student immobilized (in extreme cases, producing a phobia toward any public speaking).

## Coping and Adaptation: An Example

Let's assume that you are a college student in my class on the A-B-C model. This is the 4th of 15 sessions, and we have covered Chapters 1–4 of the text. The class contains 20 students, all training for a degree in counseling or psychology. You are sitting almost in the center of the classroom. As we start the 2-h class, I write the letters A-B-C on the board and say:

> Now that we have completed our study of much of the A-B-C model, I would like someone to stand in front of the class and present a thorough overview of all that we have learned about the model so far. I won't call on volunteers; I'll just select someone at random.

I then stop talking and scan the room in search of someone. As you sit there waiting to see whom I select, let's stop and analyze what might be going on inside of you (your mind/body experience).

Selye (1974) proposed three phases, or stages, of stress reaction in his GAS: (a) alarm, (b) resistance, and (c) exhaustion. The stimulus that triggers the alarm stage is the covert perception of a stressor in the environment. The existence of this stressor (an antecedent, $S^{Delta}$, or red light) sends a message to the covert (mind) that there is a certain probability (expectation) that danger (C– or punishment) is imminent. Said another way, individuals recognize (discriminate) something in their environment that they interpret in their covert as the signal to "Watch out! I may be in for a C– experience." In this case, the stressor is whatever there is about the environment (When? Where? Who? What? any aspect of the A) that they perceive as associated with punishment. What might be some of the stressors (S–red) in our example? We'll look at the antecedent to find out.

*When?*

At the beginning of a 2-h class

The 4th class session of 15

*Where?*

In a formal classroom

Sitting near the center of the room

In a college class

*Who?*

Dr. Kahn in the front as teacher

Nineteen other supportive students that you know casually

*What?*

Teacher writes A-B-C on board

Teacher gives instruction

Random selection; volunteers not chosen

Class notes and text are open on your desk

## GAS: Our General Adaptation System

**Y**our first response to these antecedents is covert. You size up the situation in your head and quickly determine its meaning for you. Physiologically, your covert (cognitive processing) is activated when the sensory receptors send electrochemical impulses through sensory neurons in the central nervous system to a bundle of nerve tissue called the *reticular activating system*. Located at the junctions of the spinal cord and the brain, this subcortical brain structure stimulates our first arousal to sensory impulses. This reticular formation acts as a filter, passing only novel or persistent information on to the thalamus. Housed in the limbic system, or subcortical brain, the thalamus acts as a switchboard, sending sensory impulses to the appropriate areas of the cerebral cortex, where we experience our first conscious awareness and meaning of all the sensory data flowing in from our environment.

Not only is the reticular formation responsible for selecting and censoring stimuli from the autonomic nervous system prior to its being registered in the cerebral cortex (conscious areas of the brain), but it can also transmit impulses to key areas of our limbic system, where information is screened for evidence of danger (caudate nucleus), initiates immediate feelings of anger and rage (amygdala), and is temporarily held for storage in long-term memory (hippocampus). These automatic responses of our limbic system work in conjunction with our autonomic nervous system to initiate and mobilize our fight-or-flight response. Additionally, these responses occur instantly and often unconsciously. Consequently, we can subliminally perceive and respond to various stimuli (aversive and noxious sounds, odors, sights) with anxiety while not knowing why we are anxious. This category of subliminally induced anxiety is certainly a factor in stress. However, in most instances, our anxiety (and the alarm stage) is activated by the conscious awareness of C–'s in our environment.

Your covert interpretation of the situation could vary greatly depending on:

Your past experience responding in this class with this teacher.

Your past experience with public speaking.

Your mastery of the class material so far.

Your physiological state and physical ability to perform the task.

A critical aspect of your covert interpretation is the consequences of the situation and the operant behavioral options that you could exercise in affecting the consequences that you want. If your interpretation includes the high probability of a C–, your body automatically signals the alarm reaction, and you begin to prepare for fight or flight (i.e., coping). A major task of the GAS is to determine which organ or system of the body is best able to handle the C– and then mobilize the body's resources around it.

In most nonspecific stress (a general mobilization rather than a specific organ injury or illness), a key organ that is always aroused is our skeletal muscle system. These voluntary muscles control our operant behavior necessary for effective coping. This is especially true when we literally have to fight or flee. To stimulate voluntary muscle contraction, the sympathetic nervous system becomes aroused by a complex process of activation initiated by the hypothalamus. This mobilizing action initiated during the alarm stage is undertaken by the complementary efforts of the sympathetic and parasympathetic nervous systems. Basically, the sympathetic nervous system stimulates, or turns on, certain organs (e.g., skeletal muscles) while the parasympathetic nervous system turns others off (those unnecessary for fight or flight).

Key ingredients in the activation of our central and autonomic nervous systems are the array of neurotransmitters secreted throughout our body. Our thoughts, perceptions, sensations—in fact, all of our covert behavior—occur through the electrical stimulation of billions of cells located within our brain. All of these cells, glands, and organ systems comprising our GAS must be activated (turned on and off) through electric stimulation. This electricity is carried through millions of insulated wires called *neurons*. Like a lamp attached to an electric circuit, cells, glands, and organs are connected to the body's vast circuitry of neurons, and they are turned on or off by receiving this electric current (called an *impulse*). As the electric current travels along these neurons, the body's only on–off switches are the tiny gaps, or spaces, that exist at various points along the neuron. These gaps are called *synapses*, and each synapse is filled with a chemical that normally does not conduct electricity.

When the electric impulse traveling along a neuron (called an *axon*) gets to a synapse, it must stop, somewhat as if you were traveling along a road that led to a river that had no bridge. The only way the electric impulse can cross that synapse and continue on its way is by secreting a chemical from vesicles located at the end of the axon. This chemical, called a neurotransmitter, can carry that impulse across the synapse and deposit it at just the right site (called a *receptor site*) on the other side (called a *dendrite*).

The process is somewhat analogous to a ferry that transports your car across the river to just the right dock on the other side so that you can continue your journey. The destination of the electric impulse is the cell or organ to be stimulated to either turn on or turn off. The neurotransmitter molecules actually have special shapes (like keys) that only fit certain dendrite receptor sites. The right fit (or landing at the right dock) is critical if neurotransmitters are going to serve their "ferrying" function. Consequently, we have many different kinds of neurotransmitters with different chemical compositions and functions throughout our body. As soon as the passage across the synapse is complete, the vesicles retract their neurotransmitter, close down, and await the next electric impulse. This entire synaptic crossing takes about 2000th of a second.

Through their ferrying operation, these neurotransmitters control the flow of traffic (impulses), and in so doing, determine when and where our organ systems will operate. Two crucial neurotransmitters that mobilize our autonomic nervous system are epinephrine (adrenaline) and norepinephrine (noradrenaline). Other neurotransmitters that are critical to the GAS and our covert behavior in general are: acetylcholine, which regulates visceral and skeletal muscles; serotonin, which regulates body temperature, sleep, sensory perception, and cognition that occurs in the frontal cortex; peptides, which regulate the endocrine system (i.e., glands secreting hormones into the bloodstream); endorphins (our morphine of the brain), which inhibit the neurotransmission of pain; and dopamine, a neurotransmitter operating in the brain to regulate complex body movement, our experience of pleasure, and many other emotional responses. We are still discovering new neurotransmitters and the dramatic effect that their presence or absence can have on our body and our entire human experience.

Although I have highlighted only a few neurotransmitters, I hope you can appreciate their importance to our discussion of the GAS. Now let us proceed with our overview of what occurs during this adaptation, a mobilization of the body's resources that occurs within seconds.

## Alarm

### Processes of the Alarm Stage

**1.** The hypothalamus, the master organ of the autonomic nervous system, sends chemical signals to the endocrine system, starting with the pituitary gland, executer of the endocrine system. Our hypothalamus functions as our point of integration between our thinking (cortical activity) and feeling (limbic activity) through its control of our autonomic nervous system. This control of the hypothalamus is exerted through the many hormones that are released and serve as the "shock absorbers" (Hedaya, 1996, p. 87) of the body. Under conditions of extreme stress—such as trauma, rape, military combat, severe accident, or illness—high levels of epinephrine and corticosteroids are released into the bloodstream. When the stress is unceasing and uncontrollable (as in phobias and learned helplessness, to be discussed later) the levels of cortisol become excessively high and can destroy cells that regulate our immune system and memory (hippocampal cells).

**2.** The posterior lobe of the pituitary gland secretes vasopressin into the bloodstream. This hormone constricts the arteries and increases contractile force of the heartbeat as well as blood pressure.

**3.** The stimulated anterior lobe of the pituitary gland increases its release of adrenocorticotropic hormone (ACTH), which stimulates a number of critical organs.

**4.** ACTH travels through the bloodstream to the adrenal cortex and the adrenal medulla.

**5.** One of the body's earliest responses to stress occurs when the stimulated adrenal medulla secretes adrenaline and noradrenaline into the bloodstream and throughout the body. This neurotransmitter secretion increases electrochemical activity throughout the entire sympathetic nervous system.

**6.** Adrenaline stimulates carbohydrate metabolism and causes the liver to release glucose into the bloodstream, enabling the cells to increase metabolism. A high volume of fatty acids (cholesterol) is released by the liver into the blood for cell repair and metabolism.

**7.** Adrenaline dilates the arterioles within the heart, allowing more blood to enter, accelerating the heart rate, and increasing the volume of blood circulating to the skeletal muscles.

**8.** Noradrenaline causes constriction of certain vascular channels, shifting blood away from the skin and intestinal organs and toward the skeletal muscles, heart, and brain. The blood redirected from your extremities to your heart, head, and skeletal muscles leaves your hands and feet cold. Capillaries in your head rapidly dilate to allow more blood. This latter effect may contribute significantly to migraine headaches. Blood diverted from the genitals may inhibit penile erection.

**9.** Altered blood flow relaxes the visceral muscles of the gastrointestinal tract, decreasing gastrointestinal digestion. Although hydrochloric acid secretion in the stomach decreases during short-term stress, it rapidly increases with prolonged stress. Slowed digestion and peristalsis cause the buildup of gastric enzymes in the stomach and intestinal tract.

**10.** The bronchial tubes dilate while the air passages of the lungs relax, causing respiration to increase and allowing more oxygen to move in and out. The greater volume of oxygen required for cell metabolism causes more rapid (yet shallower) respiration. This rapid increase in respiration can cause hyperventilation.

**11.** If the alarm stage is prolonged, certain (proinflammatory) corticosteroids cause tears in the arterial wall, which are then repaired with cholesterol plaques. This buildup of cholesterol on arterial walls produces arteriosclerosis, or hardening of the arteries.

**12.** Because greater levels of glucose (blood sugar) are necessary for cell metabolism (energy) during the alarm stage, the parasympathetic nervous system holds back the secretion of insulin (a hormone that inhibits glucose release) by the pancreas. Blood sugar level rises rapidly.

**13.** Noradrenaline stimulates the pupils of the eyes to dilate, allowing more light to enter the retina and thus improving our vision.

**14.** While ACTH is stimulating the adrenal cortex, the pituitary gland is also sending a thyrotrophic hormone (TTH) to the thyroid gland. Here the thyroid gland secretes thyroxin, which stimulates an increase in cell metabolism. The effects of TTH and thyroxin in increasing cell metabolism seem to accelerate as the alarm stage progresses.

**15.** The overall increase in cell metabolism causes a rapid rise in body temperature. Sensing this temperature elevation, the hypothalamus stimulates the sweat glands to increase perspiration, which evaporates and cools the body. Other glands of the exocrine system, such as salivation, are turned off, thus resulting in drying of the mouth and throat, which we might experience as "cotton in the mouth."

**16.** Finally, the release of ACTH and TTH into the bloodstream causes a decrease in the production of sex and body growth hormones.

Wow! All 16 processes (and many more) occur within seconds as the alarm stage prepares us to cope with the expected C–. Do some of these reactions sound familiar?

Returning to our classroom example, if your first (covert) reaction to my invitation to present was "Uh-oh! He's going to call on me and I'll make a fool of myself," or "If I get called on and mess up, I'll feel embarrassed and stupid," or any similar thought involving a negative consequence of being called on, you experienced the alarm reaction. You can easily tell if your muscles tightened, your heart rate increased as you inhaled more rapidly, your stomach felt like a knot, your hands felt cold and clammy and you began to perspire, and your mouth and throat got dry. You might have noticed the need to relieve your bladder, and you would have felt the tremendous need to relieve yourself of the stressor.

In teaching stress management, I have found it useful to use a subjective measurement procedure to assess the extent to which we experience anxiety. I have borrowed a measurement scale from Joseph Wolpe (1958), which he calls the Subjective Unit of Discomfort Scale (SUDS). In using the SUDS method, people assess their level of physiological arousal on a scale of 1 (no noticeable anxiety or muscle tension) to 10 (panic or acute anxiety attack). For any individual, a score of 5 represents that person's average experience of anxiety. This average is based on a period of 2 weeks or more. Notice that I did not associate a score of 1 with sleep. Many of us experience high levels of anxiety and tension during sleep. Some disorders such as bruxism (teeth grinding) and bed wetting (nocturnal enuresis) emanate from high anxiety during sleep. As the SUDS scale is totally subjective and self-reporting, each person's average score uniquely reflects them. Likewise, each person's increase or decrease on the scale reflects their subjective starting point.

Sometimes I use physiological measures of anxiety such as an electromyograph (measures muscle tension), galvanic skin meter (measures perspiration), and thermal scale (measures finger temperature) to corroborate the person's subjective experience of anxiety. With practice, most people can learn to identify their level of anxiety and quantify that level with a fairly accurate SUDS score. As you might predict, the alarm stage manifests a very high SUDS score (7–9 range); acute anxiety leading to a panic attack tops the chart (9–10); our most productive and functional SUDS level is 3–5 (depending on how severe your average is); and that calm, serene, relaxed level we would like to experience much more often is in the 1–3 range.

Just as our alarm reaction is a function of our external environment and our covert expectation for C–'s, so too is our SUDS score. If you are constantly confronted with stressors and dwelling on the C–'s associated with them, your SUDS score will remain in the 7–9 range. After a very prolonged period of stress, you will come to equate the

7–9 range as your average, and thus report this severe anxiety as a 5. At this point, you are well on the road to the exhaustion stage of the GAS.

Although we may have subtle differences in how we physically experience the alarm reaction, the general pattern of mobilization is the same. We differ somewhat in the physical cues that signal anxiety. For some, it is muscle tension in the upper shoulder and extending up the back of the neck (the trapezius muscle); for others, it is muscle tension in the head; for others, it is shortness of breath; and still for others, it might be a tight or gaseous stomach. Although the noticeable designs may differ, the point is that we all experience the alarm reaction when we perceive the expectation of punishment (some C–).

There is research (Bandura, 1986) to suggest that we experience two stages in our covert perception of a stressor during the alarm stage. The first step, referred to as *primary appraisal,* is when we become consciously aware of a C–. I call this the "uh-oh!" response, although I have used more graphic descriptors in my recognition of the presenting crises. This primary appraisal triggers the alarm reaction. The second step, *secondary appraisal,* represents how one can effectively avoid, escape, or minimize (i.e., cope with) the stressful situation. As a response to my primary appraisal, I size up the situation and my ability/strategy for dealing with the potential C– in my secondary appraisal. We could say that the primary appraisal activates the alarm reaction and the secondary appraisal either reduces my anxiety (turns off the alarm) if I feel confident in my coping skills or increases my anxiety (and moves quickly from the alarm to the resistance stage) if I feel unable to cope. We will talk a lot about secondary appraisal when we get to coping strategies in later chapters.

If, in our classroom example, you immediately perceived my instruction as a bluff, knowing you would never be called on, you might not even experience the anxiety of the alarm stage. You might have perceived my instruction as a great opportunity to show your stuff, with full confidence of your mastery of the course material, or at least confidence in your ability to entertain. In either case, you would have experienced some modest arousal or excitement, but never approach the level of mobilization encountered with anxiety.

Selye calls the positive enthusiasm, excitement, and physical arousal directed toward pleasurable and nonthreatening experiences *eustress.* (*Eu* is Greek for "good" or "well.") The excitement of a vacation, seeing a dear friend, preparing a special meal, going on a shopping spree, watching your kids play cooperatively, or making love certainly induces physiological arousal, but that arousal is very brief and never reaches the acute stage of anxiety characteristic of the alarm stage. Quite the contrary, eustress stimulates the body to activate organs and release chemicals (i.e., neurotransmitters in the brain, e.g., dopamine and endorphines) that actually induce a natural high and sense of well-being. We seek these natural highs in our recreation, relationships, and work because they feel so good and do not cause the destructive health effects created by long-term anxiety. This latter form of deleterious stress is termed *distress* (*dis* meaning "to take away, pull apart") by Selye. Distress is the experience of anxiety created by our covert expectations for C–'s, and it perpetuates the alarm stage under conditions of acute anxiety.

If our secondary appraisal adequately reassures us of our ability to cope with the C–, our anxiety dissipates and the alarm stage ends, as does our GAS. Our body returns to

## For Better or For Worse®      by Lynn Johnston

Physical arousal is not always distress. Sometimes it is eustress, and the feeling is great. (© Lynn Johnston Productions Inc./Dist. by United Feature Syndicate, Inc.)

its normal level of equilibrium. This acute stress, in which the threat is immediate and rapidly resolved, occurs frequently to all of us. With effective coping skills (and reassuring secondary appraisal), our distress is manageable and short lived. Unfortunately for many of us, our distress and its associated alarm reaction are prolonged and unabated. When our secondary appraisal fails or we are unable to avoid or escape a persistent C–, we move into Selye's second stage of GAS, resistance.

## Resistance

**D**uring the resistance stage, the body has attained peak arousal and is operating at full mobilization. Covertly and emotionally, we experience this stage as constant anxiety, tension, nervousness, stress, and discomfort. As this anxiety continues without respite, we begin to label our experience as *chronic* distress. In this stage, the sympathetic nervous system begins to direct its efforts toward those organ systems most affected by the stress. Physiological arousal directed toward resistance to the stressor becomes more specific, and biochemical resources needed throughout the body are directed toward specific organ systems. At this point, the body's homeostasis and general resistance to disease or injury are actually impaired. As the stressor continues, the resistance becomes more focused and the body begins to deplete its store of biochemical and physical resources. We are approaching physiological *exhaustion*, Selye's third stage of the GAS.

Returning to our classroom example, now that you are physically mobilized for action, your anxiety could subside for many reasons, such as:

I remove the stressor (S–red light) by rescinding my instruction.

Someone else is called on, and you emit a deep sigh of relief.

You very effectively use avoidance coping behavior by lowering your head, looking away from me, slinking down into your chair, and even requesting to go to the lavatory.

> If you believe (your covert expectation) that I want to catch someone unprepared, you might wave your hand frantically, yelling, "Me! Me! Call on me!"

> You might quickly scan your notes and renew your confidence (and competence) in the material to be presented.

For whichever reason, as the probability of a C– diminishes, your anxiety subsides; thus, the need for resistance. But let us suppose that none of the foregoing anxiety reducers occur and the following happens instead:

> In your mind, you generate all of the covert expectations for failure, embarrassment, and pain when called on, because this has happened to you before.

> You have no confidence in your mastery of the material.

> Your anxiety has become so acute that, instead of concentrating on your presentation of the material, all you can think about is how terrible this is.

> And lo and behold, you are called on!

We have all experienced the alarm and the early phase of the resistance stages many times in our lives. If the C–'s are not too plentiful or intense in our environment and if we have learned a large repertoire of effective coping operant behaviors, our anxiety will be negligible. Likewise, if the expectations for C–'s that we carry in our mind are infrequent and occur only in truly threatening situations, our anxiety will be mild and benign. To the extent that we dwell on C–'s and ruminate on all of those C–'s that we might face or have faced in the past, we will continue to experience elevated levels of anxiety.

Whether the stressor is very specific (e.g., phobias directed toward water, germs, height, social situations, etc.) or much more generalized (e.g., the extreme case of agoraphobia), the key to anxiety and the entire GAS is what we put in our mind. When we focus on C–'s, we cannot help but perpetuate anxiety. Conversely, when our mind is devoid of C–'s, we can function without the burden of anxiety and stress.

To one person, a classroom is a threatening, punishing place, but to another, it is a stimulating, supportive, and safe place to learn and grow. To this second person, it is an S–green light for involvement, experimentation, and assertiveness, but for the threatened person, it is an S–red light for those things and an S–green light only for avoidance and escape. When resistance fails and the C– continues, the body reaches *exhaustion*.

## Exhaustion

Exhaustion occurs when the resources maintaining mobilization and handling of the stressor simply become depleted and break down. Prolonged stress wears out the body, lowers resistance, and increases susceptibility to what Selye calls "diseases of adaptation." Another term used for physical illness derived from psychological (covert) processes is *psychosomatic illness*. Many diseases of adaptation have been identified with the exhaustion stage. Before listing some of them and describing the general characteristics of this stage, it is important to note that not all stress results in psychosomatic illness, nor do all these disorders result in stress. The following disorders cannot be attributed to stress alone, but the body's attempt to adapt has made it vulnerable to the whole spectrum of organic and environmental pathologies:

Allergies or increased episodes of asthma caused by an overabundance of pro-inflammatory corticoids

A weakened immune system caused by depletion of white blood cells (T-cells, B-cells, macrophages) with increased vulnerability to infectious diseases, cancer, and the acceleration of AIDS

Muscle tension headaches

Migraine headaches (vasoconstriction headaches)

Hypertension

Gastrointestinal disorder (ulcers, colitis, hiatal hernia)

Cardiovascular disorders (arteriosclerosis, tachycardia, coronary failure)

Arthritis advanced by corticosteroid depletion

Thyroid dysfunction resulting in impaired growth

As you can see from the list of 16 physiological responses occurring in the alarm stage as well as the diseases of adaptation just listed, many of these diseases develop as a consequence of a prolonged resistance stage. The body's attempt to cope under prolonged stress creates the physiological conditions that precipitate or predispose an individual to physical disorder or illness. As with a chain that breaks at its weakest link under stress, the weakest organ system of the body succumbs first. These psychosomatic illnesses are very real, and they take a severe toll upon our health in spite of the belief by many that psychosomatic illnesses such as headaches, ulcers, allergies, tachycardia, and many more are simply in your head. They may be perpetuated by covert behaviors occurring in your head, but they are just as real and can be just as deadly as a serious injury or illness.

The focus and manner of breakdown under exhaustion differ for each of us; likewise, the length of time that we can endure chronic stress (remain in the resistance stage) before we suffer the results of breakdown and illness (i.e., exhaustion) varies greatly. Past illnesses, heredity, personal habits and environmental health contribute to one's capacity to endure prolonged stress. I am sure you know of people who endure hardships and severe anxiety almost indefinitely, and others who quickly break down in the face of what appears to be a very minor stressor.

Two qualifiers affect stress endurance. The first is the subjective nature of stress. When we consider that it is the covert expectation for C–'s (i.e., fear) that creates and perpetuates our anxiety (stress response) and not our external environment per se, then a stressor appearing mild and nonthreatening to us might traumatize someone else. The prospect of a classroom presentation might prompt one student to conjure up the worst possible consequences, perceiving the experience as awful, horrible, almost catastrophic. Another student might perceive the same prospect as a great opportunity to demonstrate mastery or, at worst, a minor inconvenience. Will they experience stress differently? You know it.

The second qualifier pertains to the temporal dimension of the GAS. Because exhaustion occurs as the last stage, often long after the initial stressor provoked the alarm reaction, we sometimes fail to see the connection between the stressor and the physical breakdown. Those inconvenient colds, flus, gastrointestinal disorders, and so on that visit over holidays and vacations may have a lot more to do with term papers, final exams, and preparation hassles than we realize. How many times have we heard of individuals who seem to cope with stress perfectly, illness free, and then fall apart and get sick long after the crisis has passed? Richard Nixon seemed to survive Watergate physically unscathed, but a few months later, he developed a severe inflammation disorder. A coincidence? Maybe. It would not be coincidental, however, if the student experiencing severe anxiety in our classroom example suffered academically as well as physically.

Although mild anxiety can enhance attention, reaction time, and overall academic performance, severe anxiety impairs all three. If you experienced the same covert expectation for C–'s in all public speaking (or evaluation) attempts, you would spend most of the time in the resistance stage (with SUDS levels of 7–10). Unless you found ways of avoiding or escaping all of these stressors (e.g., remain at home and only go out under cover of night or in disguise), you will eventually break down in exhaustion. You will fail both academically and physically.

This chapter has illustrated the complex physiological reactions and their long-term consequences that enable our body to adapt and cope. But even more important than looking at physiology and biochemistry, this chapter attempts to place the body within the context of mind and environment. In so doing, I have emphasized the interrelationship and codependence between our physiology and our antecedent stimuli, covert and operant behavior, and the consequences of our actions. The ultimate appreciation and application of the A-B-C model will be based on your understanding of this functional relationship.

The A-B-C model tells us that even though much of our physiology is automatic and involuntary, our body responds to the thoughts that we generate and perpetuate in our head. These physical reactions can aid and abet our purposeful coping with stress, and they can also wreck havoc with our health and well-being if left unchecked. Our locus of control for consciously understanding our respondent behavior and formulating effective coping strategies resides in our brain, that part of the A-B-C model we call covert behavior, which is where we direct our attention next.

## Chapter Summary

**1.** Respondents are involuntary, reflexive, and physiological in nature.

**2.** Adaptation occurs when we mobilize our physiological and biochemical resources to defend against stressors and meet the demands of our changing environment as well as our physical needs.

**3.** Stress is the overall experience comprising five interrelated parts within our A-B-C model: stressor, fear, anxiety, coping operants, and unpleasant consequences.

**4.** Stressors are environmental events that signal an existing or approaching C– or ⊠+. Any change in the environment is a potential stressor if it causes us to adapt (physiologically) to deal with the change.

5. The covert expectation (real or imagined) of a C– is called fear.

6. Anxiety is the physiological arousal that we experience when our body prepares for fight or flight in the face of a C–.

7. The alarm stage of Selye's general adaptation syndrome (GAS) occurs when the person first consciously perceives the probability of a C– occurring. Physical arousal in the alarm stage is produced by the action of the autonomic nervous system and especially the sympathetic nervous system.

8. The chemicals that control the flow of electric impulses across the synapse (gap between neurons) are called neurotransmitters.

9. During the alarm stage, our anxiety increases rapidly; this would correspond to our Subjective Unit of Discomfort Scale (SUDS) score rising to 6–8 or even higher. At a score of 10, we experience acute anxiety and become immobilized, unable to function.

10. Primary appraisal tells us, "Beware, a C–!" whereas secondary appraisal tells us, "Relax, I can handle this!" or "Panic city. I don't know what to do. Help!"

11. Eustress is good stress that stimulates a sense of well-being. Distress is bad stress that creates anxiety and health problems.

12. We move into the resistance stage when our coping skills fail and the C– remains unabated. In resistance, we remain at our highest level of mobilization and arousal.

13. Exhaustion, the final stage of the GAS, occurs when the body wears out from constant arousal. Exhaustion makes us vulnerable to a broad range of "diseases of adaptation," or psychosomatic illnesses.

14. Stress and anxiety are a direct result of the C–'s that we generate and perpetuate in our covert world. Consequently, stress is subjective in that it is truly in the mind of the beholder. If we keep C–'s in our mind, we experience anxiety and all that the GAS offers; if we keep C–'s out, we do not.

**Figure 1** *The A-B-C (Cognitive–Behavioral) Model*

| (A) Antecedent | (B) Behavior | | | (C) Consequence |
|---|---|---|---|---|
| | Covert | Overt | Overt | |
| | Cognitive (Thinking) | Respondent (Physical) | Operant (Acting) | |
| Stimulus or setting event. External environments that set the occasion for behavior (thinking, acting, feeling) to occur. S^Dee = Green light. A cue that a particular behavior will result in a desirable consequence. S^Delta = Red light. A cue that a particular behavior will result in an undesirable consequence. | Subjective environment. The process and content of our thinking. Our interpretation of A-B-C as a-b-c. Includes: Attributions Expectations Self-concept Self-esteem Beliefs Attitudes Prejudices Self-talk Locus of control Images Fantasies Intrinsic consequences | Reflexive Autonomic Involuntary Biochemical Physiological changes occurring within our body. | Voluntary behavior that we choose to do or not to do. Can be: Excess = Behavior done too often or at wrong time. Deficit = Behavior done too infrequently or not when needed. | Events (external) that occur during and/or after a particular covert and/or operant behavior. Events can be: A. Desirable: 1. Positive Reinforcement present desirable = C+ 2. Negative Reinforcement remove undesirable = ⊗- B. Undesirable: 1. Punishment present undesirable, aversive = C− 2. Extinction remove desirable = ⊗+ |
| | **Emotions** | | | |

Subjective labels used to describe a specific state of being. Labels reflect the composite of our covert, respondent, and operant behavior within a specific context of antecedents and consequences.

# Chapter 7

~~~~~~~~~~~~~~

# Covert Behavior:
# Introducing the A-B-C's
# of Our Mind

~~~~~~~~~~~~~~

## Orienting Ourselves

**W**e have explored the antecedents, behavior (operant), and consequence components of our A-B-C model. In so doing, we have studied the contingency relationship that exists between operant behavior and consequences as well as the nature of antecedent stimuli which set the occasion (context) for this contingency to occur. We have studied each of the A-B-C components somewhat differentially, looking at the form and function of antecedents, behavior, and consequences as both separate and interdependent phenomena.

Antecedent stimuli set the occasion for behavior to occur, yet they derive their activation or motivational function from the anticipated consequences resulting from that behavior. Antecedent green lights elicit the expectation of a B-C+/X– contingency, whereas antecedent red lights stimulate the opposite expectation of a behavior resulting in a C–/X+.

All of these behavioral experiences, driven by antecedent environmental conditions, are processed, stored, and retrieved within the vast "in-the-head" world of our mind—a world that I will also refer to as our covert behavior. It is within this complex repository of electrochemical operations that we first recognize, ascribe meaning to, and ultimately choose to act on information about ourselves and our world. Comprising all that we can know of our past, present, and future, the subjective world within our mind provides the locus, storehouse, and executer for the complete integration of all the elements of our A-B-C experience. Our covert world is where it all comes together, and it is to this most intimate and most integrative component that we turn our attention next.

The thoughts that comprise our covert world are both reactor and initiator to the external events of our antecedents, operant behavior, and consequences. Antecedents trigger certain cognitions which, in turn, stimulate both respondent and operant behavior. This reactive function of our covert apparatus to our external environment can occur both consciously and unconsciously, deliberately and automatically, all the while facilitating adaptation to the world around us.

However, reaction and adjustment are not the only functions served by our covert behavior. As the repository of our subjective knowing of the world, our mind can initiate

**Figure 11** *Covert Behavior*

| Cognitive (Thinking) |
|---|

Subjective environment. The process and content of our thinking.
Our interpretation of A-B-C as a-b-c.

Includes:
Attributions
Expectations
Self-concept
Self-esteem
Beliefs
Attitudes
Prejudices
Self-talk
Locus of control
Images
Fantasies
Intrinsic consequences

| Emotions |
|---|

Subjective labels used to describe a specific state of being. Labels reflect the composite of our covert, respondent, and operant behavior within a specific context of antecedents and consequences.

thoughts which, in turn, can proactively influence the antecedents and consequences of our external world. As progenitor of thought and initiator of action, our covert behavior can elicit the universe of human emotions and mobilize any of the choices existing within our repertoire of operant behavior. Because our "emotional" experience is so tied to the process and content of our cognitions, I discuss emotions in this chapter. This ability of our mind to function as both servant and master of our external environment involves the integration of our entire A-B-C model into our covert creation of reality.

As with previous chapters, we will begin with a snapshot of the entire A-B-C model and then narrow our scope to its cognitive/affective component (Figure 11).

## Our Covert Operants

### Our Subjective World: The a-b-c's of Our Mind

The part of the A-B-C model that occurs within our head has been called many things. Most of us think of thinking (the process) as the generation and rumination of thought (the content), while a physiologist might refer to it as the action and product of the brain and central nervous system. A psychologist might emphasize the word *cognition*. Some might consider this vast reservoir of information—both trivial and profound—to represent our mind, while others consider our in-the-head experience to comprise our subjective representation—our apperception—of what we believe the "real" world to be.

Certainly, the world of our mind is most intimate and subjective, representing all that we know of experience. The prominent operant behaviorist B. F. Skinner (1953) considered the mind to be inaccessible to objective study and, consequently, an impenetrable "black box." Another prominent behavioral psychologist, Joseph Cautela (1970) believed that both the content of thoughts and the process of cognition were volitional and thus subject to the same principles and dynamics that govern operant behavior. Consequently, Cautela referred to cognitions as covert operants, or *coverants* for short. This conceptualization of cognition as representing the information processes and content that we can choose to inhabit our thought has garnered considerable empirical support and has advanced many therapeutic strategies targeting deliberate cognitive or covert behavioral change (Cautela & Kearney, 1993; Stein & Young, 1992). Although acknowledging that much information that exists in our mind is neither acquired, stored, nor retrieved consciously and that much remains to be learned about cognitive processes (e.g., perception, information processing, memory, and creativity, to name just a few), I find Cautela's framework for thinking to be reasonably compatible within the A-B-C model. Consequently, I will frequently refer to thoughts as covert behaviors and thinking as covert processes.

## The Antecedent–Covert Connection

Regardless of what we call the process and content of thinking, the world in our head is, at best, a subjective representation of the external world comprising our antecedents, operant behaviors, and extrinsic consequences. As we engage our external world, we constantly absorb information through our sensory modalities and central nervous system and then process it in our cerebral cortex to give it meaning. This meaning usually represents cogent explanations for such questions as:

What is happening now?

Why is this happening now?

What do I want to happen now?

How can I best respond to this experience and especially achieve what I want now?

What choices do I have now?

What will be the consequences of each choice that I exercise?

Any subtle or blatant external antecedent can elicit these covert attempts to understand our immediate experience. A chance encounter with a neighbor at the supermarket may elicit a host of ritualistic social responses depending on the relationship's level of intimacy and involvement. Casual friendship might elicit a quick greeting and promise to get together over the next holiday, a terse critique of the fortunes of a local sports team, or our old standard, "How about this weather!" The responses from a recognized relationship of longstanding interaction and friendship will set the occasion for considerably more sustained, substantive (and intimate), and physically demonstrative interaction. The former social interaction will elicit more automatic, ritualistic covert and overt behavior, whereas the latter will stimulate a much larger range of thoughts (and concomitant operant behaviors) about the nature of the relationship now, in the past, and what is wished for in the future.

Covert discrimination and assessment of the A-B-C's of the supermarket encounter can certainly transcend these socially grounded thoughts and actions and generate such thoughts as, "Wow, what a nice guy. He seems like a good neighbor to get to know." Or "I wish he'd get his muffler fixed. That racket wakes me up every morning. Maybe I should mention it now."

Thoughts even more oblique to the interaction might occur such as, "Oh damn. I am illegally parked and now I'll never get out of here." Or "I know I forgot something for dessert. Helen will scream if I have to drive back here again, and I only have 5 minutes to get to the cleaners before it closes." And so on. Regardless of how unrelated or disjointed these coverts might become as they drift away from the immediate social encounter with the neighbor, they were initially stimulated by the external antecedent of the neighbor. The degree to which our covert and overt behavior diverges from the immediate social intercourse is in part a function of the influence of other external antecedents on us (e.g., time, place, need, other events).

## Creating Our Own Covert Behavior

Our supermarket encounter illustrates how external antecedent stimuli elicit or set the occasion for many different thoughts. The thoughts, or covert behaviors, that are elicited by our external antecedents are stimulus bound, as their origin can be traced to some stimulus in the external environment.

But not all thought is stimulus bound. We have the capacity to draw on our vast reservoir of experiential, emotional, and factual memories in the creation of self-initiated thought. This uniquely human quality of covert construction enables us to transcend stimulus–response reactivity to our external environment and create thoughts spontaneously and idiosyncratically. As with stimulus-bound covert behavior, much of our self-initiated thinking struggles for acceptable explanations to the same questions and explanations that give meaning and purpose to our A-B-C experiences. Freed from their antecedent anchoring, however, self-initiated thought is bound only by our neurophysiological capacities, our cortical storehouse of past experiences, and our facility with imagination and creativity.

Whether we self-initiate the construction of our world or generate cognitive responses to antecedent conditions, our fundamental goal is to find or create meaning and purpose in the ongoing experiences of ourselves in the world that can be used to maximize our success. Our need for meaning and purpose in our experience and our cognitive understanding of it are just as powerful as any primary reinforcer. Without an understanding of our experience in the world, our mind becomes totally confused and chaotic. Stimuli are processed indiscriminately as experiences (events, people, facts, feelings, needs) that pervade our consciousness in an amorphous, ambiguous blur. Confusion and disorientation so dominate the domain of our thought that consciousness as we know it ceases to exist. In the absence of some form of consistent, coherent covert knowledge base, our actions are capricious at best and rendered paralyzed at worst. This innate need for covert meaning is cogently and eloquently explained by Jerome Frank (Frank & Frank, 1991) when he writes:

> Like all fundamental needs, the need to attribute meanings to events probably has a neurophysiological base. Reviewing extensive studies of persons with split brains, a leading neurophysiologist concludes that our brains contain a special component, located in the dominant left hemisphere of right-handed humans, that he termed the "interpreter." This interpreter "instantly constructs a theory to explain why (any) behavior occurred" (Gazzaniga, 1985). Our need to create a meaningful world is manifested by the automatic formation of certain assumptive systems or schemata (Goleman, 1985) about ourselves, other persons, and the non-human environment. The totality of each person's assumptions may be conveniently termed his or her assumptive world. (p. 24)

Regardless of whether these musings on meaning and purpose dwell on past experience, present challenges (and opportunities), or future aspirations, the substance of all this thinking embodies our reality. Let us turn to our construct of reality.

## The A-B-C's of Our Assumptive World

The assumptive world that Frank refers to represents our answers to fundamental questions about ourselves and our world: explanations and assumptions about what is safe, dangerous, important, unimportant, good, bad, and so on. Frank (1991) further believes that "these assumptions become organized into sets of highly structured, complex, interacting values, expectations, and images of self and others that are closely related to emotional states and feelings" (p. 24). From the perspective of our A-B-C model, this assumptive world comprises the aggregate of all the A-B-C's stored within our cognitive memory bank. Every antecedent that we are capable of identifying (and discriminating) with its associated behavior and consequence becomes the data base from which we give meaning and purpose (i.e., understanding) to our world. These A-B-C contingencies that we have learned experientially, vicariously, or indirectly comprise our covert (or assumptive) world and thus become the basis from which we explain past and present experiences (i.e., attributions) and predict future events (i.e., expectations).

### Our Unique Lenses for Knowing the World

The aggregate of A-B-C's that comprises our assumptive world is acquired through mechanisms of learning within a framework of innate structures, or schemata. The mechanisms or principles of learning through which we build, use, and modify this covert world have many of the same characteristics as those expediting operant behavior. Processes of covert behavior acquisition, operation, and change are generally similar for all of us. The processes of thinking through which we reactively and proactively engage our environment are fairly uniform, with differences reflected primarily in brain specialization and neuropsychological disorder. What truly differentiates each of us and reveals our uniqueness is the content of the A-B-C's that comprise our covert world. Each of the A-B-C contingencies that I carry in my head and use for understanding and acting upon the world is my interpretation of those actual (or what we might call objective) A-B-C's that I have encountered.

As with any interpretation of experience, my covert A-B-C's comprise a subjective reality that is framed and constructed through my own specially ground lenses. All of my unique life experiences provided the grinding and polishing of my covert world lenses, and these glasses enable me to see a world that is colored, sized, and configured by my idiosyncratic filters. Through these lenses, I receive, process, store, and create what I know of the world and of myself.

## Reality from Consensual Validation

**T**he distortion that inevitably results from these filters creates and maintains a covert world that may or may not match the objective A-B-C's of our external world. When filtered through these lenses, our covert world, comprising the composite A-B-C's of all that we have experienced, is actually our representation of what we believe the objective A-B-C's to be.

The A-B-C's of my supermarket experience described earlier can have at least two different (although I would hope very similar) interpretations. First, there are the objective A-B-C's of the experience, which we generally refer to as reality. The aspect of these objective A-B-C's that defines them as reality is the degree to which they can be consensually validated by other people. This requires that at least one other person describes the A-B-C's of an experience in the same way. If another person in the supermarket describes my encounter with my neighbor as totally coincidental and my neighbor as appropriately friendly, then that antecedent condition has some consensual validation and thus credible reality. If someone else also describes the encounter in the same way, the reality of the antecedent condition is even more consensually validated. Instead of conceptualizing reality as an absolute, we are defining it as relative to the degree to which an A-B-C experience receives consensual validation.

## Translating Our A-B-C's into a-b-c's

**A** second way of interpreting the supermarket A-B-C's is from the perspective of my experience. As I try to give meaning and purpose to the experience, I continually process the A-B-C's in my covert as information that I can understand and act on. But because of the distortion that naturally occurs as I interpret the objective A-B-C's through the prisms of my covert glasses, the supermarket A-B-C's in my head become only representations of the actual (consensually validated) A-B-C's. Through this innately subjective translation, the objective antecedents become the antecedents in my covert interpretation; correspondingly, the objective behaviors and consequences become subjective behaviors and consequences when interpreted through the distorted lenses of my covert world. All that I can truly know of an A-B-C experience is my a-b-c interpretation of it. Consequently, when referring to any covert experience, I will use the lowercase a-b-c to represent its counterpart A-B-C in objective reality. In effect, we can more accurately say that our covert world comprises the aggregate of all of our a-b-c's, with each a-b-c representing our interpretation of an actual A-B-C in reality.

To better illustrate this dual phenomenon of our objective A-B-C reality and our subjective a-b-c understanding of it, we can return to the supermarket. Although others might describe the A-B-C's of that episode as a brief chance meeting between two very cordial neighbors resulting in a handshake and verbal promise to get together soon, my a-b-c's of the experience may range from very similar to vastly different. In most instances, we experience considerable correspondence between our objective A-B-C's and their subjective a-b-c interpretation, which is indeed fortunate and critical if we expect to live effectively and successfully. Success in maximizing C+'s and minimizing C–'s requires us to accurately understand and comply with the A-B-C contingencies existing in our many external environments. We can often ascertain the degree of correspondence between reality and the covert a-b-c's of that reality by seeking consensual validation from others, a process called *reality testing*. We will talk more about this process later.

When the match is good, we stand the best chance of successfully negotiating our needs and objectives with the realities of the world. As our covert a-b-c's diverge and even come in conflict with the A-B-C's of our experience, we encounter anxiety, disorientation, alienation, and failure (i.e., increasing probabilities of C–'s and ⊠+'s). Dissonance between our covert and external reality can create such dysfunction in thought and action as to form the basis for neuroses and, when profoundly dissonant, psychoses—the ultimate split between the A-B-C's outside of our head and the a-b-c's within.

Without having to look at such extreme manifestations of A-B-C/a-b-c dissonance, we can use a more typical example by returning to the supermarket. If I felt particularly anxious about all the tasks that I had to accomplish that morning, I might experience any distraction or delay as preventing me from achieving my C+ (e.g., the perfect dinner party) or causing me to experience a C– (e.g., "Helen will kill me."). Compounding this anxiety might be my belief that this particular neighbor dislikes me and is deliberately impeding all that I have to accomplish. The heat and arousal of increasing anxiety combined with the turbulent anger toward a threatening, insidious foe will certainly cause me to interpret the supermarket event much more malignantly than our consensual validators. When asked by Helen to describe my experience at the supermarket, I might reply, "This obnoxious neighbor accosted me and almost caused me to get a parking ticket by detaining me forever." What is more, I might add, "And that belligerent neighbor is to blame for anything I might have forgotten." This latter attribution for my forgetting behavior is also negatively reinforced (⊠–) if such a distorted a-b-c explanation is successful in assuaging the wrath of a disappointed and angry spouse.

The A-B-C/a-b-c distinction and distortion just illustrated not only creates false (i.e., invalid) attributions but reinforces and maintains a pattern of covert a-b-c's that will continue to seek confirmation in the future as well as provide the rationale for future antagonism toward the neighbor and others. With generalization, such patterns of experience characterize and perpetuate the paranoid syndrome of dysfunction. As our covert a-b-c's are constructed and reinforced through significant life experiences, they in turn become the subjective reality through which all present experience is matched and validated and through which we respond to all future experiences. In this way, our aggregate a-b-c's become our covert world through which we filter all current and future experience.

Each contingency providing the connective tissue for each covert a-b-c illuminates our preferences for future decisions. The covert world that I took to the supermarket comprised all of the a-b-c's that I know, understand, and act on. Many of those a-b-c's were activated as I interpreted the antecedent conditions (e.g., person, place, time, object, etc.) as red lights for behaviors of patient, social interaction resulting in such undesirable consequences as failure, criticism, attack, and a probable parking ticket. These same covert antecedents would simultaneously flash the green light for terse, aggressive, antisocial behavior in anticipation of consequences of avoiding failure and attack and accomplishing my many tasks.

What is more, these same covert a-b-c's activate a pattern of physiological reactions (i.e., respondents) that supports and affirms the validity of the precipitating thoughts (Roemer & Borkovec, 1993). My covert expectation for attack will stimulate a fight-or-flight arousal (i.e., anxiety) just as surely as the sudden appearance of a poisonous snake. All that remains in ascribing meaning and purpose to this subjective experience is the attachment of an emotional label. The a-b-c's that I brought, activated, and affirmed in the supermarket might prompt me to characterize my emotional state as angry, fearful, resentful, or anxious. Whichever label I choose, it is a product of the subjective reality (covert world) from which I know, understand, and engage the world outside of my head. The nature of emotion as a distinct feeling, thought, biological state, self-assigned label, and propensity to act is cogently discussed by Goleman (1995), and I will focus on it in Chapter 12.

To summarize, capital A-B-C's represent the external world of our experience that others can see, describe, and validate. Lowercase a-b-c's represent our covert representation of those A-B-C's. Thus, A-B-C's are outside and a-b-c's are in my head.

## Levels of Consciousness

### Conscious, Nonconscious, and Automatic Thoughts

When discussing the processes and content of thinking, the first item of business is to clarify the concept of consciousness. Much of our thinking occurs at a conscious level, but a great deal is nonconscious or automatic. By "occurs at a conscious level," I mean that we are aware of the thoughts to the degree that we know when they are occurring and can express or describe them with good accuracy. Consciousness implies focused awareness on a specific thought. Because there are a multitude of thoughts (i.e., a-b-c's) that could direct our focused attention at any time, we are constantly compelled to select certain thoughts for immediate attention, or consciousness. The sentence you are now reading has your focused attention; it occupies your consciousness.

Concurrently, an infinite variety of externally stimulated and self-initiated thoughts could enter your consciousness, but are currently in your nonconscious. The external sounds penetrating your room, the condition of your chair, the casting of light from the window suggesting time and weather conditions, and a re-created memory of the supermarket encounter (I am still working through my unresolved feelings toward my neighbor) are all potential thoughts accessible to consciousness. This infinite reservoir of thoughts that remains accessible under the appropriate stimulus conditions form our nonconscious covert world.

There are many reasons for relegating and maintaining covert a-b-c's to our nonconscious. The fact that we cannot maintain focused attention on more than one thought at a time is a primary reason. Second, and certainly not insignificant from a mental health perspective, A-B-C events and experiences that are simply too painful or threatening in our a-b-c consciousness are relegated (and unfortunately, stored) to our nonconscious covert. First identified and labeled by Sigmund Freud as "defense mechanisms," covert mechanisms such as repression, projection, rationalization, displacement, reaction formation, sublimation, and compensation enable us to deny or distort A-B-C experiences to the degree that they are no longer recognizable to our consciousness.

Defense mechanisms are a normal, adaptive part of our covert functioning when their use enables us to engage the world successfully and feel good about ourselves in the process. They are especially adaptive as a coping strategy when the intolerable A-B-C experience is extant and unavoidable (e.g., the A-B-C's of an abused child).

Defense mechanisms become maladaptive and destructive when they siphon off large amounts of energy necessary for daily functioning, restrict the free and open access that we desire to have with our nonconscious experience, and leave a cadre of covert a-b-c's that disable normal, healthy functioning. The dissociative disorders manifesting amnesia and multiple identities derive from extreme reliance on repression of intolerable A-B-C experiences and are often the product of the abused child's defense mechanism.

The dissociative disorders (DSM-IV, 1994) manifesting amnesia and multiple identities may be extreme examples of maladaptive coping strategies employed under the trauma of pervasive child abuse (Terr, 1991; Dutton, 1995). When confronted with intolerable A-B-C experiences (i.e., intense and unremitting C–'s) the individual may rely on repression of the intolerable pain (emotional or physical) and learn to dissociate body from mind, lose all memory of the traumatic experiences or, in extreme cases, create a new identity (with all new A-B-C's). The DSM-IV (1994) indicates that individuals with dissociative identity disorder frequently report having experienced severe physical and sexual abuse, especially during childhood. The accuracy of these reports has been questioned, however, due to the memory distortion that results from severe stress. In any case, we can conclude with confidence that defense mechanisms often involve our purposeful manipulation of our covert a-b-c's, and can aid or hinder our successful functioning. Hans Steiner and Zakee Matthews (1996) describe the array of choices left to the traumatized child:

> If the child feels that he cannot absent himself from predictable and horrible events, then at least he can pretend that he is going somewhere else (fugue states); pretend that the events are not happening (depersonalization); pretend that the world in which they are occurring is not real (derealization); forget about them as soon as they have happened (amnesia); pretend that the abuser is at least two people—for example, an evil mother and a good mother (projected identity problems); or finally, if all else fails, the child can pretend that he is many different people but not the one being tortured right then (identity problems or multiple personality). (pp. 356–357)

We will return to covert behavioral dysfunction and emotional coping in later chapters.

## Automatic Pilot of Our Brain

**A**ccompanying conscious and nonconscious covert behavior, yet functioning independently, is a third category of covert experience called *automatic thoughts*. As defined by Beck (1976), Ellis (1984), Seligman (1990), and many others, automatic thoughts are words, phrases, sentences, or images that occur out of habit and without focused attention. For example, Tom, an employee attending a business meeting, might aggressively attack his colleague John, who questions the wisdom of one of Tom's decisions. After the meeting, Tom is perplexed by the severity of his reaction. He genuinely likes John and respects his opinion. Why the irrational response?

If we witnessed Tom's entire covert experience throughout the business meeting, we could identify the culprit: an automatic thought stimulated by John's initial question (the antecedent) and immediately provoking Tom's aggressive attack. That automatic thought as a covert a-b-c—acquired from a perfectionistic, demanding father and honed over years of "getting ahead by being the best"—was simply: "Only perfection is acceptable and must be defended at all costs." This fleeting, imperceptible thought, initially processed within his right hemisphere—or emotional brain, as we shall see in Chapter 12—had been the source of social discord throughout Tom's life, yet remained unchallenged and unalterable until brought to conscious awareness within his brain's left hemisphere.

Automatic thoughts serve us well in the performance of routine, repetitive tasks. If you have ever driven a long distance on a monotonous interstate with recollection of the landscape, speedometer reading, or fuel gauge on reaching your destination, you have employed many useful automatic thoughts. If you ran out of gas, at least one of those automatic a-b-c's needed to be more conscious. These automatic thoughts, which appear almost reflexive and enable us to make our daily routine decisions and problem-solving actions, are always close to consciousness when novelty intrudes on our routine. Deikman (1982) refers to these thoughts as "instrumental consciousness."

Automatic thoughts are considered by one prominent physiologist, Vernon B. Mountcastle (see Mountcastle, Plum, & Geiger, 1987), as internally generated neural activities from deep within the midbrain. He believes that these electrochemical impulses, or reentrants, are activated by brain cells (not by external antecedents) and sent nonconsciously to the frontal cortex where they combine with conscious information about the external environment. Automatic memory for physical (motor) activity is located within the putamen area, while our locus for procedural memory (outline sequences of action) is within the caudate nucleus. When integrated with conscious a-b-c's, these reentrants provide a command function in directing respondent and operant responses to antecedent conditions. It is through this "distributed system" that relevant information in the form of electrochemical impulses is directed throughout the many information highways of the brain. Whereas nonconscious covert thought is stored throughout the vast cortical region of long-term memory and is often inaccessible to direct retrieval, automatic thoughts are essentially subconscious and direct our most habitual and routine actions.

Throughout each day, we pursue tasks and engage in activities while directing our conscious thought to other agendas. Riding a bicycle, ironing clothes, driving a car, shaving, and painting a wall are a few examples of routine behaviors maintained by automatic thoughts. Their automaticity often allows us the luxury to contemplate more profound or stimulating conscious thoughts. As many teachers and therapists have shown, automatic thoughts are readily accessible to consciousness. A simple diversion from the routine or directed attention to our covert experience while performing a particular act brings automatic thoughts to awareness.

So there you have the three dimensions of covert behavior, or awareness: consciousness, nonconsciousness, and automatic thoughts. I have emphasized dimensions of awareness vis-à-vis levels of brain wave activity because these dimensions delineate categories in which we process and use covert a-b-c's. Although brain wave activity differentiates levels of consciousness, it is more a measure of neurophysiological activation (Pelletier, 1992). The physiological activation required of normal consciousness creates high-frequency, low-amplitude patterns of brain activity (above 13 cycles per sec) and is referred to as a beta state. An alpha brain wave pattern of low frequency, high amplitude (8–13 cycles per sec) indicates a relatively unstressed, relaxed state of consciousness. Delta waves of relatively low amplitude and frequency (4–7 cycles per sec) characterize sleep, a state of consciousness under negligible external antecedent control but potentially activated by any covert a-b-c's in our long-term memory store. Whereas brain wave activity can be altered by drugs, the covert dimensions of consciousness, nonconsciousness, and automatic thinking are impervious to drugs but significantly more critical in how we process and use our covert a-b-c's.

Now that we have looked at levels of consciousness and the relationship between our objective A-B-C's and their subjective a-b-c counterparts, we can begin to explore the covert structures and processes that form the boundaries of our covert world.

## Chapter Summary

1. Covert behavior comprises our conscious thinking and thus represents the information processes and content that we choose to reflect on in our conscious thought. The term covert behavior is the same as covert operants, a term originally coined by Joseph Cautela.

2. The world in our head is our representation of the external and internal A-B-C's of our experience. As we continually construct that covert world, we create meaning and understanding of our ongoing experience.

3. To the extent that there is an external world apart from our own covert experience of it, we call this objective world the A-B-C's of our experience. Capital A-B-C's represent the external world of our experience that others can see, describe, and validate. Lowercase a-b-c's represent our covert representation of those A-B-C's.

4. The covert processes for how we think are generally similar for all of us. The content of our covert a-b-c's is the product of our unique experience.

5. As our covert a-b-c's are constructed and reinforced through significant life experience, they in turn become the subjective reality through which all present experience is matched and validated.

6. Consciousness implies focused awareness of a specific covert thought. The external stimuli of which I am currently aware (e.g., a passing car splashing through a puddle) combined with information retrieved from my vast long-term memory storage system forms a conscious thought.

7. All information not retrieved from my memory stores or from external stimuli represents nonconscious thought.

8. Covert thoughts that comprise habitual words, images, or sensations occurring without focused attention are called automatic thoughts. Repetitive tasks such as driving a car or dialing a familiar phone number are maintained by automatic thoughts.

**Figure 1** *The A-B-C (Cognitive–Behavioral) Model*

| (A) Antecedent | Covert | (B) Behavior Overt | Overt | (C) Consequence |
|---|---|---|---|---|
| | Cognitive (Thinking) | Respondent (Physical) | Operant (Acting) | |
| Stimulus or setting event. External environments that set the occasion for behavior (thinking, acting, feeling) to occur. $S^{Dee}$ = Green light. A cue that a particular behavior will result in a desirable consequence. $S^{Delta}$ = Red light. A cue that a particular behavior will result in an undesirable consequence. | Subjective environment. The process and content of our thinking. Our interpretation of A-B-C as a-b-c. Includes: Attributions Expectations Self-concept Self-esteem Beliefs Attitudes Prejudices Self-talk Locus of control Images Fantasies Intrinsic consequences | Reflexive Autonomic Involuntary Biochemical Physiological changes occurring within our body. | Voluntary behavior that we choose to do or not to do. Can be: Excess = Behavior done too often or at wrong time. Deficit = Behavior done too infrequently or not when needed. | Events (external) that occur during and/or after a particular covert and/or operant behavior. Events can be: A. Desirable: 1. Positive Reinforcement present desirable = C+ 2. Negative Reinforcement remove undesirable = ⊄ B. Undesirable: 1. Punishment present undesirable, aversive = C– 2. Extinction remove desirable = ⊄ |
| **Emotions** | | | | |

Subjective labels used to describe a specific state of being. Labels reflect the composite of our covert, respondent, and operant behavior within a specific context of antecedents and consequences.

# Chapter 8

─────〰〰〰〰〰〰─────

# Covert Structures
# and Processes

─────〰〰〰〰〰〰─────

## Orienting Ourselves

I have used the terms covert world and mind interchangeably because they both comprise the processes of our brain and central nervous system. When we think of structures relative to this most complex human organ, we think of the 0.25-in. thick mass of 50 billion neurons comprising the four lobes of the cerebral cortex. It is here that antecedent sensory information is integrated with stored a-b-c experiences to give meaning and purpose to our constant flow of covert experiences. The integration and synthesis of information into meaningful covert experience are functions of innate biological structures that program the manner, or "style," in which information is perceived, processed, stored, retrieved, and expressed as well as the sequence in which these cognitive operations develop over the course of our life.

Our discussion of the processes and structures of covert behavior will help us understand how we think and will provide the framework for the content of our covert experience—what we think—our theme in Chapter 9. We will begin by looking at how we think. We will first examine the innate structure that programs the style in which we acquire and use our covert a-b-c's. Then we will turn to structures that program the developmental and qualitative nature of covert processes, the neurophysiology of thought, and the biology of emotion.

After studying the content of our thought in Chapter 9, we will circumscribe our investigation to those covert a-b-c's that we refer to as the self in Chapter 10. Chapter 11 will then illuminate the manner in which we judge and value our selves. Having integrated most of the A-B-C elements into our covert experience, we will incorporate the last and perhaps most crucial aspect of the human experience into our A-B-C model: emotion. But now to the structures and processes of the brain that form our covert experience.

## Hemispheric Specialization

If you move a finger in a straight line across from the top of your forehead to the back of your neck, you will have "bisected" two qualitatively different covert worlds: the right

**Figure 11** *Covert Behavior*

---

### Cognitive
### (Thinking)

---

Subjective environment. The process and content of our thinking.
Our interpretation of A-B-C as a-b-c.

Includes:
Attributions
Expectations
Self-concept
Self-esteem
Beliefs
Attitudes
Prejudices
Self-talk
Locus of control
Images
Fantasies
Intrinsic consequences

---

### Emotions

---

Subjective labels used to describe a specific state of being. Labels reflect the composite of our covert, respondent, and operant behavior within a specific context of antecedents and consequences.

---

and left hemispheres of the brain. Since first discovered by Marc Dax in 1836, it has been empirically established that our left- and right-brain hemispheres specialize in different styles of processing and using information. To quote from Roger W. Sperry (1974):

> Each hemisphere . . . has its own . . . private sensations, perceptions, thoughts, and ideas, all of which are cut off from the corresponding experiences in the opposite hemisphere. Each left and right hemisphere has its own private chain of memories and learning experiences that are inaccessible to recall by the other hemisphere. In many respects each disconnected hemisphere appears to have a separate "mind of its own." (p. 282)

Although there are specialized functions for each brain hemisphere, more recent studies (Corballis, 1983; Gazzaniga & LeDoux, 1978; Selemon, Goldman-Rakic, & Tamminga, 1995) have emphasized the interdependence of the two hemispheres. Rather than debunking the evidence for distinct functional differences, these studies highlight the overlap and compensatory relationship between the two halves of our brain. But before looking at this bilateral integration of left and right, we will look at their primary differences.

The two hemispheres of the brain that we consider the locus of consciousness combine the left and right frontal cortex. These two halves communicate through a massive bundle of 200 million nerve fibers called the *corpus callosum*. To a large extent, sensory input from the left eye and ear is processed in the right hemisphere, while the left hemisphere receives sensory impulses from the right eye and ear. In spite of common belief, there has been no definitive relationship established between hemispheric specialization and handedness (Coren, 1993).

Most of us show a preference for the left or right hemisphere as the mechanism for experiencing our covert world. Although this preference, or dominant hemisphere, is more extreme in some people, especially those with a cerebral dysfunction, it becomes less pronounced as we reach adulthood. Except for occasions of extreme stress when we return to our preferred mode of processing, most adults have been able to integrate the two hemispheres into one holistic covert experience. This preference for using one hemispheric modality in creating covert experiences is probably the result of evolutionary and biological forces. Although our preference is innate, the capacity to use both hemispheres to integrate covert experience exists for most of us. We will look at each side separately and then in combination.

## Left-Brain Functioning

The left brain processes auditory information and regulates speech.

In conjunction with speech comprehension and production, the left brain regulates language (i.e., words, sentences, linguistic symbols) to process and give meaning to covert experience. Speech comprehension is localized in the Wernicke's area of the left cortex, while speech organization and production reside in the Broca's area.

Our language system, as with our speech, is sound based and thus processed as auditory data within our left brain. In other words, when our left brain processes data, it uses the medium of language and the vehicle of speech. We talk to ourselves in our left brain. It is hypothesized that because spoken language preceded written language in both human evolution and individual development, our processing of written language occurs auditorially within our left hemisphere (Bloom & Lazerson, 1988).

As language is structured linearly, our left brain tends to think that way. Operating from a language base, left-brain functioning—or self-talk—tends to be very adroit at sequential learning, analytical problem solving, and the language-based classification of information. This latter aptitude lends itself to the convergent mastery of large amounts of information, while at the same time keeping our focused awareness (i.e., consciousness) on minute detail.

All of these left-brain proclivities of language, speech, sequencing, and analysis correspond to the tasks of learning in school. Complex verbal directions, memorization and regurgitation of facts, written expression, and a phonetic approach to reading instruction benefit from a left-brain mode of processing.

Because of their facility with language, those who show a preference for left-brain thinking tend to be more adroit in written verbal expression. Considerable research has shown that females represent the majority within this left-brain preference category.

The covert experience of left-brain processing exists as language in the form of self-talk. Covert a-b-c experiences are processed as narratives, questions, and speculations on the specific aspects of a-b-c's in the past, present, and future. The a-b-c's give structure to covert scenarios, creating such self-talk as, "I better spray the hibiscus plant in the family room. It looks like it has mites, and if I don't do something soon, I may lose it." See if you can identify the a-b-c elements of this self-talk.

Did you come up with anything like this?

antecedent = mites appearing on hibiscus plant in family room

behavior = spraying plant immediately

consequence (of spraying) = plant lives

(of doing nothing) = plant dies

Self-talk is seldom grammatically correct. Usually, we experience it as fleeting words, phrases, or disjointed narration. Our conscious self-talk may occur in more coherent, syntactic form when encountering novel or difficult situations. Driving a manual shift automobile after just learning (or being away from one for a while), preparing a difficult recipe, anticipating a formal presentation before a large audience, or even calculating your taxes may be challenging enough tasks to require deliberate self-talk or even the vocalization of thinking out loud. When not taxed to use focused awareness in overcoming a challenge, we spend much of our inner thought in fleeting sensorimotor impulses and images (in our right brain) that only become subvocal when our left brain attempts to organize and make sense of them (Joseph, 1982).

Regardless of our hemispheric preference, most of us are capable of left-brain functioning. If I ask you to name the ninth word of Lincoln's Gettysburg Address, you will probably use your left brain to answer. Try it. What is your answer? How did you get that answer? Unless you are extremely right brained and actually discriminated the ninth word from the document that you saw in your covert, you recited it to yourself. And with a good covert memory, you should have answered "brought."

Our hemispheric preference not only determines the way we process covert experience, but also the manner in which we express that experience to the external world. Our external operant behavior is our expression of how we experience (i.e., see or hear) the world in our covert. If I process experiences from an auditory language base, I express my experience in like fashion through speech and written communication. In fact, my communication includes indices of my brain preference such as "I *hear* what you mean." "It *sounds* like a good idea." and "I *told* myself."

Educators and psychologists have frequently referred to our preference for left- or right-brain processing as our "cognitive style" (Shapiro, 1965; Sternberg, 1994). There are various approaches and tests to assess our unique preference, but one simple, nonstandardized test I have found useful is the following:

You wish to invite me to your house for dinner. I will be renting a car and driving to your home from the local airport. I ask you to mail me directions. When I open the letter and gaze at your directions, what do I see or read? What do your directions suggest about your preferred modality?

Please read on and we will get back to this question after we "look" at right-brain functioning.

## Right-Brain Functioning

Our right hemisphere regulates visual perception and spatial relationships. From this modality, we process information visually and, thus, experience the covert world as pictures and images.

Because the right brain uses visuospatial integration rather than language and sound to create covert experiences, right-brain thinking tends to be nonlinear, simultaneous, and wholistic. The advantage of this processing is that we are not restricted by language to give meaning to our experiences. Our covert manipulation of visual images allows us to integrate many discrete pieces of external and internal information into the big picture. This release from the structure of language and linear thinking enables us to incorporate divergent experiences into new and unique ways of thinking. The disadvantages of not operating from a language base is the absence of a linguistic classification system in which to store and retrieve information—a critical component in memorization.

Whereas language-based left-brain thinking facilitates the integration of information, right-brain thinking facilitates the synthesis of visual and motor-based experiences (Briggs, 1988). Left-brain thinkers can describe the evolution of the safety pin in great detail, while right-brain thinkers can find 200 ways of using it. This divergent nature of right-brain thinking has been characterized as the key ingredient in creativity.

Contemporary theories of creativity define it as a process requiring a number of interhemispheric operations within an environmentally conducive context that produces a unique or distinct product (Brown, 1989). Rather than viewing creativity as a personal quality or trait, it is more accurately viewed as a repertoire of cognitive skills including breaking the perceptual and cognitive set; trying new problem-solving strategies; keeping response options open, or delaying closure; suspending judgment; using large amounts of information in broad categories; and breaking out of performance scripts or linear problem solving (Amabile, 1983, p. 363).

The execution of these skills in a supportive environment (a second ingredient of creativity emphasized by Torrance, 1975) resulting in a creative product certainly involves divergent thinking. But as Briggs (1988) points out, even divergent thinking must be complemented by convergent thinking in every demonstration of creativity. The creative process and product must occur within a cultural-historical context, with new and divergent insights drawn from the information painstakingly acquired from that context. Thomas Edison acknowledged this critical contribution of culture and hemispheric integration when he attributed his creativity to 2% inspiration and 98% perspiration. In telling Vincent van Gogh about his famous painting of his mother, James Whistler said that it took him 2 h to paint but 40 yr to learn how to paint it in 2 h (Briggs, 1988).

To the degree that we possess the capacity for both left- and right-hemispheric processing, we possess the "person" ingredients for creativity. Perhaps all that we need for an inspirational flash is the opportunity, a supportive environment, and a lot of hard work.

Our right-brain proclivity for divergent thinking may explain our common depiction of creative individuals as "visionaries" and not "self-talkers."

The right brain has no language and cannot talk by itself. Because it has no language (written or spoken) through which to communicate, it expresses itself just as it experiences the world: through the media of visual arts and nonverbal operant behavior.

Where the left brain focuses on detail, the right looks at how visual-motor stimuli fit together into the whole, or Gestalt. With this whole being greater than the sum of its parts, the right brain synthesizes experience into new meanings and new schemata.

Visual-motor integration (e.g., eye–hand coordination) is also centered in the right hemisphere. Although still speculative, one implication of this right-brain–overt behavior relationship is that right-brain thinkers might incorporate more physiological and kinesthetic information into covert visual experiences. This integration of nonverbal sensory modalities would enable the right brain to see, feel and do instead of talk about it (Gazzaniga, 1985). It may be that we experience emotion in our right hemisphere and then label it (along with planning a course of action) in our left hemisphere.

The right hemisphere is often referred to as the "emotional brain" (Gainotti, 1973; Miller, 1988). Both hemispheres of the cerebral frontal cortex have neural connections with the limbic system, brainstem, and throughout the nervous system and maintain their constant communication with each other through the corpus callosum. It is the right hemisphere, however, that appears to have the most direct and continuous interplay of sensory impulses with cells controlling visual-motor and autonomic (respondent) functioning.

Split-brain studies of individuals suffering debilitating injuries in either hemisphere (Robinson, 1986; Ross & Stewart, 1987) have found that left-brain-damaged patients experienced significantly greater levels of emotion: aggression, anxiety, depression, and general physiological arousal. Patients forced to rely on their right hemisphere experienced inordinately high levels of emotional responses that would require direct stimulation from the hypothalamus (for autonomic nervous system arousal), the amygdala (activating aggression), and even the hippocampus (locus of memory store). This right-brain-induced emotionality, prompted by the absence of left-brain mediation and moderation, included tears, yelling, cursing, agitated depression, and even physical aggression. This syndrome of right-brain emotionality was labeled by researcher Guido Gainotti (1973) as the *catastrophic* reaction.

In contrast, right-brain-disabled patients (i.e., operating only from their left brain) exhibited very flat affect and reported little arousal and concern for their disability. These patients presented themselves as doing fine and feeling unconcerned about anything, as if they were denying their emotions or were out of touch with them, which they probably were. We will return to the emotional aspects of our covert experience later in this chapter.

Right-brain preference for visual processing is further supported by research (Bloom & Lazerson, 1988) showing that individuals using sign language or a language based on pictorial symbols (e.g., Japanese, Chinese, Korean) are predominantly using their right hemisphere in that process.

By now you might have guessed that I tend to prefer right-brain functioning in creating covert experiences. I experience my covert a-b-c's as both static and moving pictures. I also pepper my speech with references such as: "It *looks* to me like . . ." "As I *see* it . . ." "Let me *picture* the problem . . ." and "I'll *show* you what I mean."

The images created in right-brain thinking tend to be in the form of moving pictures that we can experience in one of two ways. We can observe the action, as if watching a movie, or we can actually participate in the action, as if we were actors or actresses. The difference between these two perspectives has a qualitatively different effect on how we actually experience the covert a-b-c. The full experience including all of the sensory modalities necessitates the participant position. The true joy of a romp along the beach is in the doing, even if the doing is only in your head. The pain of a physical injury is also magnified as we re-create the first-person experience of the injury in our covert. The further we remove ourselves from the participant position of an experience in our covert, the less we experience its emotional component. The learning and therapeutic implications of this perspective distinction are only recently being recognized.

Our right-brain experience of the prospective demise of the hibiscus plant might consist of a few visual scenarios in which I:

See the hibiscus plant wilting as it is consumed by mites.

See myself get the spray from the garage and rescue the grateful plant with aggressive bursts of medicinal spray.

See the beautiful new blooms sprouting from my recovered treasure.

Each visualization includes all or part of the a-b-c's of my covert experience.

Again, regardless of our brain preference, most of us can experience from our right brain. You can probably tell me how many windows you have in your kitchen or which of the three lights on a traffic light signals green. You probably used your right brain to answer by seeing your kitchen and a traffic light in your "mind's eye." You used your right brain to create and manipulate a covert visual experience.

Returning to your own learning style assessment, we will renew your invitation to me for dinner at your home. If you operate from a left-brain preference, you probably wrote your directions as a narrative that reads like: "You exit the airport and go left on Route 29. Then you proceed for 3 m, past two traffic lights, and turn left at the Exxon station . . ." From the right-brain perspective, you probably drew a map and included pictures of all the important landmarks.

If you included a map with labeled landmarks and explanatory narrative, you belong to the majority, a fortunate group of people able to integrate both sides of the brain in creating covert experiences. Let us look at how both sides work together.

## Hemispheric Integration

In a healthy, normal brain, the left and right hemispheres constantly interact, channeling information through the corpus callosum to the frontal lobe of the cerebral cortex. Both hemispheres of the frontal cortex are activated during covert problem solving and planning. Proton emission tomography (PET) scans of brain utilization of glucose have also shown similar levels of brain activity when conscious thought has focused on integrative covert experiences, which combine the sight, sound, feel, touch, taste, and smell of an experience. Combining all sensory modalities into a single covert experience is called *cognitive integration*. Studies (e.g., Zilbergeld & Lazarus, 1988) have shown that maximum learning and performance of a task (e.g., creative problem solving, a complex athletic performance such as shooting a basketball) are achieved when the external operant behavior can first occur as an integrated covert experience. Antonio Damasio (1994) extended this integration of covert experience to include emotion as a critical ingredient to optimal learning and performance. We will discuss the implication of this cortex-limbic arousal system to emotion and covert functioning in Chapter 12.

Well before Damasio identified this crucial frontal cortex-limbic system link to our covert emotional experience, Walle Nauta (1971) found this interaction to be crucial in linking emotion and memory to perception and action. These connections enable the frontal lobes to maintain continuous self-regulation. In the left hemisphere, however, these emotions, motives, and perceptions of current external stimuli and action potentials (i.e., schemata) become conscious and can be directed to purposeful operant behavior. The right hemisphere may be the primary receptor for sensory and motor experiences—those physiological elements of emotion—but the left brain integrates all of the parts (physiology, external sensory information, extant memory as schemata, and aggregate a-b-c's) into the conscious awareness of a coherent covert experience. This conscious covert experience then becomes the basis for understanding, planning, and evaluating our effectiveness in dealing with the world and meeting our own needs.

The human brain has a remarkable capacity to perform integrative covert processes as well as use either hemisphere to compensate for disabilities in the other. The brain of the young child is most adaptable in employing all of its resources for learning and expression. This plasticity in bilateral functioning displayed by children may explain their facility in acquiring multiple languages. The learning of a secondary language(s) requires a greater proportion of right-hemisphere activation than is utilized in the acquisition and use of the primary or first language.

The young brain also displays the greatest plasticity in using the operations of each hemisphere to compensate for deficiencies in its counterpart. Molfese, Freeman, and Palermo (1975) have shown that if the language areas in the left cortex are damaged early in life, areas in the right cortex are able to assume their operations. Bilaterality of speech function has been reported in 15% of left-handers (Corballis, 1983), and significant proportions of stutterers have speech represented bilaterally, suggesting that a struggle for hemispheric control may actually impair speech production (Wood, Stump, McKeechan, Sheldon, & Proctor, 1980). In spite of this disadvantage, it must be concluded that hemispheric specialization and integration represent a fundamental process in the creation of covert experiences. We will now turn our attention to a second innate structure that programs the sequential development of these covert processes.

## Developmental Schemata of Covert Processes

**W**e know from our own development and frequent amazement at the thinking of youth that their covert world is qualitatively different from ours. Additional insight tells us that there is a developmental quality to the way we acquire and use covert a-b-c's. Through the work of Jean Piaget (1954, 1985), we can understand these developmental differences and explicate the structural and developmental dynamics of covert behavior.

Jean Piaget devoted his life (and the microscopic study of his children) to the investigation of innate cognitive structures that evolve developmentally to construct and continually reconstruct our own covert reality. There are three aspects of his cognitive developmental theory that have direct relevance to our understanding of the developmental and structural nature of covert behavior. The first aspect looks at the immutable cognitive processes of assimilation, accommodation, and equilibrium; the second emphasizes the evolving structures, or schemata, from which we frame our experience; and the third addresses the developmental unfolding of our covert reality.

## Assimilation, Accommodation and Equalization of Schemata

**T**o understand the processes of assimilation, accommodation, and equilibrium, we must first define the term *schema* (or its plural, *schemata*). Schemata are the innate cognitive structures by which we recognize and organize our covert world. We can understand and give meaning to our covert experience (as sensory data) because of concepts, categories, and relationships that already exist in our covert reality. In other words, schemata represent what we know about the way the world (our aggregate a-b-c's) works.

At birth, we only know the external world through the innate schemes (i.e., actions) of sucking, grasping, phonating, seeing, and hearing. The purposeful use of these schemes as instruments of sensory stimulation and tools for manipulating the environment is what I mean by the phrase "acting upon the world." These congenital schemes are the mechanisms with which we are able to engage the world on our own terms by using these sensorimotor schemes to absorb and understand the external world and our place within it. The active employment of these schemes creates the sensory infor-mation that subsequently becomes our internalized action patterns, or what Piaget called schemata.

Using our schemata as a framework for understanding, we constantly explore our world, incorporating new A-B-C experiences into existing schemata. This process of integrating external A-B-C's into matching covert a-b-c's is called *assimilation*. As long as the external A-B-C's match our existing covert a-b-c's (a confirmation of ex-pectation with experience that Leon Festinger, 1957, called "cognitive consonance"), we continue to use our existing schemata to make sense of the world.

Fortunately, as we expand our exploration of the external world, we experience new A-B-C's that simply do not match our existing schemata. Without any way of un-derstanding our new A-B-C, we are left with two alternatives: We can modify an ex-isting schema (a-b-c) so that it fits the new A-B-C, or we can create an entirely new schema that gives meaning to the new A-B-C and thus enables us to incorporate it into our covert experience. Our change in schema that results from either of these two alternatives is called *accommodation*.

## Schemata: Our Covert Action Plans

**P**iagetians believe that we construct perception through the actions through which we experience our environment. Our visual, auditory, olfactory, haptic (touch-ing), and taste schemes facilitate sensory information with which we construct our perception of reality. This perception actuates existing schemata (assimilation) and, when necessary, creates new ones (accommodation). Our subjectively constructed perceptions activate schemata that exist in our stored memory as internalized action patterns. We then direct these action patterns to objects, persons, and events. Our ac-tion on the world facilitates our covert representation of that action, with each covert representation comprising meaningful a-b-c's. These patterns of a-b-c's serve as our schemata and form our knowledge base about objects, space, time, and causality.

As a-b-c's, schemata tell us what to expect of an object or situation; they tell us what the contingency relationship is concerning the objects, people, and events in our life (Rumelhart & Ortony, 1977). For example, as children, we construct a schema for "having a cold." This schema tells us when, where, and under what conditions we can catch one (our covert a), the symptoms and treatment that we can expect (our covert b), and the anticipated consequences of the symptoms and treatments (our covert c). Our external environment is instrumental in how we construct our perception, and thus our schema, of a cold. Had we lived a few hundred years ago, this a-b-c schema would not have existed. Instead, our 18th-century schema of a cold would have re-volved around our imbalance of body humors and possession of some evil spirit. Or maybe we were just "bad."

While Piaget's contention that action must precipitate the formulation of schemata has received considerable support (Ruff, 1982), some (Butterworth, Jarrett, & Hicks, 1982) have questioned the necessity of doing to activate and develop new schemata. These information-processing theorists posit that our schemata are innate and only need appropriate discrimination of environmental stimuli to provide meaning to our covert experience. Other investigations of covert development (Damasio, 1994) posit that we are born with specialized brain mechanisms that operate from reasoning and knowledge acquisition at birth. This notion that the brain evolves with specialized functions—somewhat like modular units—has been supported by neuroanatomical studies of brain activity showing the correlation of very specific and localized electric brain activity with specific covert experiences (Damasio, 1994). When espousing an innate or developmental/constructionist orientation, both theories concur that the product of cognitive processing is an ever-expanding aggregate of a-b-c's for understanding ourselves in our world.

## Equilibrium and the Development of Self

Cognitive development and learning depend on continuous assimilation interrupted by periodic accommodations. The development of new cognitive structures or ways of knowing the world does not occur without this balance, referred to as *equilibrium*. As long as it exists, we are successful in assimilating ever-changing and expanding A-B-C's into our covert experience with the help of timely accommodations to our existing a-b-c's. Disequilibrium occurs when accommodation fails and we find ourselves with meaningless external experiences (A-B-C's). At such times, our innate need for harmony and balance (i.e., equilibrium) motivates us to create new ways (i.e., schemata) of understanding the world that will enable us to assimilate the new experience.

The 1-month-old infant experiences the external world as undifferentiated from the self; her toes, her teddy, and her mother's breasts are all part of "me." Unlike the separate identity that we will come to know (i.e., accommodate a schema for) as the "me," "I," or "self" late in life, this infantile "me" is solely a sensorimotor awareness. This sensorimotor egocentrism is the first rudiment of the self, but it is a self totally undifferentiated from every experience with the external world. Each new external antecedent is assimilated as another part of "me"—something to suck, grasp, and look at. External antecedents exist only as the infant's experience of them. The infant's covert schemata do not distinguish a from b from c. Instead, every experience is a sensorimotor encounter that satisfies physiological needs—the experience of primary reinforcement C+'s. But the infant does not covertly process (give meaning to) these primary reinforcers as consequences because the schema for causality (i.e., the contingency relationship for a-b-c) will not occur for a few months.

## Schemata As Covert a-b-c's: Developmental Factors

As antecedents such as a bottle, teddy, nightlight, mother's voice, and so on are assimilated, the infant begins to experience their absence and even begins to notice that by coordinating existing schemata (sucking, grasping, phonating, etc.) antecedents can be manipulated. These new A-B-C experiences cannot be assimilated into the old sensorimotor schemata, so new schemata are accommodated into the child's covert a-b-c. Schemata for object separateness and constancy (i.e., that A-B-C's can exist apart from my experience of them) and for causality (i.e., that my behavior can manipulate antecedents and consequences) become the basis for assimilation and equilibrium. More complex and sophisticated schemata will surely develop if opportunities continue for the young child to engage her ever-expanding and challenging environment. This sequential development of cognitive structures follows a natural progression of stages that build on the framework (i.e., covert experience) of each preceding stage.

Piaget believed that the mind constructs its own covert reality (aggregate a-b-c's) through this constant interplay of assimilation and accommodation. He further posits that this development follows innately programmed neurological growth. Just as new schemata are built from the knowledge and understanding in old schemata, the mind's capacity to accommodate increasingly complex structures follows the neurological development of the brain. Our capacity to think in abstractions and to solve problems using conjecture and hypothesis testing is a covert adult ability that Piaget refers to as "formal operations." We begin to acquire or more constructively master this ability as we enter adolescence because our neurological apparatus permits this level of brain activity and because our life experiences have created schemata that support the covert processing required for formal operations. The critical match that must be maintained for optimal cognitive development now includes the antecedent environment, the appropriate cognitive structure, and the neurological functioning of the individual. This constant interaction of environmental, cognitive, and physiological forces produces a somewhat predictable pattern of cognitive growth: a progression of stages or steps toward cognitive maturity. A brief synopsis of each stage illustrates how they build on each other.

*Sensorimotor Stage* (birth–2 yrs)—Using their congenital schemes to experience and act upon their expanding world, children become aware of themselves as separate entities from the rest of the world. This fundamental schema is the knowledge of the self and the formation of a unique identity.

*Preoperational Stage* (2–7 yrs)—Learning language enables children to use words and symbols mentally. Language becomes their covert representation of the external world of their physical experience. Objects, people, events, and places can be labeled, categorized, and stored for future reference.

*Concrete Operational Stage* (7–12 yrs)—Children's ability to compare and contrast different experiences enables them to incorporate logic, rules, laws, and predictable contingencies into their covert world. A-B-C contingencies are learned as they are experienced or told by others, and they become the law of the land. Children believe that their covert a-b-c's must be the only true reality. Perspective has not become a schema yet.

*Formal Operational Stage* (12 yrs–adult)—The adolescent can transcend the known to the unknown. The ability to manipulate possible a-b-c's enables hypothesizing and speculation. This capacity to manipulate abstract concepts brings the adolescent's covert into the realm of idealism and true perspective. Multiple perspectives, however, cause the adolescent to be self-conscious and even doubtful of the self. For the first time, things may not be the way that he or she experiences them.

Rather than present the full scope and depth of Piaget's developmental stages, I have highlighted the characteristics of each. Anyone wishing a lucid, cogent immersion into the rich complexity of his theory is encouraged to read texts by Jean Flavell (1985), Barry Wadsworth (1989), Ginsburg and Opper (1988), and any of the works by Piaget and Inhelder. Although I could never do full justice in this chapter to Piaget's many insights and contributions, my primary purpose has been to incorporate the knowledge and wisdom of his theory into an A-B-C (and a-b-c) model of the human experience—sort of my way of assimilating his model into the schemata of my own covert a-b-c's. Ideally, the assimilation that results will bring an even greater understanding and appreciation of the A-B-C model.

Now that I have placed the A-B-C model and corresponding covert a-b-c's within the context of cognitive structures and developmental processes, I would like to illustrate one example of where cognitive structures, developmental processes, and the a-b-c's might converge.

## Left-Brain Development and the Language of Covert Experience

Neurological development and especially the myelinization process proceed well beyond birth, with environmental stimulation critical for full maturity. In his study of language acquisition relative to cortical development, neuropsychologist Alexander Luria (1982) concluded that true consciousness only occurs with the acquisition of an internalized language system. In the early months of life (up to about 2 yr), we use our sensorimotor apparatus for meeting our needs and learning the rudiments of speech. Recall that this period of sensorimotor experience coincides with Piaget's first stage of cognitive development.

This prelanguage period is predominated by right-brain processing of sensorimotor experience. But without language, these right-brain experiences are neither conscious nor meaningful for rational understanding and volitional action. Without the classification and organizational structure of language, these early experiences may not even be suitable for long-term memory storage (Sullivan, 1953). This may account for our inability to recall (i.e., retrieve from memory and articulate) prelanguage experience, yet still be affected by these early right-brain experiences. This procedural knowledge of how to do some action was stored in long-term memory as sensory impulses without the organization and meaning of language (Squire, 1984). The memory of those prelanguage experiences may still exist within our cerebral cortex, but only as sensorimotor impulses.

Our left brain's attempt to organize and make sense of these sensorimotor experiences provides the impetus for egocentric speech, children's vocalizations that describe their experiences and regulate their actions (Joseph, 1982). We often hear this speech from infants as they think out loud and talk through their play activity. Sometimes they will even vocalize their action plan by announcing something like: "Uh-oh. Here comes (a), so I better (b) or (c) will happen." Gradually, through the process of assimilation and accommodation during left-brain maturation, this vocalized speech becomes subvocal and internalized. Just as Piaget saw this preoperational stage as essential for the learning of lasting and meaningful schemata, psychologist Lev Vygotsky (1982) viewed this process as the foundation of conscious thought. With language comes our ability to construct and maintain in memory meaningful and purposeful covert experiences.

This language system of developmentally expanding private speech provides the means with which we create understanding and executive purpose from the ubiquitous stimuli entering our covert apparatus. Through language, we derive and create meanings that reflect the most universal and idiosyncratic qualities of being human. Our next chapter will delve into the nature of those meanings—the content of our thought.

## Chapter Summary

**1.** The way we think is influenced by the anatomy and physiology of our brain. These innate structures determine our predisposition for processing information in various parts of the brain. Our left- and right-brain hemispheres are specialized for different styles of processing and using information.

**2.** Our left-brain hemisphere processes auditory information, regulates speech, and uses language (auditory symbols) as its modus operandi for bringing meaning, understanding, and purpose to experience. This left brain uses reason, logic, and linear thinking to maintain its executive function over problem solving and decision making.

**3.** Our right-brain hemisphere regulates visual perception and spatial relationships. Through this hemisphere, we process information visually, holistically, and without the constraints of language. Consequently, our right brain facilitates divergent thinking and creativity.

**4.** Although most of us demonstrate a preference for left or right hemispheric processing of information, by adulthood we have integrated both hemispheres into a united process of thinking about and understanding our experience.

**5.** Jean Piaget posits a cognitive developmental process through which our capacity to understand our experience evolves through interdependent stages. Building on our innate sensorimotor experience in infancy, each subsequent stage uses assimilation and accommodation to create new cognitive structures with which to understand and interact with the world.

**6.** Our knowledge and understanding of the world are stored within our memory system as schemata. As we interact with our social and physical environment, familiar experiences (objects and events) are assimilated into our existing schemata.

**5.** Novel experiences require us to alter or build new schemata to understand and act on that which is new. This alteration or addition of new schemata is referred to as accommodation and forms the basis for cognitive growth and learning.

**7.** Equilibrium is achieved when our ongoing experience is understood through (and matches with) existing schemata. The state of balance is maintained through assimilation of new information into familiar ways (schemata) of understanding the world. Contrastingly, disequilibrium creates confusion and the need to re-establish balance through accommodation and the creation of new schemata.

**Figure 1** *The A-B-C (Cognitive–Behavioral) Model*

| (A) Antecedent | | (B) Behavior | | (C) Consequence |
|---|---|---|---|---|
| | **Covert** | **Overt** | **Overt** | |
| | **Cognitive (Thinking)** | **Respondent (Physical)** | **Operant (Acting)** | |
| Stimulus or setting event. External environments that set the occasion for behavior (thinking, acting, feeling) to occur.<br><br>$S^{Dee}$ = Green light. A cue that a particular behavior will result in a desirable consequence.<br><br>$S^{Delta}$ = Red light. A cue that a particular behavior will result in an undesirable consequence. | Subjective environment. The process and content of our thinking. Our interpretation of A-B-C as a-b-c.<br><br>Includes:<br>Attributions<br>Expectations<br>Self-concept<br>Self-esteem<br>Beliefs<br>Attitudes<br>Prejudices<br>Self-talk<br>Locus of control<br>Images<br>Fantasies<br>Intrinsic consequences | Reflexive<br>Autonomic<br>Involuntary<br>Biochemical<br>Physiological changes occurring within our body. | Voluntary behavior that we choose to do or not to do.<br><br>Can be: Excess = Behavior done too often or at wrong time.<br><br>Deficit = Behavior done too infrequently or not when needed. | Events (external) that occur during and/or after a particular covert and/or operant behavior. Events can be:<br><br>A. Desirable:<br>1. Positive Reinforcement present desirable = C+<br>2. Negative Reinforcement remove undesirable = ⊘<br><br>B. Undesirable:<br>1. Punishment present undesirable, aversive = C–<br>2. Extinction remove desirable = ⊘ |
| **Emotions** | | | | |

Subjective labels used to describe a specific state of being. Labels reflect the composite of our covert, respondent, and operant behavior within a specific context of antecedents and consequences.

# Chapter 9

## Our Covert a-b-c's: What We Think About

### Orienting Ourselves

In the previous chapter, we explored the structures and processes that influence how we think. Considerations of how we process and use our covert a-b-c's lead to one of the most mundane yet profound questions of human introspection: Just what do we think about? This chapter will try to address that question. Chapter 10 will then explicate the more intimate and personal dimension of our thoughts: covert a-b-c's that pertain to and in many ways define us and form the essential structure of our self.

After I describe the various factors that influence covert a-b-c's that form the self-concept, Chapter 11 will discuss the mechanisms through which we value and make judgments about our self (or our many selves, as will be suggested). This discourse on our natural proclivity to judge our selves (using considerably harsher criteria then we often use in judging others) will preface an extensive analysis of intrinsic consequences. As will be seen, our self-judgments lead inexorably to our self as a provider (or withholder) of C+'s and C−'s. The intrinsic consequences that we consciously employ can have a profound influence on our emotions, and the a-b-c's of our experience of emotion will occupy our investigation in Chapter 12.

In their extensive investigation of the process and content of daydreaming and "stream of consciousness" (i.e., nonconscious thought), Singer (1975) found that much of our covert experience is consumed by thoughts about uncompleted tasks, plans that have not been attempted or realized, performances that are deemed inadequate to applied standards, unmet deadlines, and promises yet to be kept. We work on these thoughts by generating covert resolution and completion scenarios and by anticipating future consequences of both successful and unsuccessful action. We continue to create and rework our completion scenarios until closure (Klinger, 1971). These nagging thoughts can approach almost obsessive magnitude or they can lurk within our nonconscious thought indefinitely, only surfacing to consciousness when prompted by some external antecedent. This covert world comprises a complex of integrated processes producing and maintaining a rich and dynamic universe of subjective meanings. We will now direct our attention to this composite of covert a-b-c's that comprise the content of our thinking. But first a review of the covert component of our model.

**Figure 11** *Covert Behavior*

| **Cognitive (Thinking)** |
| --- |

Subjective environment. The process and content of our thinking.
Our interpretation of A-B-C as a-b-c.

Includes:
Attributions
Expectations
Self-concept
Self-esteem
Beliefs
Attitudes
Prejudices
Self-talk
Locus of control
Images
Fantasies
Intrinsic consequences

| **Emotions** |
| --- |

Subjective labels used to describe a specific state of being. Labels reflect the composite of our covert, respondent, and operant behavior within a specific context of antecedents and consequences.

The structures and processes of hemispheric specialization, developmental schema, and neurophysiology are essentially the same in all of us. The product of these processes—the aggregate of a-b-c's within our covert experience—is a unique creation in each of us. It defines who we are and how we experience the world. This product of our thinking has many sources, but we can classify them as coming from our external and internal environments. Just as we constantly discriminate antecedent stimuli from our external environment, we simultaneously process sensorimotor impulses throughout our body while retrieving relevant information from stored memory throughout our cerebral cortex. This continuous flow of information, or feedback, enables us to maintain a conscious awareness of our internal needs, environmental demands and opportunities, and the action plans that satisfy both. Let us see how these critical feedback mechanisms work.

## Our Cybernetic Feedback Loop

The hallmark of a healthy, fully functioning covert component is a brain that integrates all relevant external and internal sensory information into a coherent conscious experience that can be used to explain, predict, and regulate past, present, and future action (Behrends, 1986). Before we look at this, we need to understand the covert "transportation" system that delivers this external and internal sensory data to our covert processing center. This system expedites the feedback mechanism responsible for getting a-b-c's into our covert initially and then maintains the constant flow of information throughout all of our A-B-C components.

The sensory information flowing into and out of our covert processing centers, and especially our frontal cortex mechanisms for focused awareness, maintains direct lines of communication to every component of our A-B-C model. Antecedent stimuli are selectively perceived and integrated with our relevant internal memory data to give meaning and purpose to ongoing experience. The covert a-b-c's resulting from this cognitive processing provide the rationale and guidance for operant behavior. And the performance of this operant behavior impacts the external environment, creating a range of external consequences which establish new antecedent conditions, which in turn stimulate a new stream of empirical data for covert receptors to process, and so on (or until any one of the A-B-C components malfunctions). When each part of our A-B-C model serves as a receptor, processor, and activator of this dynamic flow of sensorimotor information, we can refer to the entire model as a system.

## Our A-B-C's As a Covert System

The A-B-C model meets the criteria of a living system by taking in energy and information (input) and then using its subsystems (all of the processes subsumed under covert and overt behavior) to process them for the purpose of attaining certain consequences (or outputs/outcomes in the lexicon of systems theory). This conceptualization of the A-B-C model as a living system has may benefits but is especially helpful in understanding the ways that we constantly use information from our external (A's and C's) and internal (covert and overt behavior) environments to give meaning and purpose to our experience. Our selective as well as nonconscious and automatic processing of sensory information maintains the data base that feeds our covert experience. To remain functional and effective in our external world, this covert reality needs a constant and accurate flow of information revealing what is happening now.

The subjective reality of our covert experience thrives on a constant diet of information about what is happening, both externally and internally. Were disease or trauma to interrupt this flow, our covert world would suffer such distortion and disorientation as to immobilize us. Just as a living cell, or any dynamic system for that matter, dies from insufficient input or nourishment, our covert world must be receiving its continuous, open, and accurate flow of information to thrive and avoid dysfunction.

Fortunately, the fertile gardens of our antecedents, behaviors, and consequences provide the nutrition and, at times, scrumptious menu that is promptly and accurately served at our covert table by the friendly staff of our sensory nervous system. To extend this gastronomical metaphor a bit further, in most cases, the informational food—or feedback—that is brought to our table is prompt, palatable, and nutritious. It provides all of the essential ingredients that we need for immediate meaning and purposeful action as well as the covert/overt behavioral growth that we hope to realize as fully functioning, thriving adults. Speaking of food, the cartoon illustrates the integrative, systemic nature of our A-B-C model.

Our covert experience maintains an interaction effect with our respondent and operant behavior. (Reprinted with permission of King Features Syndicate.)

## Cybernetic Regulation of Our A-B-C System

A handy way to conceptualize this "informational food," or feedback, coursing through the streams of our A-B-C system is as a cybernetic feedback loop (Churchland, 1986; Maltz, 1960; Weiner, 1948). Originating from Greek, cybernetic means "the steersman." Just as a steersman regulates direction and action through prompt and accurate feedback, our central nervous system uses feedback to regulate action and give it meaning.

Although the science of cybernetics generally focuses on mechanical control and guidance mechanisms, such as guided missiles, robotics, climate-control systems, and especially computers, Maxwell Maltz was the first to apply cybernetic principles to human action, labeling his new concept *psychocybernetics*. According to Maltz, our brain and central nervous system serve a self-regulating function through feedback from the environment to reach a known target, achieve a desired goal, or answer a question. Our covert self-regulating system is activated when a need, target, goal, or question has been consciously identified through left-front cortex activity. We retrieve action patterns from our cortical memory stores that have been successful for us in the past or we synthesize sensory and memory information in ways that will create new and, ideally, successful actions patterns.

If this process reminds you of Piaget's principle of accommodation of new schemata, your covert is moving right along with mine. Maltz further posits that much of the time, our cortical servomechanisms operate automatically (i.e., below our threshold of consciousness) by using feedback data to regulate our respondent behavior as well as all of the "habitual" operant behaviors that we have learned to do without thinking. To quote Maltz (1960):

> Once, however, a correct or "successful response" has been accomplished—it is "remembered" for future use. The automatic mechanism then duplicates this successful response on future trials. It has "learned" how to respond successfully. It "remembers" its successes, forgets its failures, and repeats the successful action without any further conscious "thought"—or as a habit. (p. 21)

Before discussing the ways that cybernetics, systems, and the A-B-C model might converge into a congruent process of learning, I will try to illustrate their interrelationship graphically.

Figure 12 presents the A-B-C model as an open, dynamic system. Our covert processing mechanisms receive input as informational feedback from every other component of the system. Perception occurs when sensorimotor impulses reach the threshold of awareness within the sensory receptors of the brain. Our perception or awareness determines whether to continue to use this new information of integration, reflection, and subsequent expression, because at this stage of cognitive processing, we try to create meaning and purpose from this sensorimotor input. True consciousness occurs as we integrate this new information with existing meanings (i.e., schemata) stored in memory. We reflect on the emerging meaning of this current covert experience as we retrieve and integrate relevant memory fragments. Our unique attributions and expectations provide structure for the emerging understanding that results from our conscious reflection. The comprehension derived from our conscious reflection is often

**Figure 12** *Information Feedback Within the A-B-C Model*

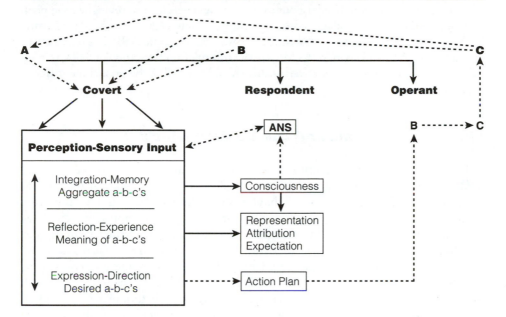

accompanied by a sense of purpose. This experience of purpose occurs whenever our new covert meaning reveals the need to express that meaning in some overt (operant) fashion. For example, reflection on a covert experience might indicate that the a-b-c's of my current experience are undesired. Consequently, continued conscious thought creates an action plan to bring about my desired a-b-c's, which provides expression of my covert reality and direction for my operant behavior.

## Change and Our Dynamic A-B-C System

The expression of our covert reality and the execution of our action plans probably involve the omission or commission of some operant behavior. At this juncture in our dynamic system, we choose to act on our external world to achieve our goal and experience our desired a-b-c's. Any operant behavior that we choose to omit or commit inevitably produces some consequence.

While our specific operant behavior is purposeful and goal directed, its most fundamental effect is change. Whether or not the resulting consequence matches our expected and desired goal, it changes our external environment, which also manifests a different configuration of antecedent conditions.

If the new information discriminated from this antecedent environment as well as from changes occurring within our internal environment reveal that our goal has been achieved (i.e., the a-b-c's are to our liking), we can shift our consciousness to other antecedents and covert realities. If, however, the new information reveals a continued or unacceptable gap between our experienced and desired a-b-c's, we re-form our integration, intensify our reflection, adjust our expression, and execute our revised action plan. This adjusted behavior produces consequences that again create change necessitating further discrimination and adjustment. In this way, our dynamic A-B-C system continues to build, grow, and change. As long as the information flow and feedback remain open and free of distortion, our covert reality should have all of the nourishment that it needs to thrive.

## The Power of Goals and Our Desired a-b-c's

A key influence on the direction of this dynamic change is our conscious explication of our desired covert a-b-c's and the corresponding operant behavior that produces them. Since our operant behavior is goal directed (i.e., designed to bring about certain desired consequences), our covert action plans comprise our cognitive strategies for achieving these consequences. As needs and desires arise within us, they manifest themselves in our covert experience as consequences that we wish to achieve.

For example, a dry, parched mouth might stimulate my conscious awareness of my need for a cold drink of water. Consuming that water becomes the consequence I wish to achieve. To achieve our desired consequences, we covertly formulate action plans that have worked in the past and have a good chance of working again. These covert strategies include the a-b-c action plans necessary for success. In this way, our desired consequence (or c in our covert a-b-c action plan) serves as the goal or objective, while the a-b portion serves as our strategy for getting there.

Returning to my example, once conscious of my desire for a drink of water, I instantaneously create the covert action plan (scenario) that will get it: In the context (antecedents) of kitchen, cupboard, sink, and refrigerator, I must perform a series of operant behaviors which result in water consumption (or cold beer, if that's what appears in my covert action plan). As a visual covert processor, I can see myself executing each step of my action plan, even to the point of imagining (covertly creating) the pleasurable sensation of consuming the nectar. This covert experience of the desired consequence enhances my motivation to perform my covert action plan.

The motivational power of perceived (covert) goals and objectives (i.e., desired consequences) for purposeful behavior change has been both scientifically (Kazdin, 1984) and clinically (DeShazer, 1984) demonstrated. This literature has consistently supported the powerful connection of desired consequences to covert action plans and subsequent operant behavior. Some of the most prominent counseling approaches, such as brief and solution-oriented counseling (Walter & Peller, 1992), capitalize on this dynamic.

## Feedback and Control

The importance of prompt, accurate, and relevant feedback to the effective function of our A-B-C system cannot be underestimated. We cannot delineate all of the rich and varied sources from which we derive feedback data. The "relatively" simple act of catching a fly ball requires precise, immediate, and acutely accurate feed-back from a multitude of sources over a minuscule period of time. Maxwell Maltz (1960) must have had Willie Mays in mind when he wrote:

> In order to compute where the ball will fall, or where the "point of interception" will be, he must take into account the speed of the ball, its curvature of fall, its direction, windage, initial velocity, and the rate of progressive decrease in velocity. He must make these computations so fast that he will be able to "take off" at the crack of the bat. Next, he must compute just how fast he must run, and in what direction in order to arrive at the point of interception at the same time the ball does. The center fielder doesn't even think about this. His built-in goal-striving mechanism computes it for him from data which he feeds through his eyes and ears. The computer in his brain takes this information, compares it with stored data (memories of other successes and failures in catching fly balls). All necessary computations are made in a flash and orders are issued to his leg muscles—and he "just runs." (p. 23)

What are the primary sources of feedback that our center fielder required to catch the ball? Here are some:

1. Antecedents =
   Crack of bat
   Position of other fielders
   Arc, direction, initial and decreasing velocity of ball
   Spin of ball
   Wind speed and direction
   Expected point ball will land
   Condition of field

2. Physiological =
   Location of glove on hand
   Body position relative to point
   of interception (sensorimotor)
   Running speed (proprioceptive)

3. Behavioral =
   (Operant)
   Action pattern in catching ball (Willie always used "basket catch")

4. Consequence =
   (Motivational)
   Reaction of fans
   Whether contract expires at end of season
   Importance of game
   Score of game

5. Antecedents with = Runner on base
   direct implications   Speed of batter
   for consequences

Whether catching a ball, solving an algebraic equation, frying an egg, engaging a friend in casual conversation, or any of a universe of purposeful actions, feedback rep-resents the flow of information that tells us how we are doing and what to do next. If it is accurate and timely, we proceed with confidence and probable success. When feedback within any part of our A-B-C system is distorted or obsolete, we feel out of sort and experience frustration in achieving our goals. Throughout this chapter, I will talk about ways that our informational feedback can be blocked, distorted, and impair our functioning. In Chapter 10 I will talk about ways to open it for the optimal performance of our A-B-C system.

### A Circle Instead of a Line

Before leaving our discussion of the cybernetic nature of our A-B-C system, a word of integration is in order. This integration of A-B-C elements does suggest a causal relationship, but not a linear one. The dynamic interaction of antecedents, covert experience, physiology, overt behavior, and consequences operates on the principle of "circular causality" (Nicoll, 1992). As a system, our dynamic A-B-C's manifest the interaction effect of all components of the model influencing all other components. A change in any one component of our A-B-C's effects changes in one or more of the others.

A particular thought can trigger an emotional response, provoke a respondent reaction, and signal the need for a desired overt behavior. Once performed, this overt behavior produces desired or undesired consequences which represent changes in the external environment. These environmental changes, in turn, provide new, if only subtly so, antecedent conditions for us to discriminate and think about. And the cycle continues.

Being an open system, change can begin at any point in this complex cycle of actions and reactions. A self-initiated thought, a biochemical change (as simple as low blood sugar when hungry or as complex as endocrine system failure), an unplanned overt behavior, or some unexpected change in our environment can each influence the cycle, initiating a change in the course of our A-B-C's. The dynamic, fluid, and complex nature of our A-B-C system offers a multitude of ways to change any part of our A-B-C experience.

Now that we have looked at some of the ways our external environment feeds data into our covert processing centers, let us turn to the part the memory plays in creating and maintaining our covert a-b-c's.

## Memory: Our Storage and Retrieval of Covert a-b-c's

**W**hether we have consummated a volitional act with conscious purpose and execution or an automatic nonconscious habit, the action patterns of learned a-b-c's are probably stored throughout our cerebral cortex and limbic system as bits of electrochemical memory traces. Although specific regions of the brain activate specialized cognitive processes (i.e., the perception of discrete sensorimotor impulses), conscious covert experiences involving the integration of new and stored information require vast, complex, and simultaneously activated circuitry. The research consensus is clear that many regions and structures in the brain are critical to learning and memory. Studies of brain function during specific memory recall indicate that the act of storing and retrieving a memory is a dynamic process involving simultaneous electrochemical interactions throughout the cerebral cortex. A memory of a specific incident, a frightening encounter, or even a friend's facial characteristics are not stored in a single location as an intact, discrete memory, but rather are stored as fragments throughout various parts of the brain.

The various sensations of smell, color, sound, taste, and so on associated with any experience each have their own storage areas. Each time we retrieve a memory, we attempt to re-create the exact state of neural circuitry that occurred at the time of the original experience. Our attempt at exact replication is, however, thwarted by purposeful and electrochemical distortion. Even in our most conscientious recollection of a memory, we create that memory anew, as we integrate multiple memory fragments into different configurations (LeDoux, 1994).

Is it any wonder that our memories seem to play tricks on us? Even if our original covert processing of an a-b-c experience corresponded almost exactly with its external A-B-C reality, our storage and retrieval of that memory alter its "reality" with each telling. As memory fragments get lost and fragments from different memories wander in, the validity of our memory a-b-c's gradually diminishes. Our capacity to enhance pleasant memories while distorting or denying painful experiences only furthers this process of memory decay and alteration. I recall very little about the oral defense of my doctoral dissertation, but I recall vivid details about my wedding day, and those details get better every year.

### The Complex Process of Remembering

The process of memory requires the reception of sensory information, processing and storing this information, and then retrieving it for subsequent expression. From a temporal perspective, this memory process involves distinct mechanisms for immediate, short-term, and long-term information retention. Immediate memory occurs for only a few seconds when you receive sensory information and immediately dismiss it from conscious awareness. The sensory impulse is either received nonconsciously or processed consciously (what we call perception), but is immediately dismissed and lost. We constantly experience this immediate memory—and loss—when inconsequential and fleeting antecedents drift through our consciousness. The number of my daughter's school bus, a trash bag along the highway, and even the oil gauge light in my car are all antecedents entering my covert world and then immediately dismissed.

Short-term memory traces are stored within a region of the limbic system (hippocampus and amygdala) referred to as a "sensory register." There they are either transferred to the cerebral cortex of conscious processing or the memory traces immediately decay. Sensory data that create some level of arousal are transferred to the cortex as short-term memory.

In studying the crucial role of the amygdala–hippocampus interaction in short-term and emotional memory, LeDoux (1994) found that the amygdala can stop sensory input from ever reaching our prefrontal cortex for conscious processing. In this way, the amygdala can hold certain sensory input "judged" to be emotionally arousing and store those electrochemical impulses in the hippocampus for short-term memory. LeDoux further posits that the amygdala is instrumental in the storage and retrieval of emotional memories and covert experiences, selectively judging the quality of our covert experience and activating every part of our central nervous system to respond to emotional alarms. This central role of the amygdala in receiving, storing, and retrieving sensory information deemed emotional is a central element of Daniel Goleman's (1995) model of emotional intelligence.

## Every Little Bit Helps

Whether visual, auditory, or tactile, the electrochemical impulses of short-term memory are probably held for processing throughout the parietal, temporal, and occipital cortex (Warrington & Wesikrantz, 1973). The smallest discrete electrochemical impulse that can be stored in memory is called a *bit*. Consequently, each bit of sensory data represents a particular aspect of information about an antecedent. A numerical digit, letter, word, name, and specific fact represent bits of information. Research on memory retention has demonstrated that we are usually able to retain about seven bits of information within our short-term memory at any one time before we begin to forget (Miller, 1956). I am not sure if it was coincidence or brilliant insight that prompted our telephone industry to employ seven-digit phone numbers. Please don't ask me to retain area codes as well. As a memory strategy, we often "chunk" bits of data together so that each bit comprises more associated parts. A word can be a bit, but so can an entire phrase such as "Now is the time"—"for all good men"—"to come to the aid"—"of their country." My social security number was always a stretch to remember until I chunked the nine digits into three bits.

Short-term memory is also known as "working memory" because it is information that we retain and use. We can use this working memory because our frontal cortex processing brings it to consciousness (Selemon et al., 1995). This retrieval process occurs much like the random access memory that we download from our computer hard drive for immediate use. It is also during this short-term memory phase that other existing information stored in long-term memory is retrieved and added to the covert processing mix. Through repetition, practice, or any of a multitude of memory technique, data in short-term memory are consolidated (probably from hypothalamic activation) into long-term memory. This consolidation involves the transformation of sensory impulses into permanent biochemical or neural structures deep within the cerebral cortex.

Although this consolidated long-term memory remains permanently stored, it is subject to reorganization and transformation as it is retrieved, used, and restored over time. Even the aggregate a-b-c's that are stored in our long-term memory are constantly being retrieved (called up to consciousness), integrated with other a-b-c's and new sensory data, and then relegated to our long-term memory store. Each time we use a-b-c's in this way, we probably transform the information they contain. As Milton Erickson (see Erickson, 1954, and Haley, 1986) discovered through his clinical experience, even our memories are subject to continual empirical influences.

## Remembering Facts and Procedures

Not only do we store a-b-c's for different durations—immediate, short-, and long-term—but we also process and store at least two kinds of a-b-c information. Procedural a-b-c's describe how to do something, while declarative a-b-c's represent factual information about people, places, objects, and events.

Squire (1987) describes declarative knowledge as information that provides a specific, accessible record of an individual's previous experience, and a sense of familiarity about those experiences. This form of factual information is processed through the thalamus, then through the temporal cortex, and probably stored throughout the lobes of the cerebral cortex, depending on its visual or auditory composition.

Procedural knowledge represents what Piaget referred to as "action patterns" that define covert experience by the a-b-c's that exist when an action is performed on the environment to achieve a purposeful consequence. You may recall that Piaget earmarked the sensorimotor period as the time when an infant's knowledge of the world, its many people, and object antecedents is limited to what the child can do to it. External antecedents have no existence apart from the sensorimotor actions that the infant performs on them. Prior to the development of language and representational covert experience at 18–24 months of age, the actual physical attributes of the external world are merely "empirical abstractions" with no quality or definition apart from the child's sensorimotor experience of them.

With language, children can covertly reflect on their experiences and begin to construct covert a-b-c action patterns that define the object (i.e., reflective abstraction) and build schemata around the object's use. One year olds have no covert a-b-c for banging a block against the side of the crib. They just bang it capriciously and reflexively. By their second birthday, they have learned that the hard, square object is called a "block" and, when banged against the crib, makes a great sound and often brings mom. They have learned a very helpful a-b-c action pattern. Stored reflective abstractions exist as declarative knowledge, while schemata serve as procedural knowledge in long-term memory.

Lynn Selemon and her colleagues (1995) have found that strong emotions can wreak havoc with our ability to keep covert information within conscious awareness (i.e., working memory), even if the information is critical to successful functioning. Emotional arousal such as fear, anger, and even joyful excitement can directly interfere with the accuracy and retention of our short-term memory. The debilitating effect of speech anxiety, our inability to clearly articulate a cogent argument in the throes of conflict, or even our difficulty remembering the names of newly introduced strangers at a party are illustrations of emotional intrusions to our covert task-oriented experience. As Goleman (1995) so eloquently puts it, "When the limbic circuitry that converges on the prefrontal cortex is in the thrall of emotional distress, one cost is in the effectiveness of working memory: we can't think straight . . ." (p. 79).

On the positive side, emotional arousal has been shown to enhance learning and the storage of experience into long-term memory. In studying the physiological effects of operant conditioning, James McGaugh (1983) found that the more valued or feared a consequence was perceived, the better the subject retained the experience for long-term memory. He speculated that the amygdala's effect on the increased secretion of the neurotransmitter norepinephrine (an exciter chemical) facilitated the consolidation of memory traces within the cerebral cortex. In other words, the more emotionally aroused the subjects became from their experience of (or even expectation for) a powerful C+ or C–, the more their biochemistry facilitated their memory and, by the same token, their learning. This line of research has profound implications for the place of physiological arousal and emotion in expedition learning and memory. It appears that physiological arousal influences the acquisition and retention of a-b-c's as significantly as covert a-b-c's can stimulate our autonomous nervous system (i.e., respondent behavior).

Covert a-b-c's provide the data from which we understand and explain past and present A-B-C experiences. From our aggregate a-b-c's, we draw conclusions and explanations for the past and present actions of others as well as ourselves. Our aggregate a-b-c's provide our attributions for causality and the A-B-C contingencies that seem to operate in our world. We will shortly turn our attention to this attributional process. But first, I must confess a final qualification concerning the content of long-term memory.

### Transcending Our Covert Experience

I have previously suggested that our aggregate a-b-c's are stored in long-term memory and accessible for downloading into consciousness as needed. Whether or not other forces within our internal or external world are influencing our covert experience—even affecting our most fundamental spiritual awareness—I will respectfully leave to your conjecture and belief. Philosophers and great thinkers throughout history have extolled universal truths, meanings, and information—a collective mind, if you will—that transcend our memories of past experiences and learned facts. Scholars and philosophers have attempted to explain the anomalies of human achievement by the existence of transcendent powers ranging from telepathy and clairvoyance, to archetypes and collective unconsciousness, and ultimately to inexplicable acts of healing and creativity.

The belief (or attribution) in transcendent, supranatural knowledge, or power as the source of genius and creative talent was held by no less than Thomas Edison, Mozart, Emerson, and Socrates. Even the eminent scientist Charles Darwin believed that his theory of natural selection came to him as a sudden, extraordinary insight while reading Malthus's theory of human population (Piirto, 1992). Parapsychologist J. B. Rhine (1964) contends that he has experimentally found an "extrasensory factor" in humans which he calls "psi." He believes that this psi knowledge transcends our sensory functions and exists qualitatively apart from our empirically learned knowledge of the world. Who knows?

While leaving this transcendent knowledge out of the A-B-C model, I enthusiastically retain the option of future inclusion upon more definitive validation. To remain truly integrative, inclusive, and practical, the A-B-C model must always be open to new feedback and the improved schemata that accommodation produces.

## Attributions: Our Explanations for Past and Present a-b-c's

Perhaps the most critical task of our covert a-b-c's is answering "Why?" Why did I fail that science test? Why didn't my car start this morning? Why did I argue with Sally yesterday? Why is it so hard to speak in public? All of these questions relate to experiences in the past, and they call for answers that explain particular contingency experiences. When I wonder why I failed that test, I am looking for a causal explanation that tells me:

under _____ testing situation (the antecedent)

I did _____ (operant behavior)

and _____ happened (consequence indicating failure)

Because:   The room was too hot.

The test covered the wrong material.

The teacher didn't like me very much.

I really didn't take the time to study.

I was just stupid in science.

My because answers to the why question represent the influences (or causes) that I attribute to my failing performance. Any causal explanation that I covertly hold for any past or present experience functions as an attribute for that experience, and the covert explanations that we formulate and maintain serve as our attributions. I embrace the attributions as reasons for why things happen as they do that shape the substance of my covert a-b-c's. Any particular attribute that I might believe, such as attributing my science test failure to the oppressive heat in the room, represents my reality, whether or not my attribute is empirically valid (i.e., can prove causality).

In addition to explaining the why for past experiences, attributes also serve as our reasons for current experiences. Why am I angry? Why doesn't this damn microwave oven work? Why doesn't he call? Why am I failing science now? All of these questions pertain to immediate experiences (i.e., a-b-c contingencies) that beg explanation. They each provide A-B-C experiences from which we covertly draw conclusions about cause and effect. Each explanatory conclusion serves as an attribute for what is happening now. If you repeat each aforementioned question and follow it with the word "because," you will provide all of the stimuli you need to create each causal attribution.

Why am I angry? Because when A, your (or it or they) C, and it made me B. Why am I failing science? Because *When we have a test (A), the room gets so hot (another A) that I get sleepy and can't concentrate (B), and I get F's on the tests* (C, probably a C–/C̶+̶).

These attributions that explain causality give meaning and understanding to experience, even if they may be total fabrications within our covert world. As I mentioned earlier with respect to defense mechanisms, our mind strives for acceptable meaning and purpose to our experience of the world. It also structures or frames covert a-b-c contingencies in ways that minimize our pain and discomfort and maximize our pleasure and self-acceptance. Although we learn our covert a-b-c's through direct and vicarious experiences, we ultimately construct our a-b-c attributions both to understand our experience and protect the integrity of our selves. We need to effectively identify and adopt the A-B-C contingencies existing in our external environment while simultaneously formulating and adopting covert a-b-c attributions that protect and reinforce our covert perception of how we want to experience ourselves. Consequently, our attributions for past and present experiences reflect our covert understanding of how the world works as well as revealing the distortions and deceptions that we employ in the service of maintaining our personal integrity and a measure of stability and cohesion in our daily experience.

### The Subjectivity of Attributions

Bernard Weiner (1986) was the first to systematically study the way we formulate and maintain attributions. His attribution theory was anchored to the fundamental proposition that how we think about and attribute causes to our successes and failures has a much greater impact on our motivation and emotions than the actual A-B-C contingencies. As a strict proponent of covert mediation of operant behavior, Weiner's research on behavioral motivation concluded that even rigorously enforced external schedules of reinforcement were superseded by individuals' covert explanations for why they received reinforcement in the manner they did.

Children who receive intermittent C+'s for producing quality work and view the B–C+ contingency as a function of effort will be inclined to work hard. Children who experience the same schedule of reinforcement but attribute their C+'s to good luck or even an easy teacher will be less motivated to put forth any strong effort. These subjective covert causal attributions will influence motivation to work depending on the degree to which children attribute C+'s to their effort (an internal construct) or to factors outside their control. The inclusion of internal–external control factors is where Weiner's attribution theory converges with Julian Rotter's social learning theory (1966).

### Attributions and Locus of Control

As with Bernard Weiner, Julian Rotter believed that covert explanations of causality (i.e., attributions) determined an individual's motivation to behave regardless of the actual A-B-C contingency existing at the time. If I maintain covert attributions that consequences (C+, ⊗–, C–, ⊗+) occur independently of my behavior, or in other words, that the C is not contingent on my B, I will be disinclined to do the B to achieve the C. Similar attributions such as luck, fate, chance, and the arbitrary actions of others reflect A-B-C contingencies beyond individual control. Rotter refers to these attributions as demonstrating an external locus of control (LOC). B–C contingencies that we perceive as within our control indicate an internal locus of control and include such causal attributions as effort, ability, talent, and resourcefulness.

Although these attributions are internalized, they differ in the degree of control (or choice potential) that we have over them and the stability with which they exist over time. Attributions such as effort and resourcefulness, with which we possess the greatest degree of direct control and judge to have the longest temporal stability, have the strongest motivational influence over our behavioral choices. Along with my belief that hard work or effort cause consequences that I desire, I must also believe that I possess this internalized attribution to the extent that I can exercise the choice of performing the behavior. This element of choice requires the behavior to exist in my repertoire whenever I choose its execution (i.e., its availability is stable over time). A behavior that I have little confidence in performing with any frequency—such as that base hit while maintaining a .002 batting average—has no stability and marginal choice potential.

My strongest attributions expressing my belief that I am responsible for my past and present behavior (and thereby my a-b-c experience) occur when my attribution reflects an internal locus of control, when that locus of control is a behavior that I can choose to perform, and when I have performed that behavior enough to ensure its stability. Conversely, those past and present experiences in which I felt the least responsible or exhibited little or no control are most likely attributed to factors having an external locus of control.

### Attributions and Our Sense of Control

While we can ascribe specific attributions to very specific A-B-C contingency experiences, such as why I broke my leg, got a speeding ticket, or received that job promotion, we can also develop a pattern or style of attribution that generalizes to an inordinately and invalidly large proportion of daily experiences. Rotter (1975) found that individuals can develop generalized beliefs that characterize most or even all experience as either out of their control or under their control. As you might imagine, these extreme attributions of control distort our covert world in most destructive ways. An extreme internal locus of control (ILOC) style causes us to assume responsibility for all past and present experiences. The more negative experiences create the more insidious forms of self-blame: guilt and shame (which I will discuss later in this chapter). Extreme and invalid ILOC's can also contribute to an overwhelming sense of control and responsibility to make things happen. Although energizing and empowering in less extreme forms, an unchecked ILOC style of attribution is a primary ingredient in anxiety and stress-related disorders.

In contrast to the self-blame and responsibility deriving from an excessive ILOC style, extreme external locus of control (ELOC) attributions render a person powerless. The belief that all of my past and present life experiences have been controlled by others and that I can attribute nothing—good, bad, success, failure, pain, delight—to my own powers of choice and action leaves me immobilized and helpless. Noted psychologist Martin Seligman (1993) has considered this extreme ELOC explanatory style as the basis for the debilitating dysfunction of "learned helplessness." These habits or styles of ELOC attribution become so pervasive as to consume our covert worldview, a covert world comprising the key manifestation of depression. Not surprisingly, this pervasive sense of powerlessness and helplessness mitigates both our pride and self-efficacy for past achievement and our motivation for future behavior. We direct our attributes and attention to the future next.

## Expectations: Predictions for Future A-B-C's

It has often been said that the best predictor of future performance is past behavior. The explanation for this prophecy of prognostication can best be found within the very fabric of our covert attributions. While our contingency attributions are answering the why questions for our past and present experience, they are building the data pool of covert a-b-c's from which we make predictions of future a-b-c's. Based on these predictions of a-b-c contingencies, we formulate (covertly) and execute (operant behaviorally) successful action plans from our past. Whether we call it learning from experience, staying with the known, or just reality based decision making, our use of a-b-c attributions in predicting future a-b-c experiences is the only game in town. Our confidence, security, sense of control, and ultimately our prospects for success in the

Expectations for C+'s bring much joy and excitement to our life. (© Tribune Media Services, Inc. All Rights Reserved. Reprinted with Permission.)

future reside in our knowledge of what to expect, which is what we have already directly or vicariously experienced.

### Motivational Aspects of Covert Expectations

Let us take one example of the power of covert expectation. If I have performed well on tests, and even more specifically science tests because I possess good intelligence and science ability (highly stable, ILOC attributions), I expect to do well on future science tests even with minimal studying. My confidence in these stable, internal attributions enables me to approach the next science test in a relaxed, optimistic manner, an approach that will improve my performance, if not my "effort" motivation.

From a scenario in which my past success in science tests is attributed to diligent study, my future science test taking will be motivated by my expectation for a diligent study–good grade contingency. In this scenario, my unstable yet internal attribution of study, over which I have considerable choice and control, provided the direction and incentive to "do it again." Not being able to rely solely on ability and intellect, my motivation to study was generated by three crucial factors: a highly valued C+ of a good grade was readily probable if I diligently expended the effort through a behavior that was under my control to perform. These three ingredients of C value, self-control in performing the B, and the B-C contingency probability are the essential elements of motivation. They define the degree to which we can take responsibility for our past as attributions, and they determine our measure of motivation to perform in the future.

Covert expectations hold the strongest influence over our actions when:

**1.** The expected C+ has high value.

**2.** The locus of control is internal for the B.

**3.** The B-C contingency has a high probability of occurring.

Perhaps you can begin to see how the dynamics of our attributions leading to our expectations establish and maintain stable and consistent thoughts and actions. This covert–overt behavioral bond is cemented even more by a phenomenon that Rosenthal and Jacobson (1968) called the "self-fulfilling prophecy." In their original Pygmalion study of teachers' expectations for students' performance, teachers taught students as they expected those students to learn. And sure enough, students performed just as teachers expected (and congruently with the way they were taught).

Subsequent studies (Dusek, 1985) demonstrated that once attributional beliefs are established (e.g., "I can't teach these students because they are severely learning disabled."), individuals behave as if the attributions were true. These validated attributions easily become the bases for their future expectations. Their behavior, in turn, is conducted congruently with their expectations and ultimately causes those same expected consequences. Thus, our prophecy of success or failure is fulfilled.

So we now have a perpetuating sequence of:

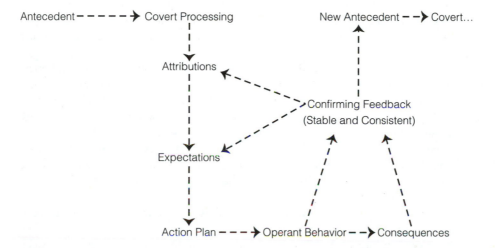

All of the elements represented in this sequence are integral to our A-B-C model and help explain why our A-B-C experience of the world is so consistent and impervious to change. Perhaps a typical anecdote might "painfully" illustrate this point.

## From Attributions to Expectations: A Painful Example

**A**s I recline on the couch immersed in the latest Anne Tyler novel, my spouse enthusiastically rushes up brandishing the local community college's latest catalog of continuing education courses. How wonderful! There is a beginners course of six 2-hour tennis lessons offered by the resident instructor, a warm and nurturing sort. "Just what I need to get you started," my spouse cooed. Being a naturally gifted athlete and inveterate tennis player, she has always cajoled and plotted to have me share her interests and develop my latent tennis skills, but to no avail. I have always been a klutz and will remain so. This sad admission was brought painfully to my and everyone else's awareness when I totally failed to hit a ball over the net in 11th grade physical education class. Since that humiliating spectacle, I have joined the "tennis challenged" and have succeeded in avoiding any activity involving a racket, net, and fuzzy-haired ball.

Against the bolstering proclamations of "aid and comfort" promised by my spouse if I'd "just give it a try," my immediate thought is an instant flashback to Mr. Frogell's physical education class. This vividly re-created horror show is again—for the millionth time—explained by my abject poverty of talent and interest in tennis. My past failure is explicably obvious. I have absolutely no ability, and what's more, I never will. Any future attempts will only validate this glaring deficiency. No! No! No!

Unfortunately, my spouse has already paid for the course and has given it to me (or was it to us, my rising anxiety was restricting my hearing) as an anniversary gift. We start next Thursday evening, and they will even loan me a racket. My covert action plans regarding this matter have always consisted of avoiding the inevitable. When an assertive "No way!" was inadequate in putting such a nonsensical proposal to rest, I found work, automotive failure and even a questionable arthritic condition to serve my avoidance needs. As my previously successful action plans fell on deaf ears, I approached Thursday evening with the vague and untested action plan that perhaps I could accidentally break my glasses or suffer some exotic injury so prone to us former athletes entering our senior years.

As might be expected, Thursday evening did arrive and Bud, our agile and energetic instructor, was just as patient and nurturing as my spouse had predicted. And I was just as klutzy as I had predicted. The racket felt alien to my palm, as were the balls alienated from that sweet spot hiding in my racket. Balls ricocheting from my racket's sour spots found the bleachers behind the court, the doorway of the physical education office, or usually the soft embrace of the net. Once, however, I managed to return a soft lob (by this point, both spouse and instructor were actually lobbing balls for me to slug) over the net in fair territory only to hear the patronizing cries of "Great return! See, you can do it."

Little did they know that there were to be no C+'s for me that night. The only consequence that held meaning and purpose was my instructor's suggestion (more like urging or even imploring) that I might consider the hiking class beginning next week as a more suitable form of exercise. He also understood that the beginners bridge class still had a few openings. And he would be glad to transfer my fees to either class or even give me a full refund if I just chose to withdraw gracefully. After a reconciling sigh from my spouse that I had given it a try, I quickly accepted his generous offer and compassionate coup de grâce.

I left the class fully confident that never again would I have to escape such humiliation; I was determined that my avoidance behaviors would work the next time the opportunity to play tennis occurred. As with so many experiences, this tennis lesson only taught me what I already knew. It validated my attributions, confirmed my expectations, reinforced an adaptive coping mechanism (covert action plan), solidified certain antecedent realities, and perpetuated a pattern of A-B-C's that I have come to accept as my own. In part, these A-B-C's and their corroborating covert a-b-c's define who I am—to myself if not to others. They describe the ways I think and act under various environmental (antecedent and consequent) conditions.

The A-B-C's illustrated in my tennis lesson represent just a small part of the vast store of covert a-b-c's that I can identify as depicting my experience. From this aggregate of covert a-b-c's, I understand, explain, and predict my experiences with the world, and from these covert experiences, I define my self. Let us explore that covert world that we have come to know as the self.

## Chapter Summary

**1.** The flow of information that maintains the dynamic interaction of our antecedents, behavior, and consequences can be conceptualized as a cybernetic loop.

**2.** Since our operant behavior is designed to maintain or attain desired consequences, our covert action plans comprise our cognitive strategies for achieving these desired states.

**3.** When we consciously think about a past, present, or future experience, we integrate current sensory data with relevant data retrieved from a vast, complex network of neurons extending throughout our cerebral cortex. This electrochemical circuitry comprises our long-term memory.

**4.** The integration of bits of associated information that have been programmed into our long-term memory through eventful or repetitive experience results in the meaningful a-b-c's of our covert world.

**5.** Our explanations for past or present experiences form our covert attributions.

**6.** I maintain an internal locus of control when I attribute the causes of actions to myself and an external locus of control when I explain causality as out of my control.

**7.** Our causal attributions for answering our past and present "why" questions provide the data pool of covert a-b-c's from which we make predictions of future a-b-c's. These predictions comprise our covert expectations.

**Figure 1** *The A-B-C (Cognitive–Behavioral) Model*

| (A) Antecedent | Covert | Overt | Overt | (C) Consequence |
|---|---|---|---|---|
| | Cognitive (Thinking) | (B) Behavior — Respondent (Physical) | Operant (Acting) | |
| Stimulus or setting event. External environments that set the occasion for behavior (thinking, acting, feeling) to occur. $S^{Dee}$ = Green light. A cue that a particular behavior will result in a desirable consequence. $S^{Delta}$ = Red light. A cue that a particular behavior will result in an undesirable consequence. | Subjective environment. The process and content of our thinking. Our interpretation of A-B-C as a-b-c. Includes: Attributions Expectations Self-concept Self-esteem Beliefs Attitudes Prejudices Self-talk Locus of control Images Fantasies Intrinsic consequences | Reflexive Autonomic Involuntary Biochemical Physiological changes occurring within our body. | Voluntary behavior that we choose to do or not to do. Can be: Excess = Behavior done too often or at wrong time. Deficit = Behavior done too infrequently or not when needed. | Events (external) that occur during and/or after a particular covert and/or operant behavior. Events can be: A. Desirable: 1. Positive Reinforcement present desirable = C+ 2. Negative Reinforcement remove undesirable = C– B. Undesirable: 1. Punishment present undesirable, aversive = C– 2. Extinction remove desirable = C+ |

**Emotions**

Subjective labels used to describe a specific state of being. Labels reflect the composite of our covert, respondent, and operant behavior within a specific context of antecedents and consequences.

# Chapter 10

## Personalizing Our A-B-C's: The a-b-c's of the Self

### Orienting Ourselves

We have studied the many elements and dynamics of the A-B-C model from a generic and objective perspective. Structures and processes of cortical function provide the framework within which we create our attributions, expectations, and covert action patterns. As we have investigated this interrelationship of structures, processes, and meanings, we have systematically traversed from the external to the internal, from the broad principle to the most private nuance of meaning, and from the A-B-C's of our environment to the a-b-c's of our covert world.

In this chapter, we again narrow our focus of study from the a-b-c's of our covert world to the a-b-c's of our self. After we explore the domain of the self, we quite naturally encounter, in Chapter 11, issues of personal value, judgment, and the spectrum of intrinsic consequences that reflect those judgments. Ultimately, our experience of self is infused with the experience of emotion, which will culminate our integration of the A-B-C model in Chapter 12. Let us review with the covert component of the model.

### The Concept of Self

The reality and meaning of the concept of self cannot be separated from time and place. From a constructionist and relativistic perspective, we might even conclude that what we are really like is a constant collision of innate human traits with cultural and historical norms. Throughout most of human history, the uniqueness of the individual, and thus any acknowledgment of a self, was not even a consideration. Until very recently, individuality and free will, with their invitation for autonomous action, were neither cultural norms nor did they exist as covert attributions and expectations. Premodern societies, and even some cultures today, have no language for or recognition of inner states, emotions, free will, and a self apart from the social milieu (Geertz, 1973; Gergen, 1991). It was not until the late eighteenth century that the individual self was recognized and studied by the new science of psychology.

**Figure 11** *Covert Behavior*

### Cognitive
### (Thinking)

Subjective environment. The process and content of our thinking.
Our interpretation of A-B-C as a-b-c.

Includes:
Attributions
Expectations
Self-concept
Self-esteem
Beliefs
Attitudes
Prejudices
Self-talk
Locus of control
Images
Fantasies
Intrinsic consequences

### Emotions

Subjective labels used to describe a specific state of being. Labels reflect the composite of our covert, respondent, and operant behavior within a specific context of antecedents and consequences.

To look at the origin of our concept of self, we need only return to that ubiquitous student of the human experience William James. His *Principles of Psychology* (1890) defined the self, or the "empirical me," as the total aggregate of all that we refer to as "us." From an A-B-C perspective, this aggregate us includes all of the ways that we experience and describe our behavior within every antecedent and consequence context. In its broadest terms, this self includes all of the following categories:

- My physical self—my body, health, strength, appearance, sexuality, and so on.
- My abilities self—my stable traits of intelligence, talents, skills, creativity, humor, and so on.
- My social self—my family, friends, enemies, and behaviors of interacting with others.
- My work self—my vocation, avocation, market value, education.
- My material self—my possessions, salary, home, car, net worth, and so on.
- My emotional self—my feelings that emerge in response to the different antecedents that I encounter.
- My spiritual self—my belief in God, metaphysical phenomena, meaning of life and death.
- My beliefs self—my attributions, expectations, and value judgments within each of these categories infused with my priorities of importance.

Another classification schema for the self is to differentiate the "self as object" from the "self as process." The self as object is essentially the self that we have been discussing (i.e., the person that I think of as "me"). The self as process represents the self as the combined processes in which we perceive, integrate, remember, reflect, plan, and construct our covert reality. In other words, our self as object represents the content of our covert a-b-c's, whereas our self as process reflects the way we process and use our covert a-b-c's. This latter self operates through the cognitive processes that we employ as we create and activate our covert action plans. Through these, we plot our interaction with the external environment to meet our needs (i.e., achieve intrinsic and extrinsic C+'s and C–'s) while activating cognitive strategies that protect and enhance our reality of self.

## The Stability of the Self

Each experience with the a-b-c contingencies stored in my covert memory is the fabric of my self-tapestry. Those b's are my behaviors just as those a's and c's are the antecedents and consequences of my past, present, and future. Drawing from the self categories listed previously, I might see my self as tall with brown hair, average in intelligence with a great sense of humor, well liked by family and friends, a hardworking teacher with a strong background in psychology, possessing a comfortable home and a beat-up old van on its last legs, a believer in a universal God who is manifest within each person, and a hot-tempered competitor who feels very sad and angry at the misfortunes of blameless victims.

The aggregate of these characterizations in conjunction with all of my other self-descriptions forms my total self-concept. But because my self-description varies significantly over place and time, this self-concept cannot retain absolute permanence, stability, or even consistency. While certain core values, such as my belief in God or abhorrence of child abuse, may only be slightly shaken even in the face of severe trauma, other images undergo greater change over time and context. My body image has and will continue to change with age, and my sense of self-efficacy will certainly vary over the many activities that I pursue.

To the degree that my external environment (antecedents and consequences) is stable, consistent, and unchanging, my covert experience of myself within it should be equally as permanent and stable. More precisely, when the antecedent conditions and consequences of my daily experience remain pretty much the same, all the characteristics that I equate with "me" conform to that consistent, reliable, known world.

Not surprisingly, studies of cultural self-concept have found that people raised in insular, static, and highly ritualized cultures—where the experience of daily life doesn't change and the only novelty is proscribed by the circadian rhythms of nature and the seasons—have measures of self-concept showing strong consistency over time, place, and antecedent experience (Taylor, 1989). Although devoid of rich diversity and challenge, this sameness provides a reassuring security that "this is who I am." Within the mundane existence of colonial village life, everyone knew their role, function, and place. Thus, the self that they knew was the self that they could reliably show the world. "In the realm of daily life one also believed in knowable selves.

Individuals possessed a basic personality or character, and in most normal relationships this essential self was made known" (Gergen, 1991, p. 83). Not so today.

## Our Many Selves

The stability, consistency, and sameness of cultural norms experienced by our ancestors no longer exist in late twentieth-century Western culture. Change, diversity, expansion, and movement have become pervasive realities in our lives. Sameness has been replaced by newness in our work, in the constantly improved products that we devour and discard, and even in our relationships. Kenneth Gergen (1991) refers to this pervasive and unremitting change as "social saturation," which occurs because:

> We are now bombarded with ever-increasing intensity by the images and actions of others; our range of social participation is expanding exponentially. As we absorb the views, values and visions of others, and live out the multiple plots in which we are enmeshed, we enter a postmodern consciousness. It is a world in which we no longer experience a secure sense of self, and in which doubt is increasingly placed on the very assumption of a bounded identity with palpable attributes. What are the consequences? How are we to respond to coming conditions? (pp. 15–16)

The self to which Gergen refers is a conglomerate of covert a-b-c's that must offer instantaneous recognition of and adjustment to an external environment of continuous change and ever-increasing complexity. The antecedents created by family and friends, the vicissitudes of work and career, decaying public institutions, 15-min celebrities and authority figures, social and political correctness, our pervasive media, and the technology fad or issue of the day are in constant flux and redefinition. Our most stable and reliable institution of family seems to reconfigure itself through marriage, work, and the multitude of seductions outside the home. Each change in the A-B-C's of our environment requires a corresponding adjustment in our covert a-b-c's both to understand what is happening around us and to construct an action plan that will meet the external environment's needs as well as our own. Just trying to discriminate all of these complex, disparate, and often contradictory antecedents is challenging enough, but our social environment expects instantaneous action with flawless results. While we are struggling with this 20-plate juggling act, we are expected to maintain the integrity of our self—be true to our selves and authentic with all others.

### A Chameleon on a Kaleidoscopic Rock

Is it any wonder that we feel fragmented and confused, experiencing and employing selves that seem designed only for the exigencies of immediate antecedents? To meet the challenges imposed by this social saturation, we strive to be all things to all antecedents. But to be all things to such diverse and contradictory antecedents requires us to perform a vast array of roles (operant behaviors), with each role prescribed by its own cadre of covert a-b-c's. We are warm, caring, and nurturing at home yet competitive and even aggressive at work. We display initiative and creativity with our department manager yet feign submissive deference to our immediate supervisor. We learn to be assertive and then patronizing on cue. We are expected to program a VCR, change a diaper, choose from 12,000 (at least) forms of entertainment, be conversant in all manner of esoteric topics, invest our income wisely, and even keep up our lawn. These challenges, often masked as opportunities, never end. Even our success leaves us feeling like a chameleon in a kaleidoscope of color.

This diversity of contrasting roles forces us to compartmentalize each role into a distinct and coherent covert and overt action pattern. While facilitating ease in stimulus discrimination and the retrieval/activation of appropriate action patterns, this compartmentalization fragments the self into disconnected and antecedent-specific (field-dependent) parts—what we might call "mini-selves." What results is a self for each occasion, with each self a genuine part of the total person that I call "me." If you ask me to reveal my self-concept, my only reply can be, "Which one?" For that composite, or holistic self, that is supposed to form the bedrock of my identity actually feels more like a sponge. Kenneth Gergen (1991) refers to this composite of differentiated a-b-c's as the "saturated self," the multiple selves that result when:

> Emerging technologies saturate us with the voices of humankind—both harmonious and alien. As we absorb their varied rhymes and reasons, they become part of us and we of them. Social saturation furnishes us with a multiplicity of incoherent and unrelated languages of the self. For everything we "know to be true" about ourselves, other voices within respond with doubt and even derision. This fragmentation of self-conceptions corresponds to a multiplicity of incoherent and disconnected relationships. These relationships pull us in myriad directions, inviting us to play such a variety of roles that the very concept of an "authentic self" with knowable characteristics recedes from view. The fully saturated self becomes no self at all. (pp. 6–7)

## The Diversity of Parts That Are Me

Unlike actors reciting scripts created by others and securing their "real" persons behind the masks of their proscribed roles, these covert selves are the substance of how we experience ourselves and engage the world. Each of the selves that comprises me is of my own creation and is as much a part of me as my eye color. I am not playing a role as much as I am discriminating the demands of my environment (antecedents) and mustering my covert and overt resources to meet the challenge. My thoughts and behavior are truly real and genuine—for the moment. I am what I need to be, and then I can choose to be what I need to be next and next and next. And my self as "strategic manipulator" is what I am able to mobilize to meet my needs and the exigencies of the moment. Since there is no consciousness of what it is to be "true to self," there can be no meaning to playing a role (Gergen, 1991). My "real self" is whomever I need to be at the moment. And so I am a composite of many parts. Each part defines my B's within the context of my A's. My values are defined by the C's that I strive for.

Viewing our selves as the composite of many interdependent yet often disparate parts is not to suggest that we are superficial, reactive automatons. Our somewhat compartmentalized selves can be completely real, congruent, and fully engaged in any moment of time. The challenges inherent in trying to negotiate successfully within a

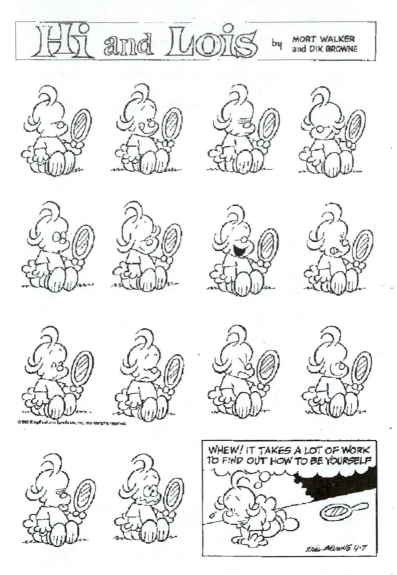

There are many selves within us. (Reprinted with permission of King Features Syndicate.)

saturated society have shaped our multifaceted, multipurpose composite self. We are forced to create and manipulate many selves for strategic purposes, not to injure or exploit others but simply to get by in the world. To experience our selves as strategic manipulators need not connote vacuous substance and insidious intent, as has been so eloquently pointed out by Erving Goffman (1963). Perhaps this multifaceted, complex, and adaptable self that we experience is simply a function of our covert evolution into a hypercomplex and expansive world where a multitude of complex and differentiated selves is the only "ticket" to successfully assimilating and ultimately accommodating the infinite bounty of life.

### Knowing, Using, and Accepting All of the Parts

Virginia Satir, one of the true bounties of family counseling has conceptualized our total person, or self, as the composite of many parts, each with its own unique features and expectations for fulfillment (Satir, 1978). Each part has proven useful to us at sometime in our life yet may get in our way at other times. My shy part served me well as a young child in a new neighborhood trying to learn the gang norms. Later on, my sarcastic part helped me jockey for a position of power within the same gang. My afraid part remained in hiding throughout most of this adolescent period and has only taken center stage during moments of safe intimacy. Most of these parts were created for strategic purposes but sometimes just hung around too long, appeared at the wrong times, or failed to appear when called on. Sometimes parts find it difficult to get along together and even try to inhibit one another.

Rather than denying and rejecting any part, Satir believes that we are most functional—at our congruent best—when all of the parts are acknowledged, accepted, and discriminately used in a harmonious and integrated manner. It takes considerable energy, effort, and even deception to reject any of these parts, and the deception can only be our own. Better to welcome all parts into the tent, where we can get to know how they have served us in the past and how we might enlist their support in the future. Even detestable parts that seem to have no redeeming value, such as our aggressive self, may be very desirable in a crisis when we must overcome opposition to achieve a critical outcome. As Satir (1978) writes, "Every part carries an aspect of energy which serves to transform it when it understands that it has choices in how and when to manifest itself and that it can cooperate with other parts rather than fighting with them" (p. 259).

### The Parts Party

To help people integrate and use all of their parts in this way, Satir directs a specific member of a counseling group to host a "parts party." With each group member serving as a separate part, the host introduces them to each other and encourages all of them to cooperate and contribute to a successful party. They are accepted for who they are and valued for how they might contribute. An additional feature of this conceptualization of a multipart, composite self is the opportunity that it provides for choice. Each part, or self, that we consciously acknowledge, accept, and create is another resource (i.e., meaning, action plan, schema) that we can choose to draw on in meeting our needs and succeeding in the world.

## Our Natural Tendencies for Self-Development

The covert a-b-c's that we internalize as our experiences both influence and conform to the images reflected in the mirror of our social environment. Beyond this environmental influence are maturational growth factors that shape the content of our a-b-c's and the covert processes we use. Two of these maturational factors have already been discussed: neurophysiological growth and the cognitive developmental mechanisms described by Piaget. The innate development of a sense of self is integral to each of Piaget's stages as individuals evolve from a sensorimotor self to a concretely egocentric self and ultimately arrive at a relativistic, flexible, yet morally principled self—the self of compatible contradictions.

### Innate Milestones of Identity Formation

A third perspective on self-development is offered by Erik Erikson (1980) along with many others (Kohlberg, 1981; Levinson, 1978; Lidz, 1976) who have either embellished his model or found a somewhat "different voice" (Gilligan, 1982). Throughout his writings, Erikson used the terms *identity* and *self* interchangeably when referring to self-perception. Erikson considered our personality to be our combined ego (i.e., covert, organizing processes) and self (i.e., object or content of our identity). Erikson's psychosocial development model proposed that self-development occurs as our ego successfully confronts a series of environmental tasks over our life span. These tasks, encountered through eight innately determined sequential stages, require us to actively engage our environment, with each sequential engagement creating covert attributions and expectations for trust, autonomy, initiative, industry, identity, intimacy, generativity, and finally integrity.

### Learning from Success and Failure

Erikson's crises, or tasks, consist of the natural behavioral expectations that our environment enforces upon us. Presuming that these tasks are developmentally appropriate, they provide antecedents that challenge and invite us to take risks, experiment, and expand our covert and operant behavioral repertoire. To the extent that we are successful, we learn these fundamental attributions and expectations about ourselves and the world around us. When our engagement with family, friends, teachers, employers, colleagues, or lovers fails, our sense of self can be shattered as our covert a-b-c's turn to mistrust, doubt, guilt, inferiority, role confusion, isolation, self-absorption and eventual despair.

But failure is inevitable for all of us. And even our most disappointing and painful experiences have something to teach about our inadequacies and vulnerabilities and about the vicissitudes of life. Unlike the shattered self that only experiences failed tasks as lessons in mistrust, doubt, guilt, and so forth, Erikson's fully integrated, optimally functioning self converts these failures into such lessons as appropriate caution, reasoned boundaries, acceptance of imperfection, humility, flexibility, adaptability, independence, and conviction of principle. In other words, our evolving self integrates all of our experience into our conscious awareness, acceptance, and activation. Thus, with trust we learn caution, with autonomy we learn to accept limitations and ask for help, with initiative we learn restraint, with industry we learn humility, and so on through each stage.

### The Formation of a Stable Identity

By the time we reach adolescence, we have assimilated and accommodated enough experience to begin evidencing a distinct, fairly integrated, and congruent sense of who we are—an actual identity. If we acknowledge all the selves that we experience and exhibit, even the most unpleasant and contradictory ones, a complex yet integrated identity enters our consciousness. What is particularly amazing is the stability and co-herence of this identity. The covert a-b-c's that we experienced yesterday actually car-ried over into today and have a good chance of being there tomorrow. This stability and continuity of a-b-c attributions and expectations enable us to categorize patterns of similar a-b-c contingencies into the relatively permanent attributions and expectations that I label as my values, beliefs, morals, and principles—my philosophy of life.

The aggregate of these covert a-b-c's now converging into this identity provides the stability and resulting security necessary for the adolescent to begin to expose and even share that emerging self with another in a relationship of intimacy. This true, mature intimacy, Erikson believes, cannot occur until this identity evolves; thus, an established identity must precede real intimacy. Carol Gilligan (1982) suggests that while this sequence may be true for males, females construct and define much of their identity through relationships and the experience of intimacy. Consequently, these developmental stages of identity leading to intimacy may be reversed for females.

In either case, the self that evolves from adolescence positions adults to employ their full range of covert and overt behaviors in the service of family (i.e., generativity) and ultimately to the benefit of humanity (i.e., integrity). Within a relatively nurturing and loving social environment, we emerge from each successive crisis with an empowering sense of who we are and how we want to be. Just as Piaget's schemata provide meaning and action patterns for knowing ourselves and successfully engaging the world, Erik-son's stages proscribe the a-b-c contingencies that make up our self-concept.

### Individuation: From Dependence to Independence to Interdependence

One dynamic of self-change that undergirds most theories of human development is our ontological movement from dependence to independence. Just as the content of the self evolves from undifferentiated to discrete and congruent, the locus of control re-flected within our covert attributions and expectations seems to progress from external to internal. When we equate an external locus of control with dependence on others and an internal locus of control with autonomy and self-sufficiency, we can readily un-derstand this developmental phenomenon. Labeled by terms such as "individuation," "differentiation," "ego," "self-actualization,"and "self-efficacy," they all share the core belief that maturation and development follow an inexorable path toward independ-ence. From the moment of separation from the womb, we struggle to discover and cre-ate our unique selves, comprising the requisite covert and overt behaviors enabling us to experience the very best in C+'s and avoiding the very worst in C–'s.

While we strive to "do it ourselves," "be our own persons," and "find our place in the world," we really do not want to give up that unconditional love, warmth, com-fort, and pervasive sense of security that we knew as infants. This dependency is most acute in infancy when the quality of the infant-mother attachment holds critical im-plications for the future growth, competence, self-esteem, and overall well-being of the child (Bowlby, 1980; Egeland and Farber, 1984). Infants whose physiological and affective needs are met through primary reinforcement from a nurturing, attentive, and accepting mother (or suitable surrogate) develop security, confidence, and self-efficacy to continue attainment of an optimal balance of intimacy and independence.

Those who fail to experience this qualitative attachment are prone to insecurity, anxiety, depression, aggression, social detachment, and in cases of severe deprivation, an acute failure to thrive (Spitz, 1945).

Unfortunately, our most profound experience of unconditional love (with absolute intimacy) accompanied our period of greatest helplessness, dependence, and vulnerability to the loss of that love. So to thwart the loss of that which was so profoundly nourishing and nurturing at birth, we began to relinquish and even resist our dependence in favor of control. With control over our needs as well as the environment's capacity to meet those needs, we might retain a semblance of that unconditional love. But control means autonomous action from an internal locus of choices. And choice implies responsibility for our own actions and the contingencies affected by those actions. Gradually, we realize that independence has its price.

### The Price of Independence

Once we assume the responsibility for control and the A-B-C contingencies influenced by that control, we naturally embrace the independence and autonomy that seem to improve the odds of success. Control, power, competence—better yet, perfection—give us the very best odds, or so we think. The dependence that seemed enough to fulfill all of our needs as very young children is now anathema to those needs. The evolving credo for meeting our needs becomes power, competence, control, independence, and avoiding dependence (with its baggage of vulnerability and helplessness) at all costs. The pure, uncensored, and spontaneous intimacy of early childhood is too enmeshed with dependence, and so it is banished from the realm of conscious pursuit.

Independence, self-sufficiency, and control over self and others are comforting fictions that become the essence of our daily striving. Neither the belligerent youth eschewing all offers of help, the rebellious teenager sneering at the hand of support and guidance, the driven executive willing to exchange his daughter's dance recital for the dance of corporate power brokering, nor the elderly woman unwilling to ask for assistance with her Alzheimer's disabled husband are willing to recognize the false dichotomy they have accepted. Their dependent "part" was denied, distorted, and essentially discarded for the illusion of achieving control and independence. Without their acknowledgment and acceptance of dependence, vulnerability, and fallibility, they lost any chance of real intimacy. Ironically, the mirage of independence and autonomy only enhanced their experience of inadequacy and failure and, perhaps most despairing of all, their rejection and disintegration of their daily selves.

### The Interdependence of All of Our Parts

The false dichotomy characterizing dependent–independent development exists whenever we distinguish contrasting parts of ourselves and then proceed to deny or distort the part that we do not like. Our strategies to deny and distort any part of our own experience, even if our purpose is to preserve and enhance our perception of self, only serve to perpetuate our incongruence and restrict our awareness of what it means to be human. We are not comprised of the greater or lesser sides of dichotomous parts, but rather the composite of all contrasting and disparate thoughts and actions, each seeking a constructive role in our daily human drama. In acknowledging and accepting every part—dependence, anger, compassion, love, hate, generosity, selfishness, resolve, resignation, spontaneity, caution, sensuality, prudishness, ad infinitum—our mission is one of balance.

Rather than seeking independence at the expense of dependence and intimacy, a goal of interdependence incorporates both into a fully congruent experience of humility with integrity, acquiescence with pride, and the capacity to both give and receive. The capacity for balance in the acceptance and expression of a fully integrated and congruent self is inherently within each of us. Our only obstacles consist of those mechanisms that we create through our misguided efforts to protect and enhance our own self-perception. We now turn to these covert coping mechanisms.

## Protection and Enhancement of Our Covert Experience

### Batter Up!

By the middle of the last inning of Jason's little league baseball game, his team was finally ahead by three runs. In spite of Jason's competent hitting and steady performance as catcher, the seasons had been a disaster. Now the team came to this last game with a record of 0–11; that's right, zip wins. Jason's father, Matt, placated his frustration and disappointment with the explanation that this was a very young team (Jason was the oldest player) and the coach was building character and good sportsmanship with his philosophy of letting every child play at least three innings and at all of the different positions. Matt congratulated the coach on his "sensitive and humanistic" approach and tried to comfort his son after each loss with like-minded platitudes. Not only was Matt a nurturing teacher and psychologist, but he was also an enlightened proponent of cooperation, sharing, and sensitivity toward others. In Matt's covert world, winning could never take precedence over the need to feel accepted and make a contribution—a conviction etched in stone when applied to children.

All that was needed, thought Matt as he watched anxiously in the stands, was to hold them for three outs and the game was won. But my God! What was the coach doing? He was replacing Jason with a novice catcher (who had played very little in the game compared to Jason's five full innings) and was sending in a first-year, untried pitcher. Upon reflection, Matt concluded that this was probably a good opportunity for these youngsters, and besides, we had a three-run lead and only needed three outs.

After the first batter was "nicked" by a pitch, the second batter watched four cautiously pitched balls bounce harmlessly around the plate and through the catcher's legs. With third and first base occupied, the next batter hit a towering blooper about 3 ft in front of home plate, a location that completely eluded the consciousness of the confused catcher. Having parlayed the elusive hit into a triple, the score stood at 7–6.

It was about this time that the spirit of "Win at any cost!" took possession of Matt's body. As he ranted and raved at the coach, even throwing a few developmentally inappropriate invectives at the dazed catcher, Matt attempted to recruit other parents in an attempt to take over the team. The next two batters were summarily walked to load the bases and still the incompetent S.O.B., #*@#* of a coach did nothing. Matt's rage was only momentarily repressed when he was warned by the umpire to "shut up or leave the field." Lacking any confederacy from the stands, Matt yelled to his son to do something. "Talk some sense to that stupid coach." Jason immediately seemed to relinquish his own frustration with the team's disintegrating play and mobilized his own humiliation and embarrassment over his father's atavistic conduct. Their mutual agony was short lived, however, as the next batter hit a clean single clearing the bases and bringing victory from the jaws of defeat to the other team.

Only when the benches were cleared, the coach's post-mortem completed, and the last folding chair tucked into the trunk did Matt regain his composure. Although successful in avoiding the coach, as designated driver, Matt couldn't avoid Jason's anger and disappointment at the loss, but Jason's feelings about his father's performance were much deeper. Since Jason refused to accept Matt's explanation of demonic possession, Matt resorted to the only rationale congruent with an acceptable image of himself as a caring, sensitive, and supportive father whose primary purpose is to create the optimal conditions for his children's success and happiness. And his son needed this win to be successful and happy. In fact, Matt concluded, all of his raving machinations were really for Jason. As John Lovitt used to proclaim as the "pathological liar" on *Saturday Night Live*: "Yes, that's the ticket!" Matt only did it to protect Jason. It felt much better to say and think this rationalization, even if his son, and later his wife, struggled to believe his fabrication. They wanted to believe, for they too had an investment in the image of self that Matt was protecting. But Matt's operant and covert behavior were simply too incongruent. Which was the real Matt?

## Constructing Our Covert Reality to Protect Our Self

In essence, Matt's infantile behavior and his verbal portrayal of the reasons for it are both a part of him. He proudly displays the image of protector of his son, but he is also motivated by many personal needs that scream for equal time. Matt's need to excel at baseball and achieve the apex of success and adoration were never quenched by his .265 batting average in high school. Although he will never realize the fulfillment of that need, he can still project the expectation underlying it on to his son and he does. But Matt's dreams and expectations for achievement and success were only part of the self that he was trying to protect during the course of the game. A second and perhaps more pervasive need surfaced after the game when he struggled to explain and reconcile the contrast between his self-perception and his behavior. This was his need to protect his self—the person he hardly recognized that day.

Our need to create a meaningful world within the structures of our covert experience is a constant priority, driving our consciousness in a relentless mission to discover (i.e., empirically identify or creatively construct) cogent attributions and expectations for our experience. Just as fundamental and consuming is our need to protect and enhance the integrity of that covert world once we have embraced it as our own.

## Our Covert Defense Mechanisms

Sigmund Freud considered the ego to represent the cognitive strategies that we consciously and unconsciously use to mediate our internal needs with the demands and resources of our environment. When our covert processes and resources (i.e., the aggregate a-b-c's that provide meaning and purpose to experience) are successful in this mediation, we experience harmony within ourselves and with our environment. Failure to mediate that balance, however, presents an immediate threat to our sense of self. That threat activates those covert strategies (i.e., ego) for the purpose of protecting and enhancing that self, and in so doing, maintaining the integrity and stability of our covert world. Our attributions and expectations, the needs and desires that we harbor, even the fears that can immobilize us all subsume our covert reality. And it is this subjectively constricted and exceedingly fragile covert reality that our ego tenaciously protects.

Freud posited the armaments at the ego's disposal for self-protection to be the array of defense mechanisms we recognize as projection, repression, dissociation, rationalization, and so forth. A massive literature already exists on these covert mechanisms, so I will discuss their general function and a few examples as they apply to covert behavior. Although employing different strategies of defense, these cognitive mechanisms protect the integrity of the self by denying or distorting parts of our covert experience of self or parts of our external environment that are too dissonant and painful. In the former defense strategy, we conceal parts of the self (i.e., covert experience) that are believed to be unacceptable to our external environment and are thus vulnerable to C−'s and the loss of C+'s. The latter strategy finds us censoring feedback from the environment that is either too threatening or incompatible with our perception of self. In both cases, the operative word is denial—denial of either our internal or external reality. Whether the rejection is of our internal experience or of feedback from others, the ultimate causality is a fully integrated, congruent self, a fluid and dynamic self that, as an open system, is accessible to both internal and external experience.

## Denying and Rejecting Parts of Our Self

So how do we go about this business of denial? To understand the ways that we deny and reject parts of ourselves, we first need to revisit the covert attributions and expectations stored within our memory banks. We have been building on that aggregate of a-b-c's since our earliest awareness of causality, and we probably have a cadre of infantile behaviors that we learned directly or vicariously to associate with C−'s and C+'s. Soiling ourselves, wetting the bed, expressing our aggression, our sexuality, or even our curiosity are likely culprits (i.e., BORCs) for the young child.

Later on, experience may teach us that any expression of our emotionality brings undesirable consequences. By adolescence, overt displays of affection, shame, guilt, fear, and sexuality are just a few of the taboo behaviors subject to social sanction and ostracism. All of the rejections, punishments, insults, and injuries that society bestows upon us for just being ourselves create a host of internal reactions from confusion and helplessness to anger and rage. But of course, these natural reactions are equally as unacceptable to others and subject to even more punishment and rejection. Increasingly, our covert experience is antagonistic to the norms of our social environment. Since our social environment is essential to our survival, we are faced with a critical dilemma. We can reject those parts of ourselves that seem to threaten our very survival, or we can accept all that we experience of ourselves and reject any social sanctions or critical feedback from others.

Our social environment's influence in resolving this dilemma is profound. In spite of our desire to be "true to self," we have got to conciliate to the norms of our social environment if we are to survive. Attribution studies have clearly acknowledged this social influence in demonstrating that we usually attribute the causes for our behavior to external circumstances, yet we attribute the behavior of others to their own internal motivations. To conform and adapt to these social norms, we need to change not only our operant behavior but also any corresponding offending covert a-b-c's. For example, while I inhibit any form of overt (operant) sexual expression (e.g., displays of affection, nudity, pornography, sexual humor, masturbation, etc.), I must also inhibit any sexual a-b-c's from my conscious awareness. Just thinking about sexual expression raises the specter of social condemnation, so the thought must be banished. In both instances of covert and overt behavioral inhibition, I am rejecting a part of myself.

Generally, it is a lot easier to inhibit the offending overt behavior than the related covert experience. Under strict antecedent stimulus control, where the antecedent red lights are flashing brightly warning of C–'s or ⊠+'s, we can usually inhibit the BORC (although, in spite of our protestations, it still remains in our repertoire). Inhibition of the thoughts and related feelings is considerably more problematic.

## Denying Our Covert Experience

An unacceptable covert experience, such as a pornographic fantasy, is not directly accessible to environmental scrutiny and punitive sanction even though it provokes covert disapproval and physiological anxiety from the anticipated C–'s associated with the thought. In fact, many taboo, or socially unacceptable, thoughts may produce incompatible intrinsic consequences of physiological arousal (C+) and self-denigration (C–). I will say more about intrinsic consequences later in this chapter.

The external environmental A-B-C contingencies that enable (or coerce) us to inhibit unacceptable operant behavior do not work as effectively on our covert behavior. These covert experiences that we deem as socially unacceptable, and thus incompatible with our safe and secure self (referred to as our "ideal self" by Carl Rogers), need to employ cognitive mechanisms for inhibition. And this is when the defense mechanisms of the ego are enlisted to direct our unacceptable covert experience away from the covert a-b-c's that we desire to represent us. The diversion of unacceptable covert experience can take various forms, but essentially it involves denying and distorting part of our experience and thus rejecting a part of our self. The following are examples:

• A common covert strategy for eliminating part of ourselves is to *project* it onto someone else. In this covert game of "hot potato," we can deny any ownership for the abhorrent part by assigning ownership to someone else. By projecting it outward, usually to people who present minimal threat, we can retain our self-integrity and self-righteously blame the targeted person. "I am not angry. You are." "What, me hostile? You're just out to get me." "I didn't fail. You just didn't do your part." "That wasn't sexual harassment. You just tried to seduce me." Sound familiar? All of us use this defense to some degree. Even groups of people use projection to defend group identity when they ascribe blame to a handy (and vulnerable) scapegoat.

• When we are unable to eliminate unacceptable parts of self by projecting them onto others, we find ways to distance ourselves from them internally. One of the most blatant and severe ways is a defense mechanism referred to as *dissociation*. This desperate form of self-defense occurs when a traumatic or catastrophic experience is simply too painful and abhorrent to be allowed into conscious awareness, much less a feature of our conscious self. Typically, a childhood trauma such as severe abuse or neglect is enough to activate this covert strategy. Once activated, this mechanism creates a new and separate category of experience in which to place the traumatic memory. Once separated from the conscious self, the traumatic experience can then be assigned to a new and discrete self created just for that purpose. Sometimes it is the "old, original" self that is assigned to take on the traumatic experience, and a new and acceptable self is created for general conscious cognitive functioning. If trauma continues unabetted, this covert mechanism for survival can continue to create new selves in a desperate attempt to maintain the integrity of a functional, conscious self. Individuals employing this dissociative reaction to intolerable experience usually present the clinical syndrome of multiple personality disorder. In line with our previous discussion of the importance of parts integration, therapy is designed to help these folks integrate all of their separate selves into a coherent, cohesive, and conscious whole with all parts welcome.

• Another covert strategy for self-protection is to completely banish the unacceptable experience from conscious awareness. In this banishment or *repression* strategy, instead of creating a separate self that assumes ownership of the unwanted part, we actually keep it from entering our consciousness. A variation on the familiar adage "Out of sight, out of mind" might translate to the repressor as "Out of mind, out of self." When it works, this covert denial strategy relieves us of all guilt and responsibility— and memory—for the unacceptable thought or feeling. "It is just not me" becomes the operative refrain. The disadvantage of repression, especially if it works, is that the banished part is very difficult to access and reintegrate into a congruent self. Additionally, because long-term memory retrieval and decoding are so fraught with error and so susceptible to social influence and subjective interpretation, it is difficult to decipher the content of the original experience. This issue has received considerable attention lately with the phenomenon of repressed memory therapy.

• When we cannot hide our unacceptable covert experience somewhere out of consciousness and cannot give it away to someone else, an alternative is to distort the experience and render it unrecognizable to ourselves and others. Commonly known as *rationalization*, this self-protection mechanism doesn't deny that a thought, feeling, or behavior occurred; instead it very creatively and consciously distorts the original experience until it conforms to the acceptable self. Of course, to rationalizers, this is never a deliberate distortion, but rather represents a reasonable explanation for their overt and covert behavior. Because the strategy of rationalization may be so automatic and the reconstruction of the experience so exquisitely fabricated and sincerely delivered, rationalizers firmly believe their re-creation of reality. The believability of this rationalized version of reality is continually reinforced as we vociferously convey our story to others, but even more so as we covertly rehearse and ruminate on the version that fits our desirable self.

Recall my little league anecdote and you will quickly recognize this common form of self-defense. Matt possessed a fairly well-integrated, congruent, and functional self that he experienced with pride and integrity. As the baseball game began to unravel, certain parts of Matt's composite self began to enter his consciousness. These were the parts that we could label as competitive, hypocritical, perfectionistic, selfish, arrogant, hostile, and irrational (perhaps the worst part of all for this learned professional), and they were in direct and blatant conflict with the self that he embraced so proudly. It was his need to defend his deteriorating self that mobilized these most distasteful parts. The sense of helplessness, frustration, and defeat that rapidly arose within Matt may have provoked an even more fundamental need for self-control, thus mobilizing worse parts of his defense repertoire. In any case, the Matt that he experienced was anathema to the self that he knew and wanted to maintain. Unable to deny the fact of his actions, he pursued the only defense he knew, which was to rationalize his behavior. By framing his actions as motivated by his intense concern for his son's success and well-being, Matt assuaged some of his internal conflict and resolved the cognitive dissonance between his belief about himself and his behavior. Although protecting his self, Matt's rationalization probably did little to restore his credibility with Jason and mom.

## Cognitive Dissonance: The Search for Compatible Parts

**M**y last list entry introduced a concept of covert defense and self-preservation that warrants further discussion. This is the theory of cognitive dissonance introduced by Leon Festinger (1957). Festinger's extensive research and review of the literature led him to conclude that all individuals strive for internal consistency. Our opinions, attitudes, and beliefs about ourselves and others exist in consistent and persistent clusters. Covert attributions, such as our belief that honesty is the best policy, a good education is critical to success, never disclose your credit card number over the telephone, Japanese automobiles are always the best in value and quality, and smoking is very unhealthy all sustain their credibility and influence over us as we consistently behave in consonance with their message.

According to Festinger, we seek out experiences and information that conform to our covert beliefs (i.e., attributions, expectations, values) about the world. Preferring the term "consonance" to consistency, he posited that attainment of this congruence between our thoughts and actions or between contiguously held thoughts is a motivating force. A feeling of harmony, balance, and control (at least predictability) occurs when consonance is achieved.

By and large, we are able to maintain a state of consonance because our overt behavior follows our covert attributions and expectations, thus confirming our beliefs (and illustrating the self-fulfilling prophecy described previously). We even seek out evidence and selectively discriminate information from our environment that supports our covert reality. As Frank and Frank (1991) point out, we are constantly "filtering information through assumptive systems that emphasize confirmatory experiences. Contradictory information is either ignored or quickly forgotten" (p. 32). This confirmatory bias (Meichenbaum & Gilmore, 1984) that we all share maintains our sense of stability and security within an unpredictable and ambiguous world, but taken to the extreme, it severely restricts our freedom of thought and action. Consonance may be comforting, but dissonance is our real catalyst for change.

Feedback from our external environment is replete with information that challenges and contradicts those attributions and expectations that we hold so dear. According to Festinger, the dissonance that we experience when two meaningful thoughts are incompatible or when a thought is incompatible with an action creates a "psychological discomfort" that motivates us to reduce the dissonance and regain our experience of consonance. Before we discuss dissonance reduction, let us look at a few examples of cognitive dissonance.

### Covert–Overt Behavioral Dissonance

| Covert | Overt |
|---|---|
| Smoking is bad | Smoking a cigarette |
| Honesty is best | Complimenting Aunt Sue on her unpalatable spaghetti dinner |
| Southerners are slow | The president of my bank built his own home and grew up in Georgia* |
| Never give away credit card number | Must reserve valued concert tickets with payment over phone |
| I am patient and caring | I rage at handicapped driver for driving under speed limit |
| Japanese cars are best | Purchase used Chevy for son |
| Teenagers are irresponsible and lazy | The high school car wash makes $1500 for homeless center* |

### Covert–Covert Dissonance

| Covert | Covert |
|---|---|
| Value sanctity of life | Support death penalty for child murderers |
| Value gender equity | Believe moms should stay home with young children |
| Government largesse is bad | Support government subsidy of my flood insurance |

The dissonance that we experience from any of these examples can only be reduced through a process of change in either part or in our acceptance of incompatible parts. Here are our options.

### Change Our Overt Behavior

This option presents all of the difficulties extant in operant behavior change. Quitting smoking, confronting Aunt Sue about her abysmal cooking, losing that cherished ticket, and remortgaging the house to afford that Chevy each conform to a covert belief, but might create consequences of even greater pain and discomfort.

### Change Our Covert Behavior

Sometimes we resort to rationalization as we re-create the covert reality of an experience to conform to our overt behavior. We might convince ourselves that smoking is bad except when it is with low tar and nicotine cigarettes and that giving your credit card number over the telephone is okay if you get the name and address of the recipient. At other times, especially if we are receptive to external feedback, we reassess our belief (attribution, expectation, value judgment) and revise it accordingly. Upon reflection, I might conclude that sensitivity to the feelings of others sometimes takes precedence over abject honesty, American cars have bridged the quality gap with their Japanese counterparts, and I have the capacity (i.e., part) to be impatient and inconsiderate.

The two dissonance examples marked by asterisks illustrate that we can also encounter incongruities between our covert beliefs and the external reality around us. Our confirmatory bias can often inflict us with all sorts of myths, prejudices, stereotypes, and aprophilic fantasies, none of which could pass empirical validation. And we must be open to empirical validation if our dissonant covert beliefs are to change. The kind of change that restores our consonance with ourselves and the world doesn't require a thorough, painstaking investigation of every piece of evidence. The only empirical evidence that we need is what we receive when we open ourselves up to our immediate and direct experience of ourselves and our environment. Through this open conduit of immediate feedback, I can't possibly believe that "teenagers are irresponsible and lazy" because I experienced evidence to prove otherwise. And southerners? Well, that guy from Georgia could run rings around anyone that I know.

### Learn to Live with Dissonance

As dissonance is a constant reality of our human experience, the most functional and liberating path to consonance is to accept incongruity and contradiction as natural parts of life. After all, acknowledging and accepting ourselves for all that we are—contradictions, ambiguities, and inconsistencies included—are the bases for realizing a truly integrative self. Dissonant covert beliefs are ultimately nothing more than disparate parts of who we are, each needing to be put in its proper place. Even old and obsolete covert and overt behaviors that have long lost their validity and utility can have a place in the archive of our self. If nothing else, they can at least show us who we were and how far we have come.

## Self-Valuing: Judgments We Make About Self

N ow that we have looked at the substance of covert experience as reflected in our attributions and expectations and the cognitive mechanisms that we use to perceive, integrate, store, retrieve, and manipulate those aggregate a-b-c's, we can consider the ways that we judge and e-value-ate those experiences. Our self-concept represents the process and content of those covert experiences as they characterize us, and the qualitative judgments that we render about self define our self-esteem. Just as the content of our covert a-b-c's can, at best, comprise our subjective representation of external reality (i.e., A-B-C's), the judgments that we make about ourselves are susceptible to even larger increments of error. Straight-A students may be covertly aware of their academic standing, yet may still judge that performance to be inadequate and consequently demean themselves for incompetence. The judgments that we make about ourselves, the values that we place on our thoughts and actions, and ultimately the consequences (i.e., C+'s and C–'s) that we present to ourselves determine the quality of our life and our motivation to learn and grow.

As we delve into the realm of covert self-valuing, it is important that we first define belief, attitude, and value. From these operational definitions, we will move to covert self-valuing mechanisms with particular emphasis on intrinsic consequences vis-à-vis the extrinsic consequences discussed in Chapter 3. Then we will be ready to explore the effects of covert valuing with respect to self-esteem, self-efficacy, and motivation to behave. Conclusions and extrapolations from our discussion of covert valuing will lead to an exploration of the emotions within the context of our A-B-C model. So on to some definitions.

### Covert Valuing Definitions

The dictionary defines belief as "an acceptance of something true; an opinion, expectation, or judgment about something; confidence in the truth of something." From the covert behavioral component of the A-B-C model, I will define a belief as a conscious covert experience (description) combined with its attribution (explanation) and related covert expectations. In most instances, our beliefs explicitly or implicitly carry our qualitative judgments about the importance or value associated with the belief (i.e., its description, attribution, and expected action or consequence).

Through direct experience or vicarious learning, we accumulate beliefs about everything and anything from the mundane to the profound, the obvious to the obscure, and the personal to the universal. My belief in environmentalism includes my description of what it is, my attribution for why it should (or should not) occur, and my expectations for what will happen if it does (or does not) occur. Translated to a personal level, this belief includes how (description) I recycle trash each week, why (attribution) I choose to do it, and what (expectation) will happen if I continue the practice. And of course, this belief is infused with value judgments about the goodness, worth, or importance of my experience of environmentalism.

Owing to the complex and idiosyncratic nature of human experience, there are no limits to the number, variety, and substance of the beliefs that we embrace, maintain, and expose to others. Whether it is our belief in dental floss, the appropriateness of managed healthcare, the sanctity of human life, or the nature of spirituality and a higher power, they each comprise a description of what we mean, some attribution for why it exists as we perceive it, expectations for how that belief will influence our future, and value judgments about the importance or rightness of following the particular belief.

Although we hold beliefs about most phenomena in our life, the intensity and commitment with which we embrace, retain, and even espouse our beliefs vary on a continuum. My belief in dental floss may change as I experience the ravages of a childhood without flossing (and I may espouse my new belief to my children, although I doubt that I would join an organization espousing universal flossing). My beliefs about managed care weigh a bit heavier in my covert valuing and might prompt a more substantive commitment for adoption from me. Moving along the value continuum, it must be apparent to anyone following the controversies over abortion and capital punishment that beliefs about the sanctity of life are firmly embraced and rigorously (if not aggressively) espoused. And the belief in a higher power penetrates our most fundamental attributions and expectations for our future, in this life and beyond. So powerful is this latter belief that more wars have been fought under the banner of religious belief than any other cause.

## The Power of Belief

These four components of a covert belief—description, attribution, expectation and value—are crucial in understanding the relationship between our beliefs, our emotions, and our motivations to behave. Even when devoid of empirical validation, our beliefs can stimulate emotional experiences that mobilize our physiological resources and motivate our operant behavior in the most fundamental and inexplicable ways. In our struggle to bring stability, comprehension, and some sense of control in this world, even when that control is as illusional as our comprehension is delusional, we often adopt, create, and embrace beliefs that are neither logical, valid, nor in the best interest of us or those around us. Certain a-b-c beliefs sustain such insidious emotional states as anxiety (e.g., an external locus of control for life-threatening C–'s) and depression (e.g., an extreme external locus of control for C+'s which are generally beyond our grasp). These emotional states, in turn, can motivate such dysfunctional behaviors as phobias and suicide, respectively. We will talk about the emotional and behavioral casualties of certain beliefs later in this chapter.

As the value and importance of certain beliefs increase, those beliefs provide the rationale and direction for our actions and the justification for the actions' consequences. In consonance with the self-fulfilling prophecy, they actually create consequences that confirm each component of the beliefs. The "Hawthorne" effect experimentally demonstrated by Rosenthal (1969) and the "demand characteristics" identified by Orne (1969) illustrate the power of covert attributions and expectations over the performance of subjects under experimental conditions.

## The Placebo Effect

**R**elated literature that demonstrates the power of belief in mobilizing us to action, even when that belief has no empirical support to do so, looks at the "placebo effect." Comprising an inert substance of no known biochemical benefit (e.g., a sugar pill or some attention alternative to a proscribed treatment), a placebo exerts significant effects when embraced by the subject as any other valid and established treatment. As early as 1943, Kraines reported that the stronger a patient believed in a particular cure, the greater the chances of resolving problems effectively. Since then, numerous researchers have documented the power of the placebo effect in facilitating salutary therapeutic treatment gains. This treatment effect can only be explained by assuming that the belief influences the body's biochemistry much like actual medication (Kabat-Zinn, 1990). Although the power of faith, suggestion, and belief has certainly evoked miraculous cures and behavior changes over the course of human history (Siegel, 1986), we are only beginning to purposely harness this powerful placebo effect to medical and psychological interventions.

In spite of the success that Peter Pan experienced in his belief that he could fly and Dorothy's equally as successful belief in the power of the ruby slippers, the causative power of the placebo, myth, and apocryphal anecdote has received scant support from the scientific community. This is changing, however, as the inspirational, psychoneuroimmunological, and motivational properties of beliefs receive empirical validation (Cousins, 1989; Kabat-Zinn, 1990; Pelletier, 1977; Siegel, 1986; Talmon, 1990; among many others).

## Attitudes: The Action of Beliefs

**O**ur beliefs and attitudes are usually thought of as synonymous covert phenomena, and yet an important distinction is indicated. While a belief is our covert experience, meaning, and value about something in life, our attitude is an overt manifestation of that belief. The dictionary defines attitude as "the manner of acting, feeling, or thinking that shows one's disposition, opinion, or belief about something." We carry our beliefs in our head and express and display them in our attitudes of respondent and operant behavior. My belief about abortion becomes an attitude when I actually campaign for a pro-life political candidate or picket an abortion clinic. The more I value my belief, the more blatantly it shows in my face, body, and actions, revealing a certain attitude.

## Self-Esteem and Our Valuing of Self

**W**hile our covert processes are attempting to give order and meaning to the raw data from our sensory and motor neurons, we are continually making value judgments about the covert a-b-c experiences that emerge from those data. It is not sufficient to subjectively re-create our ongoing experiences with the world to match the a-b-c's in our head with the A-B-C's of our external reality. We then inveterately have to subject those a-b-c's to our covert "scales" to see how they measure and compare to our covert standards of acceptability, worth, importance, and value. Our judgments of our a-b-c's constitute our covert process of self-valuing. As we apply standards, we make judgments and assign value according to the disposition of those judgments. The values that we assign to our self represent the qualitative core of our self-concept— our self-esteem.

The dictionary defines value as "the worth of a thing. The quality of a thing that makes it more or less desirable, useful, important." To value is "to think highly of; to esteem; to prize." Thus, value as a noun is an entity that exists in varying amounts. My public speaking voice commands a high value when I perform before an audience, but my singing voice offers value only when immersed in a hot shower, and then only to me. As a verb, value is a judgment or decision that I deliberately make about the worth, importance, or significance of something. I think highly of, esteem, and prize things about myself that measure up to my standards of value. I love to sing in the shower and prize moments when my voice is indistinguishable from Plácido Domingo or James Taylor. Well almost.

I can choose to value a part of myself even when its extrinsic or attributed value is markedly less. The intrinsic value of my singing voice in the shower supersedes any extrinsic value that it might command. Conversely, I can choose to demean and de-value a part of myself even in contradiction to the high value that others might place on it. In each instance, my self-valuing (covertly) produces consequences that directly impinge on my self-esteem, my emotions, and my approach to life. How we self-value is profoundly more important to our self-esteem than the extrinsic value that might be attributed to any particular part by others. Let us look more closely at this intrinsic process of self-valuing.

## Intrinsic Consequences

There is extensive literature (Gross & Drabman, 1982; Kahn, 1989; Watson & Tharp, 1993) on the effects of self-administration of consequences on covert and overt behavior. In most cases, however, these studies employed self-administered extrinsic C's. In contrast, self-evaluation leading to intrinsic consequences occurs as a natural covert experience. While extrinsic consequences, as described in Chapter 3, certainly maintain a strong contingency over our thoughts and overt behavior, at a more fundamental and intimate level, the covert judgments that we make about our thoughts and actions maintain the most profound effect on those covert and overt experiences (Bandura, 1986).

Chapter 3 introduced the principle of intrinsic consequences and suggested that covert and overt behavior is motivated or inhibited as much by the consequences we provide in our covert processing as by any external contingencies that we might experience. The characteristics that set intrinsic consequences apart from extrinsic consequences are inherent in the subjective, intimate, and idiosyncratic nature of our covert experience. Extrinsic consequences occur in our external environment and are observable and measurable (with some creative observation). They predictably occur within a

B-C contingency and usually include the behavior of other people (except when self-consequation of extrinsic C's is employed). Few of these conditions characterize intrinsic consequation. We will use an example of intrinsic positive reinforcement (C+) to illustrate this distinction, although any of the four categories of extrinsic consequences (i.e., C+, X–, C–, X+) is just as applicable to covert intrinsic consequation.

### The Picnic and the Invisible C+'s

Let's suppose that my wife is invited to a picnic held by friends at the school where she teaches. She of course asks me to come along but prompts me to dress casually and wear my sneakers because a "noncompetitive" softball game is planned. The picnic day arrives and as the softball game commences, I quickly realize that most of the players are 20 years my junior and excessively eager to display their athletic prowess before their colleagues and spouses. I, on the other hand, want to preserve a little dignity and avoid reinjuring my scarred knees and arthritic shoulder. Playing shallow right field, I haltingly reach for two ground balls that go through my legs toward the real right fielder. I also narrowly escape colliding with the speeding projectile (i.e., softball) when I allow a line drive to drop a few feet to my left. Throughout this display of public ineptitude, my extrinsic consequences consisted of "competitive ostracism" (i.e., the C– of a 25-year-old jock positioning himself right in front of me) and team denial (i.e., the X+ of stunned silence from my teammates).

Little did they know that my covert was fully activated in constructing lavish intrinsic positive reinforcers for my every effort. The smell of the grass, the warm sun at my back, and the nostalgic feel of padded leather between my fingers were incredibly reinforcing; it really felt good. As each hit ball began its arc to the outfield, I could picture myself as the graceful, sure-footed and strong-armed 15 year old I once was—or remembered that I was—plying my adolescent trade in the fields of my youth. Wow! What a rush.

What's more, I punctuated each attempt to catch, throw, run, or even back up a play with covert self-talk that consisted of "Hey, I almost got that ball. Pretty good. Two more feet and I would have caught it." "Wow, I got that ball to second with just three bounces, and I'm doing great for 50. Wait till these kids get older." When I hit dribblers to the pitcher during my two trips to the plate, I continued the course of my intrinsic C+'s in the absence of any noticeable extrinsic consequences. My two at-bats offered much to value and, consequently, ample opportunity for intrinsic reinforcement. First, I hit the ball—twice! Then, I ran out each grounder and almost beat the throw the second time. And finally, the feel of the bat, the contact of bat and ball, and the intimate connection of batter and pitcher were exhilarating, the kind of innately reinforcing experience that illustrates the essence of intrinsic positive reinforcement.

An objective analysis and post-mortem of my softball experience by an external observer might easily conclude that I played poorly, experienced only C–'s and X+'s, and had a lousy time. As a result of this awful embarrassment, the external observer might conclude that I will never play softball again and that my self-esteem (relative to softball sports, competition, social interaction—however far I choose to generalize my "failure") has suffered severely.

But you and I know differently. My experience of the entire picnic was replete with intrinsic positive reinforcers in spite of the absence of extrinsic C+'s. Let me define some terms and then we can identify those intrinsic elements that made for such a successful day.

## Intrinsic Positive Reinforcement

**A** pleasant or desirable covert experience associated with (or physiologically stimulated by) a particular thought or action functions as intrinsic positive reinforcement. The covert experience serves to motivate the performance of that thought or action in the future. Just as there are levels of extrinsic positive reinforcement, there are also similar intrinsic levels. Let's start with the most basic.

• *Primary Intrinsic C+'s:* In the same way that primary extrinsic C+'s are physiological in nature, primary intrinsic C+'s are physiological states of excitation or relaxation that we experience as desirable. We may refer to these as states of joy, pleasure, bliss, mellowness, or even as being "in a zone." Regardless of our subjective label, these physiological states are our natural, direct, and internal reactions to certain thoughts and actions. Elevated levels of dopamine, adrenaline, endorphin (our body's natural opiate drug), and the host of neurotransmitters activating arousal and attention can also induce pleasurable and desirable feelings and thus serve as primary intrinsic C+'s. A walk through a pristine forest in fall, a vigorous set of tennis, the enchantment of a Gershwin rhapsody, and the sounds of a joyful family reunion are a few experiences that include large measures of primary intrinsic C+'s. Their pleasures are brought about by the body's own chemistry and require no extrinsic drug or environmental response.

The biochemical change crated by ingesting drugs and medications may be experienced as C+'s (or even as ⊠–'s), but their source and maintenance are external. The primary intrinsic C+'s that enrich our lives and sustain some of our most enduring (and endearing) behavior represent biochemical changes that naturally result when we exercise our body's optimal potential.

• *Secondary Intrinsic C+'s:* Most of the covert C+'s that we experience and present to ourselves are not the physiological by-products of our actions, but are instead judgments we make about our thoughts, our actions, our appearance, or any of the parts that we associate with being who we are. Usually these judgments occur in the form of self-talk, which, as you'll recall from previous chapters is a covert monolog in which we monitor certain thoughts and actions (which we experience consciously as covert events), make judgments about them, and then reveal those judgments through self-referencing self-talk. Although we could experience this entire covert self-judging visually (we could see ourselves succeeding, performing well, achieving our standard of performance, or receiving accolades from others), we generally experience secondary intrinsic C+'s auditorially by talking to ourselves.

Regardless of whether our self-judgments occur as subvocal praise or condemnation or appear as their visual counterparts, these appraisals of self exert an extraordinary influence over our self-esteem and willingness to act. The judgments that we make about our selves exert considerable power over our thoughts and actions and ultimately serve as the final arbiter over our self-worth and value. We turn to the influences of these self-judgments in the next chapter.

## Chapter Summary

**1.** The aggregate of all the a-b-c's that I associate with me in conjunction with all my other self-descriptions represents my total self-concept.

**2.** Because each of our experiences evokes a unique a-b-c schema and prescribes a specific a-b-c action pattern, our self-concept will, in turn, be situational and diverse over our many experiences. Our selves are thus the composite of many interdependent yet often disparate parts. Our "true" self is the composite of our many different selves.

**3.** We construct our covert a-b-c's in a manner that protects and enhances our various selves. In this way, we look for evidence that supports and validates the self that we desire.

**4.** Intolerable experiences or parts of our selves that we judge as unacceptable may cause us to deny or distort their existence. We selectively ignore evidence that challenges or contradicts our desired self-concept.

**5.** We naturally seek harmony between our thoughts and actions. When confronted with a clear discrepancy (dissonance) between two thoughts (beliefs) or between a belief and an operant behavior, we experience anxiety and seek to resolve that dissonance. We solve this cognitive dissonance by changing a belief or even an operant behavior so as to ring harmony into our covert–operant behavioral system.

**6.** Our values represent the qualitative judgments that we make about our covert a-b-c's. While certain a-b-c's can be good or right, others can be bad or wrong.

**7.** Beliefs are our value judgments about an entire class of a-b-c's, such as stealing, helping others, or ingesting drugs.

**8.** An attitude is an overt (operant) manifestation of a covert belief. We maintain beliefs in our head but we display those beliefs in our operant behavior, which reveals our attitude about the beliefs.

**9.** Just as there are extrinsic consequences to our behavior that encourage (C+, $\cancel{C}$–) or discourage (C–, $\cancel{C}$+) our continued behavior, there are also intrinsic consequences that motivate or inhibit our actions.

**10**. Intrinsic consequences are inherent within our behavior, such as the natural high of a satisfying hobby, or they may represent self-judgment about the worth or value of a particular thought or action.

**Figure 1** *The A-B-C (Cognitive–Behavioral) Model*

| (A) Antecedent | Covert | (B) Behavior | Overt | (C) Consequence |
|---|---|---|---|---|
| | | Overt | | |
| | Cognitive (Thinking) | Respondent (Physical) | Operant (Acting) | |
| Stimulus or setting event. External environments that set the occasion for behavior (thinking, acting, feeling) to occur. | Subjective environment. The process and content of our thinking. Our interpretation of A-B-C as a-b-c. | Reflexive Autonomic Involuntary Biochemical Physiological changes occurring within our body. | Voluntary behavior that we choose to do or not to do. | Events (external) that occur during and/or after a particular covert and/or operant behavior. Events can be: |
| $S^{Dee}$ = Green light. A cue that a particular behavior will result in a desirable consequence. | Includes: Attributions Expectations Self-concept | | Can be: Excess = Behavior done too often or at wrong time. | A. Desirable: 1. Positive Reinforcement present desirable = C+ |
| $S^{Delta}$ = Red light. A cue that a particular behavior will result in an undesirable consequence. | Self-esteem Beliefs Attitudes Prejudices Self-talk Locus of control Images Fantasies Intrinsic consequences | | Deficit = Behavior done too infrequently or not when needed. | 2. Negative Reinforcement remove undesirable = ℂ̶ B. Undesirable: 1. Punishment present undesirable, aversive = C– 2. Extinction remove desirable = ℂ̶ |

**Emotions**

Subjective labels used to describe a specific state of being. Labels reflect the composite of our covert, respondent, and operant behavior within a specific context of antecedents and consequences.

# Chapter 11

~~~~~~~~~~

# Our Judgments
of Self

~~~~~~~~~~

## Orienting Ourselves

It is not enough that we are constantly framing the a-b-c's of our covert experience in terms of attributes that define us. We then evaluate what we find. Each new experience is mined for those precious nuggets of information that enhance our understanding of who we are and what makes us unique. Our language centers are continually flowing through our cybernetic feedback system scanning for information that reveals who we are and how we are doing. New information might disclose attributes never before realized, but more frequently it reveals data that simply confirm what we already know.

My hair is brown. I enjoy French-fried potatoes. My right knee aches during cold, rainy weather. I can become very impatient and irritable when caught in a traffic jam. Each attribute or characteristic that I apply to my self was learned and is maintained through principles described in previous chapters. Some of these descriptions remain as parts of my identity, sustained in my covert as idiosyncratic characteristics of how I am or can be.

Most of our self-applied attributes and adjectives are subjected to our covert "court" of self-judgment. Our covert judicial system applies standards of value, goodness, and acceptability to many concepts and characteristics that we have come to know as "us." In so doing, we transcend the description (i.e., brown hair, gimpy knee, impatient driver, etc.) and formulate a judgment about that description. Brown hair might now become good vis-à-vis gray hair, but a gimpy knee might be judged as a weakness, and impatience in driving might be viewed as very bad for a counselor to display. Over time, these concepts of self that are subjected to our covert appraisal become the bases for the level of esteem and value that we ascribe to our selves. In effect, our covert valuing system translates our self-concept into our self-esteem. This process of covert valuing is the focus of this chapter. Again, the covert component of our model will serve as our reference.

**Figure 11** *Covert Behavior*

---

**Cognitive
(Thinking)**

---

Subjective environment. The process and content of our thinking.
Our interpretation of A-B-C as a-b-c.

Includes:
Attributions
Expectations
Self-concept
Self-esteem
Beliefs
Attitudes
Prejudices
Self-talk
Locus of control
Images
Fantasies
Intrinsic consequences

---

**Emotions**

---

Subjective labels used to describe a specific state of being. Labels reflect the composite of our covert, respondent, and operant behavior within a specific context of antecedents and consequences.

---

## Judgments from Others

In one sense, the C+'s that we receive from others and from our external environ- ment reflect the judgments that others make about us. When their response is a C+, their judgment is perceived by us as favorable or positive. A compliment or recogni- tion from our employer implies that our boss judged our performance according to some standard and concluded that we fell within the acceptable/good/successful or some such positive range, at least for that behavior. In contrast, a criticism from our boss (i.e., a C– such as, "That was terrible!") or to be completely ignored (i.e., $\cancel{X}$+) would be experienced as undesirable and imply that the boss judged our behavior to be unacceptable/bad and valueless.

Inherent within most of the social feedback that we receive as C+, $\cancel{X}$–, C–, or $\cancel{X}$+ is the element of judgment. Over the course of constant extrinsic consequences from others, and especially that significant feedback from those most prominent in our so- cial environment, we begin to internalize those consequences and the judgments imbedded within them. In the case of extrinsic C+'s, we begin to positively reinforce ourselves for behaviors (or parts of ourselves) that produced C+'s from others.

Five-year-old Jennie, apple of her mom's eye and recipient of extensive recognition for being so pretty, verbally "pats herself on the back" when glancing in the mirror wearing that new party dress. She likes what she sees and tells herself so. Mom's standards for physical appearance and criteria for pretty have been learned and adopted by Jennie. In the process of internalizing mom's extrinsic C+'s and creating her own covert affirmations of her beauty, Jennie also internalized mom's standards for beauty and the inclination to judge herself and others on the basis of those standards. The product of this internalization of extrinsic C+'s is a covert valuing system that becomes the mechanism and standard for Jennie's own intrinsic secondary positive reinforcement.

Just as each part of Jennie experienced extrinsic C+'s throughout her young life, her covert valuing system fabricates comparable standards of acceptability or worth for those very same parts. If her charm, wit, beauty, and assertiveness experienced ample extrinsic C+'s, then in all probability, her overt valuing system would also judge those parts to be positive (good, worthy, special, important, desirable, etc.) and prompt her to tell herself whenever they were brought to her consciousness. Perhaps not as overt as Maria's pronouncement of "I'm so pretty and witty and bright" in the musical *West Side Story*, Jennie's covert pronouncements are just as intrinsically positively reinforcing and emanate from an internalized valuing system from which she continually judges herself.

## Our Covert Valuing System

In the same way that we can experience the pleasure and satisfaction of positive reinforcement (C+), the relief of negative reinforcement ($\cancel{C}$–), the fear and discomfort of punishment (C–), and the disappointment and frustration of extinction ($\cancel{C}$+) when they occur as external consequences of our actions, we can also create the same array of consequences as part of our covert experience. Whenever we judge our thoughts, actions, and any part of what we consider our self, we invariably place a value on its performance or appearance. Our covert valuing system provides a calibrated "acceptability scale" for assessing our thoughts and actions and then judging our worth, value, success, and importance on the basis of these covert assessments. With each portion of feedback that we process about ourselves, we employ one of our vast store of covert self-assessments in what I have termed our *covert valuing system* (CVS). We use this scale as our basis for determining whether the part of us under scrutiny meets the standard of acceptability—thus warranting intrinsic C+—or falls below our internalized standard of acceptability and the obligatory intrinsic C–/$\cancel{C}$+ that we invoke for "not measuring up."

Our covert valuing system serves as our repository for all of the standards that we initially observed and experienced from our external environment and then internalized. Once internalized, this CVS provides the mechanism for both judging ourselves and for issuing reinforcers or punishers for the disposition of those judgments. Figure 13 depicts this covert valuing system.

This covert valuing system (CVS) is calibrated from 0 to 10, representing the range of quantitative or qualitative performance in which I might experience any of my parts. As I have used the term previously, part refers to any covert or overt behavior,

**Figure 13** *Covert Valuing System (CVS)*

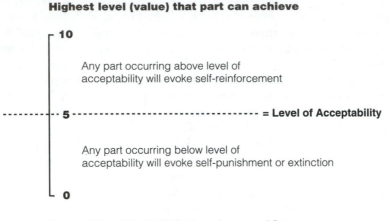

**Highest level (value) that part can achieve**

10

Any part occurring above level of
acceptability will evoke self-reinforcement

5 = **Level of Acceptability**

Any part occurring below level of
acceptability will evoke self-punishment or extinction

0

**Lowest level (value) that part can achieve**

characteristic, or attribute of my self. My hair color, tennis serve, and family of origin are each a part of me. A rating of 0 represents the lowest level of performance that I could possibly experience from any part of my self. To fall at the 0 level reflects a total absence of skill, performance, or quality on that particular attribute.

A rating of 10 reflects the apex of any attribute or behavior. It is the absolute standard of excellence that is achievable by anyone. Perfection is achieved at this level when a consensus agrees that this achievement is the best that could possibly be achieved. A violin concerto by Isaac Stern, a bowling score of 300, SAT scores of 1600 or a Nobel Prize winning scientific discovery can each serve as criteria for perfection, and consequently rank at the 10 level.

The median score of 5 on this scale indicates the average on this particular attribute or behavior. Note that this average is the level achieved by *most* people with respect to any part under assessment. This average ranking is norm referenced and signifies that on some objective measure an equal number of people will fall above and below that level of performance. Throughout our day we usually succeed in accomplishing our tasks adequately (at the 5 level). Sometimes we excel, performing well above the average, and sometimes we experience our selves at the lower ranges of the CVS sale. The essential point to understand about the vertical (or ordinate) axis of the CVS is that it displays a calibrated continuum of performance or attribute from absolute worst (lowest possible) to absolute best (highest possible).

The number that I assign each CVS, although subjective and arbitrary, reflects the range and diversity with which I have experienced that particular part in others or in my environment. Some parts, like income, golf score, or grade point average, can be calibrated quantitatively so that the range from 0 to 10 represents a numerical performance. A grade point average of 4.0 would receive 10 on my CVS while a golf score of 200 would hover close to 0.

Other parts of my self are qualitative in nature and produce CVS ratings of more categorical or dichotomous dimensions. When rating my sense of humor, patience with my children, automotive repair skill, expertise in presenting a lecture, or other such part, I use more subjective criteria for a specific rating. A 10 for any one of these parts could range from "yes, I let my kids finish a task without interrupting them" to "keeping everyone in uproarious laughter." My ranking of 10 usually reflects the ideal or perfect level at which any part could be performed. Here are a few examples of parts and how they might be calibrated from 0 to 10.

Tennis serve    10 = Perfect serve with speed, accuracy, and topspin
                 0 =  Miss the ball with the racket

Thick, dark hair  10 = Dark brown
                   0 =  Completely bald (no hair of any color)

Education       10 = Medical degree
                 0 =  Dropout

Cooking skill   10 = Gourmet
                 0 =  Unable to boil water

The numerical range that I assign to any particular behavior (or part of myself) serves as my covert standard or criterion against which I measure and then judge my performance at a specific time. A glimpse at my CVS for my performance at the picnic softball game can illustrate how my CVS enabled me to have such a C+ experience in spite of my play and feedback (C–/C+) from others.

First of all, the range of performance that I used as my covert standard was fair and realistic. My performance could have fallen anywhere between refusing to play at all (a rating of 0) to major league hitting and fielding (a rating of 10). Along this continuum, I performed at a level approximating 2 or 3. So if my performance was so far below my optimal, or ideal, performance of 10, how was I able to enjoy and feel so good about the experience? My level of acceptability provides the key.

If you turn back to Figure 13, you will notice a dashed line extending horizontally through 5. This line represents the level of acceptability relative to the range of performances from 0 (worst) to 10 (best).

The level of acceptability placement that I choose (e.g., 2, 7) for any particular behavior (or part) identifies the point at which I deem my performance to be either acceptable or unacceptable. Behaviors that rank above my level of acceptability are acceptable and warrant intrinsic positive reinforcement. Conversely, behaviors that fall below my level of acceptability are unacceptable and unworthy of intrinsic C+'s. What's more, I may judge parts of myself to be so deficient and below my level of acceptability that they elicit intrinsic punishment (C–).

To judge my behavior as acceptable or not, good or bad, a success or a failure, valuable or worthless, I need to measure it against a standard that differentiates these qualitative judgments. That standard comprises my CVS and the level of acceptability that I assign for any particular part of my self. My covert valuing system comprises the range in which I could possibly exhibit any part of myself (e.g., any performance from 0–10 that could possibly characterize my softball experience) and the level of acceptability that I would place along that performance continuum. The judging and subsequent self-reinforcement or punishment occur when I actually match my behavior to my CVS. The results of this covert match determine the nature and extent of intrinsic consequences that I experience. To reiterate, the process of self-valuing, matching, and judging consists of the following steps:

1. A range (created from 0 to 10) of possible behavioral performances is formulated and stored within my covert memory. This objectively determined range reflects the worst to the best level of achievement that could be attained by any particular part of myself (behavior or attribute).

2. I behave or display some attribute.

3. A level of acceptability is ascertained for each performance or part of myself. This level represents the standard that I hold for myself for that particular behavior. This level may be set before, during, or after I perform. While my standard of performance is objective and norm referenced, my level of acceptability is subjective, arbitrary, and self-determined.

4. As I behave or experience different parts of myself, I consciously match my performance against my covert standard (level of acceptability) for that particular behavior. On some tasks for which I have acquired a high level of self-efficacy, my level of acceptability will appear relatively high—well above the normative average of 5. Inconsequential tasks for which a minimum performance is expected—and deemed adequate—might result in a level of acceptability well below 5.

5. When the part of myself that I experience achieves or exceeds my level of acceptability, I provide myself with intrinsic C+'s (and ⊠–'s). When the part of myself under consideration falls short of my level of acceptability, intrinsic C–'s and ⊠+'s occur.

## Choosing Our Level of Acceptability

**T**hrough the processes of social learning and the internalization of external contingencies and social norms discussed in Chapter 5, we acquire the information used to construct our covert valuing system. Just as the range of behaviors appearing in my CVS is constructed from my experience with the external world, to a large extent, the placement of my level of acceptability also reflect the norms of my social environment. Our life experiences teach us how we could be, just as our ongoing experience shows us how we are. Seldom do we attain the apex (ideal) of all possibilities. Instead, we generally experience ourselves somewhere between best and worst. Fortunately, we do not have to attain perfection or even the extrinsic C+'s of social acclamation to recognize and reinforce our own parts. Sometimes we do not even have to be very good. Our CVS allows us the discretion of choosing what parts we want to reinforce in ourselves. We can choose where we place our level of acceptability. For reasons that I will explain shortly, my level of acceptability for my performance in the softball game hovered around 2. My expectations were low and my C+'s were abundant.

As I have said, my level of acceptability for the picnic softball game hovered around 2 or 3. Consequently, I easily and consistently experienced myself at or above 2. Just the act of being on the field attained my level of acceptability and provided considerable intrinsic C+'s. As I took to the field and consumed myself with the joy of simply playing the game within my own capability, I could not help but exceed my level of acceptability at every turn. It felt so good to experience those parts of myself that I had kept dormant yet valued so much in my youth that the experience was truly worth doing, even if done poorly. Because my level of acceptability was so low, I had every opportunity and reason to reinforce myself intrinsically, even when my external consequences were devoid of C+'s.

In the distant past, when my legs, shoulder, and reflexes were new, my level of acceptability for these behaviors would have been much higher, and I would have had to perform exceedingly well to intrinsically reinforce myself. Over the years, my CVS range of behaviors has not changed, but my level of acceptability has. As a result of this reasonable developmental change in my standard for self-acceptance, I am able to participate enthusiastically in intrinsically reinforcing activities with the expectation that similar activities will be just as reinforcing in the future.

## The Subjective Nature of Our CVS

The C+'s that we experience from our external environment are subjective and derive their motivational power from the value we place on them, and the same can be said for intrinsic C+'s. Moreover, the C+'s that we receive from others do not necessarily equate to the C+'s that we give ourselves.

Regardless of how positively reinforcing the external world responds to my behavior (or any part that I consider to be me), if I do not process that feedback in like manner, I experience that part of me as unacceptable and unworthy of C+'s. For example, the contribution that I make to my colleagues in solving a difficult problem might be received with their admiration and praise, but might fall short of my own level of acceptability. Consequently, I may conclude that I have failed and denigrate myself accordingly. This disparity between my experience of extrinsic C+ and intrinsic C+ for the same behavior or attribute might be manifest as a feeling of guilt, dishonesty, or phoniness. The world may think that I am a competent, clever person, but I discount their praise in favor of my intrinsic judgment of incompetence and stupidity when I fail to attain my level of acceptability. Only when I achieve my level of acceptability can I truly experience the empowerment and motivational force of intrinsic positive reinforcement.

## The Motivational Effects of Our CVS

We all like to feel good about the self that we display to the world. Likewise, we are much more likely to learn and choose behaviors that rank at or above our level of acceptability regardless of where that level falls on our CVS. Positive reinforcement, whether achieved extrinsically or intrinsically, powerfully motivates future behavior. As a source of self-acceptance and motivator for future action, intrinsic C+'s are far more essential than any extrinsic consequences. Positive reinforcement from others is certainly a powerful influence, but it loses its power and significance when we fail to incorporate those extrinsic C+'s into our own intrinsic reinforcers. My self-judgment is the ultimate arbiter of whether I have succeeded or failed and whether I will chance subsequent efforts in the future. Even in the face of C−'s and ⊗+'s from a hostile and rejecting environment, my CVS allows me a measure of self-esteem through the mechanism of intrinsic positive and negative reinforcement. The energizing effect of achieving our level of acceptability is to be expected when we realize that covert expectations for intrinsic C+'s are as powerful in motivating our behavior as are our expectations for extrinsic C+'s. Let us look more closely at the motivational properties of our CVS.

As we think, feel, and interact with the external world, we constantly receive feedback on the nature of these covert and overt experiences. This feedback reveals significant information about how our external environment experiences and values our various parts. Over the course of our lifetime, we have experienced a multitude of extrinsic consequences from our external environment in response to most of those overt actions (and less so for the covert ones). We received many C+'s for some behaviors, perhaps many C−'s for others, and hardly any consequences at all for still others. To the extent that these contingencies, or simply contiguous associations, were consistently experienced over time, they were internalized and incorporated into our covert attributions and expectations. Where mom and dad once celebrated our athletic prowess or artistic creativity with generous portions of primary and secondary C+'s during our early years, we came to celebrate our own manifestations of these parts as we grew older. Once encountering (or even depending on) mom's C+'s for drawing a picture or investigating the wonders of the backyard, these same creative expressions and risk-taking behaviors became positively reinforcing in and of themselves. The act of doing the behavior created its own internal consequences that were separate from and even independent of any external consequences from the environment. Artwork produced for external praise and recognition in early childhood gradually attained a level of intrinsic satisfaction and value.

The same dynamic of intrinsic reinforcement (and thus motivation) can be said for the high of the distance runner, the rush of the thrill-seeking skydiver, or the bliss of the aficionado immersed in a favorite hobby. In each instance, the act of performing the operant behavior triggered biochemical changes that naturally and intrinsically felt good. Additionally, we probably accompanied these operant behaviors with covert self-talk replete with positive self-references such as: "Great job . . . I'm doing fine and having a wonderful time." Regardless of the behavior, the presence of an intrinsic C+ ensures a continued motivation "to just do it."

An opposite motivational effect occurs when our operant behavior is accompanied by negative or aversive covert experiences. When a particular behavior (or even the covert expectation of a b-c experience), such as public speaking or performing a difficult task, triggers severe anxiety, we quickly learn not to perform that behavior. To the extent that the physiological response of anxiety is experienced as a C−, we associate that behavior with intrinsic punishment and decrease its performance accordingly.

To add to our misery, we may even produce our own covert C–'s in the form of negative self-talk such as: "I can't to this." "I'm so stupid." "That was terrible." "What a failure." "I'm such a worthless fool." and so on ad nauseam. Whether the physical discomfort is accompanied by our own negative self-references (i.e., our negative judgments of self) or each occurs separately, the effect is to decrease or eliminate the offending behavior. Intrinsic C–'s exert a powerful influence over our covert and overt behavior. Let us look further at the covert experience of punishment.

## Intrinsic Punishment

Our thoughts and actions can be experienced negatively when they result in physiological pain or discomfort or when we cast a negative judgment on the thought or action in question. In the physiological case, often brought on by anxiety-inducing thoughts or actions or by the ingestion of noxious drugs, the intrinsic C– is physiological and autonomic in nature. Obsessive thoughts about extrinsic C–'s (e.g., physical injury or abuse by others) automatically provoke our autonomic nervous system to acute levels of anxiety. Although these acute levels of anxiety (i.e., our SUDS level) are our body's general adaptation to stress, their physiological experience can only be characterized as a C–.

Likewise, most addictive drugs (e.g., heroin, cocaine, alcohol, tobacco, and even caffeine) start as a physiological C+ but quickly become a C– as our body establishes greater tolerance levels and withdrawal symptoms. Under advanced states of drug addiction, removal of the physiological pain of withdrawal is enough to sustain the addictive habit. Many of those addicted to opiates or alcohol have long ceased to experience any C+'s from their substance of choice; their addictive behavior is instead motivated by the escape from pain (thus ⊠–) that briefly results from their next score.

We experience intrinsic punishment much more frequently when we "judge" ourselves (any of our parts) as inadequate, unacceptable, and somewhere below our covert level of acceptability. Whenever we consciously experience ourselves as less than we should, must, or ought to be and then castigate ourselves for our inadequacy, we are creating intrinsic punishment. I have deliberately used the word "creating" because this form of intrinsic punishment is the result of a conscious, volitional judgment and decision that we make about ourselves. When we drag out our covert measuring sticks to assess the quantitative and qualitative nature of how we experience ourselves, we choose the standards of acceptability against which these parts are judged as well as the substance of what we tell ourselves about how well we measure up. Whenever we experience negative self-references (usually in the form of self-talk) that denigrate, castigate, belittle, demean, criticize, or in any way cast a negative judgment about any part of ourselves, we are making a choice based on our judgment that we have failed to attain some internalized standard of acceptability.

Does any of this self-talk sound familiar "I look terrible in shorts because my legs are too fat." "How stupid of me to forget my father's birthday." "The B that I got in my geometry class only shows how dumb I am in math." "What a failure I've become; 2 years on the job and still no promotion." "I hate feeling afraid and timid in front of guys." "Why would any girl want to go out with a nerd like me?"

These negative self-references have the same basic ingredients of intrinsic punishment. They each derived from judgments that were made when a part of our experience of self was found to be deficient when matched with a covert standard of acceptability. The actual standard employed in each instance was learned and internalized to form a subjective and quite arbitrary judgment. Leg size, grades, promotions, dating success, and even periodic memory loss retain no absolute value. The particular value placed on the manifestation of each part is strictly a subjective judgment call. Based on other standards I could have learned and internalized, I might have judged my B grade as a major achievement, my employment history as indicative of job security and perseverance, my nonassertiveness as caution and selectivity, and even my large legs as just fine for getting me around.

Choosing to provide intrinsic punishment for parts of ourselves that we find deficient is a painful and debilitating pattern of covert behavior that can render us severely anxious and even immobilized if taken to extremes of scope and frequency. Just as intrinsic C+'s motivate us to think and behave in increasing measure (and feel good about in the process), intrinsic C–'s cause a decrease in the behaviors we deem unacceptable. Additionally, intrinsic C–'s create even higher expectations for experiencing comparable B–C–'s in the future, thus elevating our anxiety level. Ultimately, intrinsic C–'s cause us to feel bad about that part of ourselves. Intrinsic extinction also depresses the scope of our behavior and the tenor of our emotions.

## Intrinsic Extinction

We can provide intrinsic C+'s for ourselves and we can also deny ourselves any form of self-reinforcement. A covert world devoid of positive self-references and intrinsic reinforcers is a realm of thinking and feeling under extinction. Under conditions of covert extinction, our covert and overt behavior occurs without those crucial motivating C+'s that we provide for ourselves. Thoughts and actions receiving no intrinsic C+'s cease to become a source of self-acceptance, value, and esteem. Even if our external world continues to value, praise, and extrinsically reinforce certain parts of our selves, if we fail to internalize, confirm, and validate those C+'s, we lose our motivation to display those parts. Without this motivation to think, feel and behave, we stop doing them. Our thinking becomes narrow and repetitive, our emotions become flat and hollow, and our actions diminish in scope and intensity. A great deal of the covert and overt experience of who we are is diminished under the rubric of extinction, and the starvation that we experience from a stringent diet of self-reinforcement is as debilitating as if life's basic nutrients were withheld from our body. Intrinsic extinction leaves us without hope, optimism, an expectation for pleasure, and an empowering sense of self.

## Depression As Covert Intrinsic Extinction

While intrinsic punishment fills our thoughts with specters of C–'s and the anxiety associated with the experience or expectation of C–'s, covert extinction actually drains our enthusiasm and hope for life's pleasures, rendering us emotionally flat and unaroused. When we cease to experience the intrinsic C+'s in everyday behavior and cannot find reason to positively reinforce ourselves for what we do and who we are, our lives lose a sense of value and purpose. Although we may go through the motions of daily routine, we do so without joy and vigor. The mobilizing and energizing forces of anticipation of C+'s simply do not occur, and we find ourselves unable to generate the energy and reason to do much of anything. Consequently, we find ourselves doing less and less.

Likewise, as the scope and intensity of our actions decrease, we find less behavior (or fewer parts) to actually self-reinforce. This insidious spiral of declining activity and covert extinction can propel us along a continuum from transitory "downtime" to the depths of despair. We all know this continuum as depression, whether our actual encounter with it is a brief period of the blahs or the pervasive immersion into hopelessness leading to thoughts of suicide.

Our inability to experience intrinsic positive reinforcement, whether momentarily or chronically, can stem from a learned cognitive style that accentuates an external locus of control for any C+'s that might be experienced and any actions that might succeed in bringing about any C+'s. This external LOC encompasses both the attributions for the causes of C+'s as well as the expectations of any future C+'s. The more pronounced this covert distortion becomes, the stronger the sense of helplessness and hopelessness that consumes one's entire covert experience. This helplessness (Maier & Seligman, 1976) and hopelessness (Abramson, Metalsky, & Alloy, 1989) that we consider to be the covert ingredients of depression can have varied sources. While many prominent researchers and clinicians emphasize the nurture (i.e., learning) side of the covert extinction phenomenon, other studies (Weiss, Simson, Ambrose, Webster, & Hoffman, 1985) point to the biological etiology of this pessimistic experience of ourselves in the world.

Robert Hedaya (1996) cites a number of brain imaging studies suggesting that dysregulation of neurotransmitter dopamine within our accumbens nucleus, the pleasure center located in our limbic system, is a major cause of severe depression. While abnormally low levels of dopamine are associated with depression, inordinately high levels accompany states of mania and an unrealistic sense of optimism and well-being. Regardless of its etiology (nature or nurture), tenure (chronic or acute), or severity (mild sadness, dysthymia, or bipolar depressive psychosis), the result of a covert world devoid of intrinsic C+'s is individuals who care little about themselves, their future, and their capacity to experience the C+'s that make life worth living.

## Intrinsic Extinction and Our Level of Acceptability

Intrinsic extinction can readily be understood within the context of our covert valuing system. When everything I do (or any part of my experience of self) falls below my level of acceptability, and any C+'s that I might experience from my environment appear unwarranted or independent of my actions, I cease to self-reinforce. Whether or not I concurrently castigate my "perceived" inadequacies with intrinsic punishment, my self-imposed restriction of C+'s provides the basic ingredients for depression and low self-esteem. Regardless of how accomplished I am (as perceived by others), if my

**Calvin and Hobbes**

Happiness and self-C+'s often require us to accept the B's that we actually do, even if short of our dreams.
(© 1995 Watterson/Dist. by Universal Press Syndicate.)

covert judgments of myself consistently fall below my level of acceptability, I will experience intrinsic extinction. Perfectionists whose level of acceptability constantly hovers above 8 or 9 seldom experience intrinsic C+'s unless they constantly achieve perfection. As admirable as the attainment of perfection might be in theory, the reality for most of us is the experience of a broad range of selves, with some parts deserving of C+'s for only the highest level of achievement and other parts for just occurring. We will return to the topic of perfectionism later in this chapter. But first a word about imperfection: the reality in most of our lives.

As a teacher, I maintain a relatively high standard in evaluating my classroom performance, and thus in granting myself C+'s. Most of the time my high level of acceptability matches my teaching performance. Occasionally, however, a lesson will "bomb" or I will be unable to motivate or help a student. It is during these down times that I confront the choice of castigating myself for poor teaching or finding reason to lower my level of acceptability. In choosing the former, I settle for a period of self-doubt and the blues, knowing that my mood will lift within a few successful teaching experiences. Choosing the latter, I must re-frame my performance as acceptable under the circumstances. Through this re-framing, or rationalization process, I am able to explain (or attribute) my performance as caused by factors outside of my control (my students were tired, the room was too hot) or by factors that are not a true measure of my ability (so I had a bad class, we all do; even the best hitters have 0 for 5 games). As a mediocre tennis player, a low level of acceptability would enable me to positively reinforce the simple completion of an entire set, a performance at the 3 or 4 level. In the unconditional positive reinforcement category, I have lots of parts that warrant C+'s simply for being. Physical characteristics for which I have no responsibility or control, comforting habits that hurt no one yet produce nothing of particular value, hobbies and interests that I intrinsically enjoy yet reveal my total ineptitude, and even my ability to sustain a pulse rate are all parts of myself that deserve the very lowest level of acceptability. If I can always give myself C+'s for maintaining my pulse rate, I will never experience a day without some C+'s, as long as my experience is conscious and alive. I have often found comfort and encouragement in William Purkey's belief that if something is truly worth doing, it is worth doing poorly (Purkey & Novak, 1984). This recognition of the value of trying and simply doing for the sake of doing are crucial to our experience of intrinsic positive reinforcement, our maintenance of a positive self-concept, and ultimately our sense of optimism and purpose in life.

The fact that we experience our selves as falling at or above our level of acceptability does not necessarily mean that those selves (covert and overt behavior) are productive, valued by others, or even meeting a social standard of morality. To experience ourselves within the acceptable range of our CVS only provides the occasion for self-acceptance and esteem. I may behave as an arrogant prig, aggressively bullying my way through life, and come to value (and intrinsically reinforce) my violent or obnoxious behavior. Each successful act of intimidation might prompt my self-aggrandizement and enhance my self-esteem as a powerful figure. In contrast, gestures of compassion or benevolence would fall well below my level of acceptability. Violent youth offenders do not suffer from low self-esteem, but rather process their violent behavior as evidence of strength, power, and control—all falling well above their level of acceptability. In contradicting the prevailing belief that violent aggressive bullies suffer from low self-esteem, Baumeister, Smart, & Boden (1996) illustrate the subjective and amoral nature of our CVS. Where we experience ourselves within our CVS is a function of personal choice, not an objective standard of virtue and morality. The world is replete with self-hating heroes and pompous criminals. Perhaps our occasional hubris might best be challenged by reasoned adjustments in our levels of acceptability.

## Optimism, Pessimism, and the Orientation of Our CVS

**O**ur self is the aggregate of all of our parts. Our self-esteem represents our judgment about the worth, value, goodness, and competence of that self. Positive self-esteem and the experience of intrinsic positive reinforcement are synonymous.

The intrinsic C+'s that are so integral to self-esteem and the motivation to approach life with optimism and enthusiasm are a direct function of how we position our level of acceptability within our CVS. Ideally, our level of acceptability coincides with our operant behavior (and other parts of our self) in such a way that intrinsic reinforcement is our usual covert experience. The match between our perception of self (i.e., all of our parts) and our level of acceptability ensures a healthy, positive self-esteem and a strong expectation for continued success. But what happens when our level of acceptability is too low (i.e., 1–4)? Do we become complacent and continually settle for mediocrity? Does a low level of acceptability deplete our aspirations and destroy our motivation to do well? Not necessarily.

Keep in mind that intrinsic C+'s positively reinforce behavior in the same manner as extrinsic C+'s and that positively reinforced behavior recurs or even increases in frequency under similar antecedent conditions. This dynamic explains the motivational effects of even the lowest level of acceptability. I will use a cooking example to illustrate this point.

Let us say that I cook an abysmal meal for my family, perhaps undercooking some dishes and rendering the others unpalatable. My wife prudently decides to begin her long-delayed diet early into the meal and my kids scramble for the leftover pizza in the refrigerator. No extrinsic C+'s are forthcoming from this bunch for my culinary efforts. As I dive into the repast of chewy potatoes and "blackened" meatloaf, I marvel at my creative machinations of fire and food. Sure, it's not up to the standard of our typical fare. But it's a real dinner, and I cooked it myself. My level of acceptability is real low on this one, and I have attained it with morsels to spare.

Because I attained my level of acceptability as a novice cook, I felt successful in my efforts and enthusiastically attempted other recipes (while my wife and kids added their own options to the family menu). Each attempt, though modest in scope and difficulty, taught me new skills and familiarized me with the nuances of culinary art. I even envisioned the day when my family might return to my table and delight in my creations. Each new effort was reinforced by my ability to achieve my level of acceptability, and each new effort improved my skill and confidence. With time, my level of acceptability for the chef part of me gradually rose. But at no time did I allow it to climb out of easy reach. When my culinary risk taking took the express lane to the garbage can, I just reinforced myself for trying. And on those rare occasions when my efforts did produce a "superb" meal that approached 7 or 8 on my CVS, I simply continued to reinforce myself while enjoying the praises of my astonished family.

Although I might have attained a relatively high level on my CVS, my level of acceptability remained fluid and relatively low. Although I could continually reinforce myself for attaining 3s and 4s (and even an occasional 2), I improved my skills and continued to enjoy the experience. Had I left my level of acceptability at my highest level of attainment, in this case 7 or 8, I would not have continued on a path of success and improvement; in fact, I might have relinquished the entire cooking endeavor to my wife. Exceptionally high levels of acceptability promote perfectionism, and perfectionism leaves no margin for error.

## Perfectionism and Our Level of Acceptability

Perfection is the achievement of the highest degree possible. Behaviorally, it means to be completely skilled or informed and able to perform an action without defect or flaw. Individuals who set exceedingly high goals or standards for themselves or for others are thought to be perfectionists. When viewed within the context of our CVS, perfectionism is the practice of maintaining our levels of acceptability at the top rungs of our scale. As we approach 8, 9, and 10, we are approaching perfection as the criterion for intrinsic C+'s. With levels of acceptability at the highest rungs, we leave very little margin for intrinsic C+'s and considerable room for intrinsic punishment and extinction. Perfectionists may succeed gloriously in the attainment of perfection but are highly vulnerable to the pain and discouragement of intrinsic C+'s and C−'s when they fail to measure up.

The effects of extrinsic punishment and extinction on the decline of operant behavior can be just as pronounced when the two aversive consequences are experienced intrinsically. When any behavior (or part of our selves) is consistently devoid of intrinsic C+'s and even provokes intrinsic C−'s, the probability of performing that behavior declines, and thus we become less motivated to perform that behavior in the future. If our criterion for intrinsic C+ is perfection the probability is fairly high that we will not succeed (unless, of course, we attain perfection with relative ease and frequency, an experience that very few of us encounter).

For those very gifted and unique individuals who do attain perfection and its concomitant intrinsic C+ with some degree of regularity (and expectancy), their covert experience will continue to motivate their efforts. For the remainder of us, the attainment of perfection is slim at best, and as our only level of acceptability, it leaves us dissatisfied and lacking. In reference to my earlier cooking anecdote, had I maintained my level of acceptability within the 7–10 range, I would have quickly acknowledged my failure and given up. Even when I did attain a rare 7 or 8, my ongoing intrinsic C+ and motivation to try were sustained by maintaining my level of acceptability in the 3–5 range. I did not need to attain perfection to feel good about my performance or myself.

Our discussion of the undesirable characteristics of perfectionism is not meant to imply that we should strive for mediocrity and renounce standards of excellence. We all want to perform at our best and we all need to achieve certain levels of excellence in some of our attributes or behavior. To strive to be the very best at our vocation, our relationships, and even our hobbies is an essential ingredient to growth and change. The primary point is that we can maintain our levels of acceptability at readily attainable positions while we strive for excellence. When so much of our unhappiness and self-criticism is a function of unattainable levels of acceptability, is it any wonder that so many of us simply give up and refuse to try?

Rather than motivate conscientious effort and risk taking, perfectionism often leads to surrender and withdrawal. Why try when the probability of perfection is negligible? We have all known highly competent and accomplished perfectionists who ultimately relinquish their struggle for perfection by giving up entirely. The creative musician who will not play, the talented athlete who will not compete, and the brilliant writer who cannot finish a paragraph are often the tragic victims of a perfectionistic CVS.

A more common example of this sad preoccupation is bright, gifted students who have chosen the course of least effort rather than the challenge of success. The saddest aspect of their choice is that instead of lowering their level of acceptability to coincide with their diminished performance—and experience some measure of intrinsic C+— they leave their level of acceptability at the top of their scale and resigned their fate to intrinsic extinction and punishment. Frankly, I would much rather reinforce myself for a deficient behavior or attribute than never feel that I warranted intrinsic C+'s. As I said earlier, some days I find it comforting to reinforce myself for maintaining a pulse rate. For when all else fails, I can probably maintain my pulse.

## Our Orientation to Success or Avoidance of Failure

**A** motivation to perform and achieve that derives from a high expectation of intrinsic C+'s is a *success orientation* (Atkinson, 1983). But the covert expectation for extrinsic and intrinsic C+'s is not the only dynamic that motivates our behavior. Covert, intrinsic negative reinforcement (i.e., $\cancel{C}$–'s) also motivates us in powerful but insidious ways. The covert experience of punishing, castigating, or criticizing ourselves for failing to attain our level of acceptability is certainly unpleasant. Intense

Perfection—that elusive expectation that keeps us from celebrating what we actually have. (Reprinted with permission of King Features Syndicate.)

and frequent forms of covert self-abuse are very powerful intrinsic C–'s, and their avoidance or escape can provide very strong motivation. This motivation to avoid intrinsic punishment (i.e., to avoid self-criticism, denigration, and the terrible things that we say and feel about ourselves when we fail to attain our level of acceptability) can be a primary orientation toward life (Atkinson, 1983). This avoidance orientation finds us motivated by the desperate desire to avoid the pain of intrinsic C–'s rather than the expectation of intrinsic C+'s. Under an avoidance orientation, we may never positively reinforce ourselves and give ourselves praise, recognition, or a pat on the back because our level of acceptability for intrinsic C+'s is unattainable. Instead, what might be attainable if we just work hard enough is the avoidance of failure and its accompanying wrath (from self and others). The critical objective for our behavior under this covert valuing system is avoiding failure rather than attaining success.

Is your behavior more oriented toward achieving success (C+'s) or avoiding failure (C–'s)? If your answer is avoiding failure, you may accomplish a great deal, but your only satisfaction will derive from your belief that you avoided or escaped from another bad experience. Where are the extrinsic and intrinsic C+'s in those experiences? Remember, even though both positive (C+) and negative (C–) reinforcement motivate us to behave, only the former gives us the satisfaction of competence and self-efficacy (Clifford, 1990).

Throughout our discussion of the many facets of our CVS, the common thread that ran through each covert experience was some form of judgment. Whether stemming from catching a ball, cooking a meal, commenting at a meeting, writing a sentence, looking at my reflection in a mirror, or any of the myriad parts that I might display, each covert reality is replete with self-valuing judgments. The nature of those covert experiences and the disposition of those judgments are likewise framed with physical sensations and covert labels that we know as emotions. Our experience of emotions involves integrating all of the elements operating without our covert reality; consequently, our exploration into this uniquely human phenomenon of emotion can best (and only) be left for last. Our attention to the A-B-C's (or more accurately, our covert a-b-c's) of human emotion will conclude our story of the A-B-C model.

## Chapter Summary

**1.** Our covert valuing system serves as our repository for all of those standards that we initially observed and experienced from our external environment and then internalized.

**2.** This covert valuing system provides levels of acceptability for assessing our thoughts and actions and then judging their worth, value, importance, or success.

**3.** Each time we use our covert valuing system, we make a positive or negative judgment about where we experience ourselves relative to our level of acceptability.

**4.** When we fall above our level of acceptability, we provide ourselves with intrinsic C+'s/X–'s. When we fall below our level of acceptability, we self-punish or deny ourselves any intrinsic C+'s.

**5.** The intrinsic consequences that we create for ourselves are subjective in nature and may or may not correspond to the extrinsic consequences that we receive from our environment.

**6.** The most significant and motivating C+'s that we experience are the ones that we give ourselves.

**7.** Excessive intrinsic X+'s can lead to depression. Excessive intrinsic C–'s can cause intense fear and anxiety.

**8.** Frequent and attainable intrinsic C+'s lead to a sense of self-efficacy, positive self-esteem, and strong motivation to "do" and strive to achieve.

**9.** Perfection in any behavior or attribute is the attainment of a 10 on our CVS. Perfectionism is the practice of placing our level of acceptability at this level of perfection. Consequently, perfectionism leaves no margin for error in giving ourselves intrinsic C+'s. Anything below a 10 is unacceptable, and undeserving of C+'s (or deserving of intrinsic C–'s).

**10.** While achievement of success (intrinsic C+'s) is a strong motivator to behave, the avoidance of failure (i.e., intrinsic X–) can be just as motivational, but is much less enjoyable.

**Figure 1** *The A-B-C (Cognitive–Behavioral) Model*

| (A) Antecedent | | (B) Behavior | | (C) Consequence |
|---|---|---|---|---|
| | Covert | Overt | Overt | |
| | Cognitive (Thinking) | Respondent (Physical) | Operant (Acting) | |
| Stimulus or setting event. External environments that set the occasion for behavior (thinking, acting, feeling) to occur.<br><br>$S^{Dee}$ = Green light. A cue that a particular behavior will result in a desirable consequence.<br><br>$S^{Delta}$ = Red light. A cue that a particular behavior will result in an undesirable consequence. | Subjective environment. The process and content of our thinking. Our interpretation of A-B-C as a-b-c.<br><br>Includes:<br>Attributions<br>Expectations<br>Self-concept<br>Self-esteem<br>Beliefs<br>Attitudes<br>Prejudices<br>Self-talk<br>Locus of control<br>Images<br>Fantasies<br>Intrinsic consequences | Reflexive<br>Autonomic<br>Involuntary<br>Biochemical<br>Physiological changes occurring within our body. | Voluntary behavior that we choose to do or not to do.<br><br>Can be: Excess = Behavior done too often or at wrong time.<br><br>Deficit = Behavior done too infrequently or not when needed. | Events (external) that occur during and/or after a particular covert and/or operant behavior. Events can be:<br><br>A. Desirable:<br>1. Positive Reinforcement present desirable = C+<br><br>2. Negative Reinforcement remove undesirable = C̶<br><br>B. Undesirable:<br>1. Punishment present undesirable, aversive = C−<br><br>2. Extinction remove desirable = C̶ |

**Emotions**

Subjective labels used to describe a specific state of being. Labels reflect the composite of our covert, respondent, and operant behavior within a specific context of antecedents and consequences.

# Chapter 12

～～～～～

# Our Covert Experience
# of Emotion

～～～～～

## Orienting Ourselves

It would take a monumental effort to try to synthesize and distill the scientific literature on the topic of human emotion. Moreover, it would be well beyond my capacity to bring coherence to the infinite ways in which our poetry and prose address the
subject. Suffice it to say that the scientific community has a cogent, lucid understanding of the biochemical/behavioral elements of emotion, although it does not approach
the eloquence with which our poets capture the essence of this most human state of
experiencing. In this chapter, I will consider features of emotion and feeling that fit
naturally within our study of the A-B-C model. Once again, a glance at the relevant
parts of the model.

## Emotional Memory and the Biology of Temperament

Any discussion of the A-B-C's of human emotion must begin with the biological
foundation that forms the basis for our earliest experiences of life. This foundation comprises our genetic pool, which influences how we perceive and act on the
world. Our genes provide the basic instructions for our biological processes, which in
turn determine the manner in which our brain anatomy and physiology process information from every part of our external and internal environment. These innate (genetic) regulations of our brain chemistry influence our covert world, and consequently,
the manner (action plans) with which we engage our external world. This biologically
based dimension of our covert and overt behavior has been referred to as *temperament*
(Cloninger, Svrakic, & Przybeck, 1993).

Our temperament represents our genetic predisposition to think and behave. It results from the way our brain processes neurotransmitters, hormones, and the other
chemicals so crucial to our thinking and our experience of emotion. Because temperament and emotion are so integrally connected, our temperament has been framed as
the wellspring of our emotional memory (Hamer & Copeland, 1998). Genetically determined brain chemistry orchestrates our emotional behavior by regulating our limbic

system—locus of our most powerful drives—moods, and nonconscious covert activity. Within this emotional center of the brain are the roots of fear, aggression, lust, and pleasure (Hamer & Copeland, 1998). From birth, these emotional responses (i.e., emotional memory) are expressed in patterns of thinking, feeling, and behaving that define our particular temperament. Inordinately high or low levels of some neurotransmitters resulting from dysregulation can result in excessive fearfulness (i.e., high harm avoidance) or fearlessness (i.e., high novelty seeking or low harm avoidance). Likewise, neurotransmitter dysregulation can result in excessive dependence on pleasure (i.e., high reward dependence) or an absence of motivation for C+'s of any kind (i.e., low reward dependence and novelty seeking). These innate tendencies form the basic temperaments that have been identified by behavior geneticists and psychologists (Cloninger, 1987; Hamer & Copeland, 1998; Kagan, 1994). Let us look at how three of these temperaments might influence our covert experience of emotion.

The biological roots of temperament have been extensively studied in children (Kagan, Reznick & Snidman, 1988) as well as adults (Cloninger, Adolfsson & Svrakic, 1996; Zuckerman, 1995). Although there is some disagreement about the core traits of different temperaments, researchers have identified three independent temperamental qualities: (1) harm avoidance; (2) reward dependence; and (3) novelty seeking. Each of us displays some degree of each of these temperamental qualities, for each quality we have can fall along a continuum from low to high. A review of each temperament will show their individual variability as well as some of their interrelationship.

**1.** *Harm Avoidance* This temperament reflects our reactivity to aversive stimuli. High levels on this quality cause feelings of fear, anxiety, and worry. This inborn aversion to antecedent stimuli creates and maintains high expectations for C−'s and produces a behavioral response style called inhibition (Kagan, 1994). While high levels of human avoidance cause fearfulness, shyness, and pessimism, low levels are associated with uninhibited optimism, confidence, risk taking, and high levels of novelty seeking (Cloninger, Svrakic, & Przybeck, 1993).

**2.** *Novelty Seeking* The intensity of response (arousal) in expectation for or response to novel stimuli characterizes this temperament. Arousal and pleasure in response to past, present, or future C+'s/C−'s determine the degree to which we are novelty seeking. High levels on this quality exhibit exhilaration in response to novel stimuli, activities, and experiences. The high expectation for C+'s (and the belief that most experiences will produce them) activates behavior and causes the novelty seeker to explore, take risks, and act (often impulsively without consideration of the negative consequences). Novelty seekers tend to be disorganized, unpredictable, intolerant of structure, and easily bored. Low levels of novelty seeking manifest rigid consistency, compulsive routine, and indecisiveness. Moderate levels produce reflective decision making, reliability, and cautiousness (Hamer & Copeland, 1998).

**3.** *Reward Dependence* Reward dependence also relates to the expectation and experience of C+'s/C−'s, but describes more closely the addictive quality that connects specific B-C+/C− contingencies. High reward dependence reveals persistence and craving for gratification, extreme sensitivity to rejection and addictive preoccupation with the desired C+/C−. The individual is inordinately motivated to maintain previously reinforced

**Figure 11** *Covert Behavior*

| **Cognitive (Thinking)** |
| --- |

Subjective environment. The process and content of our thinking.
Our interpretation of A-B-C as a-b-c.

Includes:
Attributions
Expectations
Self-concept
Self-esteem
Beliefs
Attitudes
Prejudices
Self-talk
Locus of control
Images
Fantasies
Intrinsic consequences

| **Emotions** |
| --- |

Subjective labels used to describe a specific state of being. Labels reflect the composite of our covert, respondent, and operant behavior within a specific context of antecedents and consequences.

behavior at any cost (Cloninger, Svrakic, & Przybeck, 1993). People low on reward dependence are unmotivated by external C+'s. Because social approval and other forms of social C+'s are inconsequential to someone low on this temperament, they will display nonconformity, independence, and social detachment to the point of antisocial aggression. Extreme forms of this temperament can range from substance addiction at the high end to anhedonia and severe depression at the low extreme.

I will close this discussion of temperament with a temperamental qualification. Although these qualities of temperament inform our emotional memory from birth, they are not the sole program for the A-B-C's of our experience. While the behavior geneticists and researchers cited previously appreciate the biological bases for our temperament, and thus for our thoughts and actions, they fully recognize the place of nurture in the formula for human experience. Hamer and Copeland (1998) highlight this critical relationship of nurture and nature when they say:

Just because a person is born with a particular temperament, however, doesn't mean there is a simple set of instructions or blueprints. Nor does temperament mean that people are "stuck" with their personalities from birth. On the contrary, one of the marvelous features of temperament is built-in flexibility that allows us to adapt to life's hurdles and challenges. Growing up means not only learning the ways of the world, but also how to deal with yourself. Psychologists call this more flexible aspect of personality "character." (p. 7)

We now turn our attention to the emotional dynamics of our character that inform and enrich our covert experience.

## Emotion: An Integrative Covert Experience

**D**aniel Goleman (1995) refers to our covert experience of the world as comprising two separate yet interdependent realities: the rational experience of our neocortex and the emotional experience of our limbic system. Both experiences "operate in tight harmony for the most part, intertwining their very different ways of knowing to guide us through the world" (Goleman, 1995, p. 9). Goleman (1995) concludes that "ordinarily there is a balance between emotional and rational minds, with emotion feeding into and forming the operations of the rational mind and the rational mind refining and sometimes vetoing the inputs of the emotions" (p. 9). According to Goleman (1995), these two aspects of our covert experience are interconnected through our brain circuitry, with "feelings essential to thought, and thought to feeling" (p. 9). This conclusion is especially instructive, for it suggests that the terms "feelings" and "thought" might be used interchangeably with "emotion" and "rationality," respectively. To better clarify and distinguish the elements that comprise our emotional experience, I will use "feeling" and "thought" to represent our conscious experience of emotion. We experience emotion only by feeling sensory stimulation and thinking about the sensation.

Our illustration of the dental appointment that introduced the A-B-C model in Chapter 1 is an example of feelings and thoughts stimulating each other in the production of emotion. I will highlight the anecdote and then analyze each component.

The appointment example begins with a postcard from the dentist that it is "checkup time again." Let us say that this antecedent stimulus was accompanied by "bumping into your dentist at the local supermarket" just a few days after you began to experience a severe toothache. In response to these stimuli (A's), we generated three different behavioral options that ranged from making the appointment immediately, delaying it temporarily, to refusing to even consider it. Each choice presented its own series of physical and behavioral actions and consequences, and each scenario generated its own cadre of emotions. Before we identify the array of emotions, we need to define their basic elements.

## The Physiology of Emotion: Feeling

**L**ong before our thinking brain became what it is today, we felt what it was to be human. Starting from our sense of smell, we began to understand and interact with the world through the modalities of sight, sound, touch, and taste. These sensory impulses coursing through our primitive central nervous system found their locus and command center in the ring of neurons capping our brain stem called the *limbic system*. Within this bundle of neurons, the raw sensory impulses passing through our nose, eyes, ears, tongue, and skin were integrated, transformed into meaningful signals, and even stored in primitive memory areas.

Two parts of the limbic system were particularly crucial in the integration and transformation of sensory data, as they still are today: the amygdala and the hippocampus. Although all sensory impulses entering our limbic system pass through the thalamus, raw electrochemical sensations are translated into usable messages in the amygdala, the next stop in the sensory journey. Working in conjunction with the memory storage centers of the hippocampus, the amygdala's extensive web of neural connections allows it to store information from past experiences, compare new sensory data with previously stored information, and stimulate the body's autonomic nervous system response to a potential threat. Through its capacity to stimulate key centers of our respondent behavior (i.e., the physiological arousal mechanisms of our autonomic nervous system described in Chapter 6), the amygdala can trigger arousal even before our neo (frontal) cortex formulates conscious meaning to the incoming sensory message. As Goleman (1995) explains, "The amygdala can have us spring to action while the slightly slower more fully informed—neocortex unfolds its more refined plan for reaction" (p. 18). Painful, aversive, or even intensely joyful experiences are imprinted in these critical limbic areas in such a way that the amygdala records the intensity of the feeling while the hippocampus registers the specific sensory patterns that accompany the feeling (LeDoux, 1994).

## The Amygdala–Hippocampus Partnership

Thus, we have an "emotional" partnership in which the hippocampus retains the content (specific context and perceptual patterns) of emotional memories while the amygdala stimulates our physiological arousal associated with those memories. This partnership of unconscious emotional responses operates to record and store original experiences as physiologically arousing and to subsequently stimulate (mobilize) our autonomic response whenever elements of the stored memory are stimulated and recognized in our hippocampus. The greater the intensity of feeling the more rapidly the amygdala–hippocampus dyad mobilizes the body's response. Our amygdala first responds to life-threatening emergencies that instantaneously elicit our fight-or-flight response and then works with the hippocampus to store the memory for future reference. This reaction serves as our early warning system and first defense against threatening stimuli from our external environment. Its rapid, almost reflexive response occurs without our conscious awareness.

Our autonomic response of arousal and mobilized action enables us to cope with the crisis of a real or imagined C– even before our conscious mind can integrate and interpret sensory data arriving in our left frontal cortex. Although the intense feeling of anxiety and arousal first arises from our amygdala, the accompanying thought of imminent danger (conscious covert expectation for C–) trails behind. An abrupt injury, excessive noise, life-threatening crisis, aversive encounter with another person (or animal, e.g., a neighbor's dog), or any traumatic experience registers in this feeling memory of our amygdala–hippocampus even before it is perceived and understood by our frontal cortex.

Once recorded in our feeling memory, we can then use our frontal cortex to reflect on the experience. It is only during this conscious reflection stage that we "label" the feeling and give meaning to the experience. Our rational coping strategies are also considered at this stage of emotional experience. Only upon reflection of the feeling and contextual parts of the experience do we conclude that we are scared, angry, elated, sad, or any emotional label. Because our amygdala–hippocampus partnership can trigger very strong physical arousal without conscious attention by our thinking brain, we can refer to the amygdala–hippocampus partnership as the "feeling" part of emotion in contrast to the "thinking" part of emotion that occurs within our frontal cortex.

## Feelings and the Dental Appointment

So how does this unconscious partnership relate to our reaction to the dental appointment? Since painful, noxious, or threatening experiences are registered by our amygdala–hippocampus centers as feeling emotions, it is quite possible that an early childhood experience with dental pain still exists within our feeling memory. The pain of a decayed tooth, dental filling, or extraction that once provoked the autonomic response of anxiety and mobilization for fight or flight can imprint a feeling memory that needs only the slightest reminder to reestablish its prominence over our physiology. Sights, sounds, smells, tastes, and sensations associated with the original experience are enough to stimulate our entire alarm reaction. The faint sound of a drill, smell of dental materials, sight of a dental chair (or even little cups with serrated edges), or sensation of metal objects in your mouth are enough to trigger acute anxiety.

Perhaps at an earlier time, especially at the time of your original experience, this early warning system was necessary or helpful to your well-being. As illustrated in our discussion of the general adaptation system, physiological arousal is critical to effective coping, but only when the C– is real and imminent. Arousal during combat, a severe accident, intense competition, or a challenge to our survival is critically valuable. Unfortunately, arousal that stems from only the memory of those events can immobilize us as well as be injurious to our health.

## Feelings and Our Memory of Pleasure

Fortunately, it is not just strong negative feelings that occupy our emotional emergency. At the other end of the continuum, unconscious emotional memories can also be created by strong positive feelings of elation and pleasure. The peak experiences of joy experienced during our earliest years of life, even before our acquisition of language, are programmed into our amygdala–hippocampus circuitry.

Our feeling emotion is diligent in matching current experience with those in the emotional memory of our amygdala–hippocampus. This constant matching is strictly associative and without rational thought. "When one key element of a present situation is similar to the past, it can call it a 'match'—which is why this circuit is sloppy: it acts before there is full confirmation" (Goleman, 1995, p. 21). These unconscious feeling emotions cause us to "react to the present in ways that were imprinted long ago, with thoughts, emotions, reactions learned in response to events perhaps only dimly similar, but close enough to alarm the amygdala" (Goleman, 1995, p. 21). Our experience of these feeling emotions can range from joyous bliss to sheer terror. This subtle matching of present to past might result in an inexplicable experience of déjà vu or could induce the acute anxiety of a posttraumatic stress disorder (LeDoux, 1989). In either case, the neural alarm of our autonomic nervous system sounded before our thinking brain could reflect on and understand the real nature of the experience. This alarm function needs further discussion.

These emotional states triggered by our feeling memory can also serve as an early warning system, revealing our gut feelings about a particular experience. Often referred to as intuition, these activated emotional memories alert us to potential danger or pleasure. When triggered by some antecedent stimulus, these bodily sensations signal caution in a course of action or heightened anticipation of some inexplicable sense of pleasure. Although unconscious at their inception, these feeling emotions may continue to build until their intensity breaks the threshold of awareness and consciousness. At this point, the physical manifestations of feeling emotion draw our attention to our increased perspiration, respiration, and heart rate, muscle tension, dry mouth, and many other physiological substrata of our autonomic nervous system. We are now ready to acknowledge that we are highly anxious and fearful of seeing a dentist for our painful tooth. With consciousness, we are able to integrate our feeling emotion into the vast network of critical activity that comprises our ability to reflect, solve problems and strategize about our dental dilemma. This journey from unconscious to conscious emotion takes us to the frontal cortex regions of our brain to see what happens to our emotions when we consciously think.

## Bringing Our Emotions to Consciousness: Thinking

**M**uch has already been said in this text about the role of our cerebral cortex and especially the differential function of our two hemispheres in the conscious processing of emotion. We refer to these two connected hemispheres of our brain as our frontal cortex. They usually work in tandem to take in information from our thalamus and then try to make sense of it. In the frontal cortex, perceived information is recognized and used in conjunction with long-term memory information stored throughout various cortical areas to give meaning to an experience. When necessary, our frontal cortex uses this meaningful information to plan and organize actions toward a goal. When the meaning of an experience evokes an emotional response, such as an old friend or a signal of conflict with an enemy, our frontal cortex incorporates the emotional response into the meaning of the experience. In fact, the emotional (feeling) response of the amygdala gives the experience its richness and vitality, framing its qualitative and subjective meaning. Without the affective response of the amygdala, our lives would be devoid of feeling and emotion. However, without the contribution of our frontal cortex, our experience would have no conscious meaning or understanding. We feel emotion in our amygdala, but we understand and label it in our frontal cortex. The nature of this conscious meaning derived from our frontal cortex is a function of the specific hemisphere in which information is processed. To understand this differential function of our two hemispheres, we need to revisit each.

The visual nature of our right-brain processing contrasts to the auditory/linguistic workings of our left hemisphere. As important as this left–right distinction is to our style of learning, problem solving, and thinking about ourselves, hemispheric specialization is crucial to our conscious experience of emotion. Due to the extensive interconnectedness of our sensory, motor, and limbic structures to our right hemisphere, it should not be surprising that our right hemisphere plays a significant role in our experience of emotion. And so we will first turn to our right brain's role in conscious emotion.

Studies of the physical and biochemical circuitry between the amygdala and the right frontal cortex have revealed a direct partnership in the experience of strong emotion (Damasio, 1994; LeDoux, 1994). These studies suggest that intense arousal at the amygdala–hippocampus level activates regions of the right neocortex, which register in our consciousness as intense fear or anger. This emotional awareness serves as our first consciousness recognition that a strong emotion is experienced. Of course, the explanation, meaning, and even labeling of that emotion does not occur until the physical sensations are communicated to the left hemisphere. Until then, the stimulation provoked in our right brain is experienced as intense arousal. In unconscious reaction, that elevated arousal could express itself as rage, aggression, or excitement.

For example, the imperceptible (unconscious) odor of gasoline might trigger our amygdala–hippocampus to retrieve a childhood memory of an automobile accident involving a gasoline fire that resulted in severe pain. The arousal activated by the amygdala might elicit an autonomous nervous system response enabling us to fight or flee from the feared experience. As our feeling emotion is elevated (i.e., our SUDS level rapidly climbs), the intense emotion stimulates the right hemisphere to perceive and consciously recognize that something is not right. Even before giving meaning to that something in our left brain, we might consciously experience the intense emotion as debilitating or enraging. In terms of their function, we can say that the amygdala at the unconscious level works with the right hemisphere at the conscious level to switch on our emotions. The job of our left frontal cortex is to give meaning to that emotion, to regulate its intensity, and when necessary, to switch off our emotional experience.

True to its mission of understanding and rationally regulating our covert and overt world, our left frontal cortex tries to comprehend and moderate our emotions, enabling us to function successfully and feel good about the process. When intense arousal threatens to immobilize us, our left brain tries to analyze the perpetrator, then formulates and executes a strategy either to remove the threat or at least remove the threatening experience from consciousness (i.e., defense mechanisms used to deny or distort intolerable, subjective realities). The tool for this executive task conducted by our left brain is language.

## Complex Covert Partnerships in Emotion

When our amygdala–right-brain partnership renders us emotionally aroused, anxious, or upset, our left brain processes the experience to better understand what is going on. This processing draws on all the existing schemata (understandings) that are

The antecedents that provoke our emotions are idiosyncratic, just like us. (Reprinted with permission of King Features Syndicate.)

stored as long-term memory networks throughout our cerebral cortex that could help us know what is happening and what we can do about it. As we access (retrieve) the relevant schemata, we use our language system to reflect on their relevance and utility. We also use language to label our emotional experience as anger, fear, resentment, confusion, jealousy, happiness, joy, and so forth, again using language to better understand and address our emotional feeling. Our emotional labels reflect both the intensity of our feeling and the context from which we give the emotion meaning and explanation.

Our capacity to consciously process information symbolically and linguistically in our left brain enables us to think about our emotions' source, meaning, and implications for future action. Our right brain registers feeling while our left brain brings the feelings to conscious reflection and meaning, the thinking component of emotion. Through the vehicle of language, our left brain is able to integrate long-term memory, current experience (in our "working memory"), and future intention with the emotionality that defines us as human. And only through this integration do our feelings inform our emotions, and our emotions in turn give qualitative meaning to our experiences and actions. When our left brain labels our strong arousal in the presence of a growling dog as emotions of fear and panic, it is immediately capable of analyzing the danger and formulating a strategy of fight or flight. Our feelings inform emotions (and their linguistic labels) that activate cognitive problem solving crucial to our survival and well-being.

More subtle but just as indicative of emotional thinking are the gut reactions and intuitive sensations that inform us of potential danger, opportunity, good fortune, and an array of present and future experiences that could endanger or enrich our lives. Fortunately, the feeling emotions of our amygdala–hippocampus–right-brain circuitry provide the bases for emotional learning that continually educates our conscious reality. Only through emotional learning can our subjective judgments and values influence our actions.

When my rational, analytic, and problem-solving left brain listens to my emotional right brain, it is able to apply emotional context and meaning to my actions. The first task of my left brain is to understand the existing emotion. What am I feeling? What is my body trying to tell me about its reaction to something of which I may not even be aware? Why does my heart race when called to speak in class? Why the tension in my neck and upper back when I notice April 15 on the calendar? What does it mean when these same reactions occur as I pack my bags for my first visit to an exotic vacation spot?

## Feeling, Thinking, and Labeling Emotion

In each instance, my limbic–right-brain partnership is informing my left brain of existing states of arousal. But without the context and analytic reason provided by the left brian, my experience of these feeling emotions is strictly physiological, with varied arousal that ranges from exhilaratingly pleasant to excruciatingly aversive. Once the level of arousal is registered in my left brain, I can begin to consciously understand the emotion. Pulling from relevant long-term memory stored within the billions of neuron networks throughout my cerebral cortex, I begin to connect similar experiences from my past with what I perceive in the present. With analysis of this memory plus external sensory and feeling data, an explanation (or what some might call a story) begins to emerge in my consciousness. Constructed linguistically, this explanation provides the context and meaning of the emotion.

We might think of our left brain as our locus of conscious problem solving, decision making, and strategic control over our internal and external world. As our sentinel for stability and self-control, our left brain takes the role of mediating crises and our emotional arousal (i.e., fear, anger) in response to crises. As you may recall from our discussion of defense mechanisms, our left brain might even formulate extreme strategies of denial and distortion to cope with distress and maintain a subjective reality of stability and safety. From the mildest forms of rationalization to extreme dissociation with the self, a primary function of our left brain is to protect us from debilitating states of emotion.

To this end, some neurophysiologists (Damasio, 1994; Gainotti, 1972) view the left brain as the "off" switch for distressing emotions derived from amygdala–right-brain circuitry. Through deactivating neurotransmitters, the left brain seems to inhibit strong negative feelings like fear and aggression that occur in our right brain. These neurophysiologists cite numerous studies in which stroke patients with an impaired left brain and fully functioning right brain experienced intense emotions of worry, fear, and rage. In contrast, patients with a disabled right frontal lobe experienced inordinately frequent states of calmness, detachment, and passivity. Apparently, the absence of our left-brain function renders us emotionally overwhelmed with distress, whereas the diminishing influence of our right brain leaves us feeling flat and emotionally deprived.

To be fully functioning, we need the balance of emotional feeling by our right brain and emotional thinking of our left brain. Human emotion is neither the raw feeling of arousal and discomfort nor the symbolic labeling of what we think we are experiencing. Rather, our emotion represents what we feel and what we think we feel within our universe of external environments.

When the blatant or subtle sensory messages of tooth discomfort enter our amygdala–hippocampal complex of neurons, we instantaneously experience arousal in our SUDS. Simultaneously, our amygdala signals our right brain of impending danger, and we become consciously aware of feelings of fear, anger, and distress. As these feelings of impending pain or even doom build in our right brain, they quickly cross a threshold of awareness and signal our left brain to the rescue. Using its powers of rational problem solving our left brain first tries to understand the nature and meaning of the feeling by applying emotional labels such as scared, anxious, depressed, and angry. With clearer meaning and understanding of our emotional response to the situation, our left brain calculates action patterns and coping strategies that enable us to successfully avoid and escape the stressors of present pain and expected agony at the dentist's office. And so we pick up the phone, dial the number, and wait anxiously for an answer.

## The A-B-C Model: Closing the Circle

With our executive decision to schedule the dental appointment in spite of our high anxiety and covert expectation of pain, we come full circle in our explication of the A-B-C's of our experience. Our initial depiction of the dental appointment in Chapter 1 offered a preview of one way to understand a typical human experience through the lens of the A-B-C model. This first exposure to the model offered only the surface elements of this rich and complex framework for looking at ourselves within our many environments. With each succeeding chapter, we narrowed our focus to each component of the model while simultaneously building the fabric of interdependence that all components maintain.

Even while each element of the A-B-C model was studied in depth, we realized that, no matter how complex and distinct, each could only be understood and appreciated in relationship to all of the others. Although our study of the A-B-C model was linear and sequential, the dynamic operation of the A-B-C's was clearly integrative and holistic. And since the locus of integration occurred within the massive network of neurons comprising our brain, we also integrated the entire A-B-C model through analysis of our covert experience. With this integration complete, we can reflect on the depth, scope, and complexity of the A-B-C's of our experience and begin to consider the ways we can use this knowledge to enhance our lives.

## Chapter Summary

**1.** Temperament represents our innate predisposition to think, feel, and behave in certain ways. Researchers have identified temperament styles reflecting novelty seeking, harm avoidance, and reward dependency. Each of these styles determines how we experience intrinsic and extrinsic consequences.

**2.** We experience emotion through feeling sensory stimulation and then thinking about the sensation. The amygdala–hippocampus partnership enables us to identify emotionally arousing stimuli, store this information in short-term memory, and then activate our autonomic nervous system in preparation for an aroused response.

Later, in the "emotional" experience, our amygdala–hippocampus system sends this information to our frontal cortex for conscious reflection and problem solving.

3. Because our hippocampus–amygdala partnership can trigger very strong physical arousal even without conscious attention by our thinking left brain, it constitutes the feeling part of emotion in contrast to the thinking part of emotion within our left frontal cortex.

4. Strong positive feelings of elation and pleasure can make their imprint in our emotional memory located within our amygdala–hippocampus circuitry. Even the faintest smell, taste, sound, and touch reminiscent of past pleasure can evoke those same blissful sensations. Only later might our left brain label the experience as joyous, exciting, relaxing, nostalgic, erotic, and so on.

5. While our right frontal cortex (hemisphere) switches our emotions on, our left frontal cortex gives meaning to that emotion, regulates its intensity, and switches the intense emotional arousal off.

6. Through language, our left brain is able to integrate long-term memory, current experience (in our working memory), and future intention with the emotionality of our right-hemisphere–limbic system. In this way, our left brain is the fundamental locus for integrating all of the relevant a-b-c's associated with a given experience.

7. Once integrated, our left brain uses its language capacity to label the subjective, emotional features of the experience.

# References

Abramson, L.Y., Metalsky, G.I., & Alloy, L.B. (1989). Hopelessness, depression: A theory-based process-oriented sub-type of depression. *Psychological Review, 96,* 358–372.

Amabile, T. (1983). *The social psychology of creativity.* New York: Springer-Verlag.

Ashton, H. (1992). *Brain function and psychotropic drugs.* New York: Oxford University Press.

Asterita, M.F. (1985). *The physiology of stress.* New York: Human Sciences Press.

Atkinson, J.W. (1983). *Personality, motivation and action.* New York: Praeger.

Bandura, A. (1969). *Principles of behavior modification.* New York: Holt, Rinehart & Winston.

Bandura, A. (1986). *Social foundations of thought and action: A social cognitive perspective.* Upper Saddle River, NJ: Prentice Hall.

Bandura, A. (1997). *Self-efficacy: The exercise of control.* New York: W. H. Freeman.

Bandura, A., Ross, D., & Ross, S. (1963). Vicarious reinforcement and imitative learning. *Journal of Abnormal and Social Psychology, 67*(6), 601–607.

Bateson, G., Jackson, D., Haley, J., & Weakland, J. (1956). Toward a theory of schizophrenia. *Behavioral Science, 1,* 251–264.

Baumeister, R. F., Smart, L. & Boden, J. M. (1996). Relation of threatened egotism to violence and aggression: The dark side of high self-esteem. *Psychological Review, 103*(1), 5–33.

Beck, A. (1976). *Cognitive therapy and the emotional disorders.* New York: International Universities Press.

Behrends, R. (1986). The integrated personality: Maximal utilization of information. *Journal of Humanistic Psychology, 26,* 27–59.

Bloom, F.E., & Lazerson, A. (1988). *Brain, mind, and behavior.* New York: W.H. Freeman.

Bowen, M. (1978). *Family therapy in clinical practice.* New York: Aronson.

Bowlby, J. (1980). *Attachment and loss* (Vol. 3). New York: Basic Books.

Briggs, J. (1988). *Fire in the crucible: The alchemy of creative genius.* New York: St. Martin's Press.

Brown, R.T. (1989). Creativity: What are we to measure? In J.A. Glover, R.R. Ronning, & C.R. Reynolds (Eds.), *Handbook of creativity* (pp. 217–246). New York: Plenum.

Butterworth, G., Jarrett, N., & Hicks, L. (1982). Spatiotemporal identity in infancy: Perceptual competence or conceptual deficit? *Developmental Psychology, 18,* 435–449.

Cannon, W. (1932). *The wisdom of the body.* New York: Norton.

Cautela, J. (1970). Covert reinforcement. *Behavior Therapy, 1,* 33–50.

Cautela, J., & Kearney, A. (Eds.). (1993). *Covert conditioning casebook*. Pacific Grove, CA: Brooks/Cole.

Churchland, P. (1986). *Neurophilosophy: Towards a unified science of the mind/brain*. Cambridge, MA: MIT Press.

Churchman, C. (1979). *The systems approach*. New York: Dell.

Clifford, M. (1990). Students need challenge, not easy success. *Educational Leadership*, 48(1), 22–26.

Cloninger, R. C. (1987). A systematic method for clinical description and classification of personality variants. *Archives of General Psychiatry*, 44, 573–588.

Cloninger, R. C., Adolfsson, R., & Svrakic, M. (1986). Mapping genes for human personality. *Nature Genetics*, 12, 3–4.

Cloninger, R. C., Svrakic, D. M., & Przybeck, T. R. (1993). A psychobiological model of temperament and character. *Archives of General Psychiatry*, 50, 975–990.

Comings, D. E. (1990). *Tourette syndrome and human behavior*. Duarte, CA: Hope Press.

Corballis, M.C. (1983). *Human laterality*. New York: Academic Press.

Coren, S. (1993). *The left-handed syndrome*. New York: Vintage Books.

Cormier, W.H., & Cormier, L.S. (1991). *Interviewing strategies for helpers*. Pacific Grove, CA: Brooks/Cole.

Cousins, N. (1989). *Head first: The biology of hope*. New York: Dutton.

Damasio, Antonio. (1994). *Descartes' error*. New York: Gorret/Putnam.

Deikman, A. (1982). *The observing self: Mysticism and psychotherapy*. Boston: Beacon Press.

DeShazer, S. (1984). *Keys to solutions in brief therapy*. New York: Norton.

*Diagnostic and statistical manual of mental disorders* (4th ed.). (1994). Washington, DC: American Psychiatric Association.

Dusek, J. (1985). *Teacher expectations*. Hillsdale, NJ: Erlbaum.

Dutton, D. G. (1996). *The batterer: A psychological profile*. New York: HarperCollins.

Egeland, B., & Farber, E.A. (1984). Infant–mother attachment: Factors related to its development and changes over time. *Child Development*, 55(3), 753–771.

Ellis, A. (1984). *Rational-emotive therapy and cognitive therapy*. New York: Springer.

Ellis, A. (1993). Fundamentals of rational-emotive therapy. In W. Dryden & L.K. Hill (Eds.), *Innovations in rational emotive therapy* (pp. 12–38). Newberry Park, CA: Sage.

Erickson, M. H. (1954). Pseudo-orientation in time as a hypnotic procedure. *Journal of Clinical and Experimental Hypnosis*, 2, 161–283.

Erikson, E.H. (1980). *Identity and the life cycle*. New York: Norton.

Festinger, L. (1957). *A theory of cognitive dissonance*. Evanston, IL: Row, Peterson.

Fish, R., Weakland, J., & Segal, L. (1982). *The tactices of change*. San Francisco: Jossey-Bass.

Flavell, J. (1985). *Cognitive development* (2nd ed.). Upper Saddle River, NJ: Prentice Hall.

Frank, D.F., & Frank, B.F. (1991). *Persuasion and healing: A comparative study of psychotherapy*. Baltimore, MD: Johns Hopkins University Press.

Gainotti, G. (1973). Emotional behavior and hemispheric side of lesion. *Cortex*, 8, 41–55.

Gazzaniga, M.S. (1985). *The social brain: Discovering the networks of the mind*. New York: Basic Books.

Gazzaniga, M.S., & LeDoux, J.E., (1978). *The integrated mind*. New York: Plenum.

Geertz, C. (1973). *The interpretation of cultures*. New York: Basic Books.

Gergen, K. (1991). *The saturated self*. New York: Basic Books.

Gerin, W., Litt, M., Deich, J., & Pickering, T. (1996). Self-efficacy as a component of active coping: Effects on cardiovascular reactivity. *Journal of Psychosomatic Research*, 40(5), 485–493.

Gilligan, C. (1982). *In a different voice*. Cambridge, MA: Harvard University Press.

Ginsburg, H., & Opper, S. (1988). *Piaget's theory of intellectual development* (3rd ed.). Upper Saddle River, NJ: Prentice Hall.

Goffman, E. (1963). *Stigma*. Upper Saddle River, NJ: Prentice Hall.

Goldiamond, I. (1965). Self-control procedures in personal behavior problems. *Psychological Reports, 17,* 851–868.

Goleman, D. (1985). *Vital lies, simple truths: The psychology of deception.* New York: Simon & Schuster.

Goleman, D. (1995). *Emotional intelligence.* New York: Bantam Books.

Gross, A., & Drabman, R. (1982). Teaching self-recording, self-evaluation, and self-reward to nonclinic children and adolescents. In P. Karoly & F. Kaufer (Eds.), *Self-management and behavior change: From theory to practice* (pp. 285–315). New York: Pergamon Press.

Haley, J. (1986). *An uncommon therapy.* New York: Norton.

Hamer, D., & Copeland, P. (1998). *Living with our genes: Why they matter more than you think.* New York: Doubleday.

Hanson, G.B. (1995). *General systems theory beginning with the whales.* Washington, DC: Taylor & Francis.

Hedaya, R. J. (1996). *Understanding biological psychiatry.* New York: W. W. Norton.

Hoffman, L. (1993). *Exchanging voices: A collaborative approach to family therapy.* London: Karnac.

Hutchins, D. E., & Cole, C. G. (1992). *Helping relationships and strategies.* Pacific Grove, CA: Brooks/Cole.

James, W. (1890). *The principles of psychology.* New York: Holt.

Joseph, R. (1982). The neuropsychology of development: Hemispheric laterality, limbic language and the origin of thought. *Journal of Clinical Psychology, 38,* 4–33.

Kabat-Zinn, J. (1990). *Full catastrophe living.* New York: Delta.

Kagan, J. (1994). *Galen's prophecy.* New York: Basic Books.

Kagan, J., Reznick, J. S., & Snidman, N. (1988). Biological bases of childhood shyness. *Science, 240,* 167–171.

Kahn, W. (1989). Teaching self-management to children: An empirical study of the paradigm. *Elementary School Guidance and Counseling, 24*(1), 37–46.

Kazdin, A.E. (1984). Covert modeling. In P.C. Kendall (Ed.), *Advances in cognitive-behavioral research and therapy* (Vol. 3, pp. 103–129). New York: Academic Press.

Klinger, E. (1971). *Function of fantasy.* New York: Wiley-Interscience.

Kohlberg, L. (1981). *Philosophy of moral development.* New York: Harper & Row.

Kraines, S. (1943). *Managing your mind: You can change human nature.* New York: Macmillan.

LeDoux, J. (1989). Indelibility of subcortical emotional memories. *Journal of Cognitive Neuroscience, 1,* 238–243.

LeDoux, J. (1994). Emotion, memory and the brain. *Scientific American, 270*(6), 50–57.

Levinson, D. (1978). *The reasons of a man's life.* New York: Ballantine.

Lidz, T. (1976). *The person: His and her development throughout the life cycle.* New York: Basic Books.

Luria, A. R. (1982). *Language and cognition.* New York: Wiley.

Maier, S.F., & Seligman, M. (1976). Learned helplessness: Theory and evidence. *Journal of Experiential Psychology: General, 105,* 3–46.

Maltz, M. (1960). *Psychocybernetics.* New York: Pocket Books.

McGaugh, J. L. (1983). Hormonal influences in memory storage. *American Psychologist, 38,* 161–174.

Meichenbaum, D., & Gilmore, J.B. (1984). The unconscious: A cognitive-behavioral perspective. In K. Bowes & D. Meichenbaum (Eds.), *The unconscious reconsidered.* New York: Wiley.

Miller, G. A. (1956). The magical number seven, plus or minus two: Some limits on our capacity for processing information. *Psychological Review, 63,* 81–97.

Miller, L. (1988). *The emotional brain.* New York: Ballantine.

Mischel, W. (1971). *Introduction to personality.* New York: Holt, Rinehart & Winston.

Molfese, D., Freeman, R., & Palermo, D. (1975). The ontogeny of brain lateralization for speech and non-speech stimuli. *Brain and Language, 2*, 356–368.

Mountcastle, V.B., Plum, F., & Geiger, S.R. (Eds.). (1987). *Handbook of physiology* (Vol. 5). Bethesda, MD: Physiological Society.

Nauta, W. (1971). The problem of the frontal lobe: A reinterpretation. *Journal of Psychiatric Research, 8*, 167–187.

Nicoll, W.G. (1992). A family counseling and consultation model for school counselors. *School Counselor, 39*, 351–361.

O'Leary, K.D., & Wilson, G.T. (1975). *Behavior therapy: Application and outcome*. Upper Saddle River, NJ: Prentice Hall.

Orne, M.T. (1969). Demand characteristics and the concept of quasi-controls. In R. Rosenthal & R. Rosnow (Eds.), *Artifacts in behavioral research* (pp. 147–179). New York: Academic Press.

Pelletier, K.R. (1977). *Toward a science of consciousness*. New York: Random House.

Pelletier, K.R. (1992). *Mind as healer, mind as slayer*. New York: Delta/Seymour Lawrence.

Pert, C. (1987). *Noetic science review*. New York: Random House.

Piaget, J. (1954). *The construction of reality in the child*. (M. Cook, Trans.). New York: Basic Books.

Piaget, J. (1985). *The equilibrium of cognitive structures: The central problem of intellectual development*. (T. Brown & K. L. Thampy, Trans.). Chicago: University of Chicago Press.

Piirto, J. (1992). *Understanding those who create*. Dayton, OH: Ohio Psychology Press.

Premack, D. (1965). Reinforcement theory. In D. Levine (Ed.), *Nebraska Symposium on Motivation* (pp. 123–180). Lincoln: University of Nebraska Press.

Prigogine, I. (1984). *Order out of chaos: Man's new dialogue with nature*. New York: Bantam Books.

Purkey, W., & Novak, J. (1984). *Inviting school success* (2nd ed.). Belmont, CA: Wadsworth.

Rhine, J.B. (1964). *Extrasensory perception*. Boston: Humphries.

Rice, P.L. (1987). *Stress and health: Principles and practices for coping and wellness*. Pacific Grove, CA: Brooks/Cole.

Robinson, R.G. (1986). Post-stroke mood disorder. *Hospital Practice, 21*, 83–89.

Roemer, L. & Borkovec, T. (1993). Worry. In D. Wegner & J. Pennebaker (Eds.), *Handbook of mental control* (Vol. 5, pp. 346–382). Upper Saddle River, NJ: Prentice Hall.

Rosenthal, D. (1969). Interpersonal expectations: Effects of the experimenter's hypothesis. In R. Rosenthal & R.L. Rosnow (Eds.), *Artifact in behavioral research* (pp. 181–277). New York: Academic Press.

Rosenthal, R., & Jacobson, I. (1968). *Pygmalion in the classroom*. New York: Holt, Rinehart & Winston.

Ross, E., & Stewart, R. (1987). Pathological display of affect in patients with depression and right frontal brain damage: An alternative mechanism. *Journal of Nervous and Mental Disease, 175*, 165–172.

Rotter, J. (1966). Generalized expectancies for internal versus external control of reinforcement. *Psychological Monographs, 1* (No. 609).

Rotter, J. (1975). Some problems and misconceptions related to the construct of internal versus external control of reinforcement. *Journal of Consulting and Clinical Psychology, 43*, 56–67.

Ruff, H. (1982). Role of manipulation in infants' responses to invariant properties of objects. *Developmental Psychology, 18*, 682–691.

Rumelhart, D., & Ortony, A. (1977). The representation of knowledge in memory. In R. Henderson, R. Spiro, & W. Montague (Eds.), *Schooling and the acquisition of knowledge* (pp. 47–68). Hillsdale, NJ: Erlbaum.

Satir, V. (1972). *Peoplemaking*. Palo Alto, CA: Science and Behavior Books.

Satir, V. (1978). *Your many faces*. Millbrae, CA: Celestial Arts.

Schneidman, N., McCabe, P., & Baum, A. (1992). *Stress and disease processes*. Hillsdale, NJ: Erlbaum.

Selemon, L. D., Goldman-Rakic, P. S., & Tamminga, C. A. (1995). Prefrontal cortex and working memory. *American Journal of Psychiatry, 152*, 5.

Seligman, M. E. (1975). *Helplessness: On depression, development and death*. San Francisco: W.H. Freeman.

Selye, H. (1974). *Stress without distress*. New York: Lippincott.

Selye, H. (1976). *The stress of life* (rev. ed.). New York: McGraw-Hill.

Shapiro, D. (1965). *Neurotic styles*. New York: Basic Books.

Siegel, B.S. (1986). *Love, medicine and miracles*. New York: Harper & Row.

Singer, J. (1975). *The inner world of daydreaming*. New York: Harper & Row.

Skinner, B.F. (1953). *Science and human behavior*. New York: Free Press.

Sperry, R. (1974). Lateral specialization in the surgically separated hemispheres. In F. O. Smitt & F. Worden (Eds.), *The neurosciences: Third study program*. Cambridge, MA: MIT Press.

Spitz, R. A. (1945). Hospitalism: An inquiry into the genesis of psychiatric conditions in early childhood. *Psychoanalytic Study of the Child, 1*, 53–74.

Squire, L. P. (1987). *Memory and brain*. New York: Oxford University Press.

Stein, D.J., & Young, J.E. (Eds.). (1992). *Cognitive science and clinical disorders*. San Diego: Academic Press.

Steiner, H., & Matthews, Z. (1996). Psychiatric trauma and related psychopathologies. In H. Steiner (Ed.), *Treating adolescents*. San Francisco: Jossey-Bass.

Sternberg, R. (1994). Allowing for thinking styles. *Educational Leadership, 52*, 36–40.

Sullivan, H.S. (1953). *The interpersonal theory of psychiatry*. New York: Norton.

Talmon, M. (1990). *Single session therapy*. San Francisco: Jossey-Bass.

Taylor, C. (1989). *Power of the self*. Cambridge, MA: Harvard University Press.

Terr, L. (1991). Childhood traumas: An outline and overview. *American Journal of Psychiatry, 1*, 148, 10–20.

Toffler, A. (1984). *Future shock*. New York: Bantam Books.

Torrance, E.P. (Ed.). (1975). *Issues and advances in educational psychology: A book of readings* (2nd ed.). Itasca, IL: F. E. Peacock.

Von Glassersfeld, E. (1984). An introduction to radical constructivism. In P. Waltzlawick (Ed.), *The invented reality* (pp. 17–40). New York: Norton.

Vygotsky, L. (1962). *Thought and language*. Cambridge, MA: MIT Press.

Wachtel, P. (1977). *Psychoanalysis and behavior therapy: Toward an integration*. New York: Basic Books.

Wadsworth, B. (1989). *Piaget's theory of cognitive and affective development* (4th ed.). New York: Longman.

Walter, J., & Peller, E. (1992). *Becoming solution-focused in brief therapy*. New York: Brunner/Mazel.

Warrington, E.K., & Wesikrantz, L. (1973). An analysis of short-term and long-term memory defects in man. In J.A. Dentsch (Ed.), *The physiological basis of memory*. New York: Academic Press.

Watson, D., & Tharp, R. (1993). *Self-directed behavior*. Pacific Grove, CA: Brooks/Cole.

Watzlawick, P. (1990). *Munchhausen's pigtail*. New York: Norton.

Weiner, B. (1986). *An attributional theory of motivation and emotion*. New York: Springer-Verlag.

Weiner, N. (1948). *Cybernetics*. New York: Wiley.

Weiss, J.M., Simson, P., Ambrose, M., Webster, A., & L. Hoffman. (1985). Neurochemical basis of behavioral depression. *Advances in Behavioral Medicine, 1*, 253–275.

Wolpe, J. (1958). *Psychotherapy by reciprocal inhibition*. Stanford, CA: Stanford University Press.

Wood, F., Stump, D., McKeechan, S., Sheldon D., & J. Proctor. (1980). Patterns of haloperidol medication: Evidence for inadequate left frontal activation during stuttering. *Brain and Language, 9*, 141–144.

Zilbergeld, B., & Lazarus, A. A. (1988). *Mind power: Getting what you want through mental training*. New York: Ivy Books.

Zuckerman, M. (1995). Good and bad humors: Biochemical bases of personality and its disorders. *Psychological Science, 6*, 325–333.

# Author Index

# Subject Index

TO THE OWNER OF THIS BOOK:

I hope that you have found *The A-B-C's of Human Behavior: An Integrative Approach* useful. So that this book can be improved in a future edition, would you take the time to complete this sheet and return it? Thank you.

School and address: _____

Department: _____

Instructor's name: _____

1. What I like most about this book is: _____

_____

_____

2. What I like least about this book is: _____

_____

_____

3. My general reaction to this book is: _____

_____

4. The name of the course in which I used this book is: _____

_____

5. Were all of the chapters of the book assigned for you to read? _____

    If not, which ones weren't? _____

6. In the space below, or on a separate sheet of paper, please write specific suggestions for improving this book and anything else you'd care to share about your experience in using the book.

_____

_____

_____

_____

_____

Optional:

Your name: _____ Date: _____

May Wadsworth quote you, either in promotion for *The A-B-C's of Human Behavior: An Integrative Approach* or in future publishing ventures?

    Yes: _____ No: _____

    Sincerely,

    *Wallace J. Kahn*

---

FOLD HERE

NO POSTAGE
NECESSARY
IF MAILED
IN THE
UNITED STATES

# BUSINESS REPLY MAIL

FIRST CLASS      PERMIT NO. 358      PACIFIC GROVE, CA

POSTAGE WILL BE PAID BY ADDRESSEE

ATT:    *Wallace J. Kahn*

**Wadsworth Publishing Company
10 Davis Drive
Belmont, California 94002**

---

FOLD HERE